DISCARDED

CONSUMPTION AND DEPRESSION IN GERTRUDE STEIN, LOUIS ZUKOFSKY AND EZRA POUND

Consumption and Depression in Gertrude Stein, Louis Zukofsky and Ezra Pound

Luke Carson
Department of English
University of Victoria
Canada

First published in Great Britain 1999 by
MACMILLAN PRESS LTD
Houndmills, Basingstoke, Hampshire RG21 6XS and London
Companies and representatives throughout the world

A catalogue record for this book is available from the British Library.

ISBN 0-333-71451-2

 First published in the United States of America 1999 by
ST. MARTIN'S PRESS, INC.,
Scholarly and Reference Division,
175 Fifth Avenue, New York, N.Y. 10010

ISBN 0-312-21662-9

Library of Congress Cataloging-in-Publication Data
Carson, Luke.
Consumption and depression in Gertrude Stein, Louis Zukofsky, and Ezra Pound / Luke Carson.
p. cm.
Includes bibliographical references and index.
ISBN 0-312-21662-9
1. American literature—20th century—History and criticism.
2. Consumption (Economics) in literature.   3. Stein, Gertrude, 1874-1946—Knowledge—Economics.   4. Zukofsky, Louis, 1904-1978—Knowledge—Economics.   5. Pound, Ezra, 1885-1972—Knowledge—Economics.   6. Modernism (Literature)—United States.
7. Depressions in literature.   I. Title.
PS228.C65C37   1998
810.9'355—dc21   98-8143
                                                                                    CIP

© Luke Carson 1999

All rights reserved. No reproduction, copy or transmission of this publication may be made without written permission.

No paragraph of this publication may be reproduced, copied or transmitted save with written permission or in accordance with the provisions of the Copyright, Designs and Patents Act 1988, or under the terms of any licence permitting limited copying issued by the Copyright Licensing Agency, 90 Tottenham Court Road, London W1P 9HE.

Any person who does any unauthorised act in relation to this publication may be liable to criminal prosecution and civil claims for damages.

The author has asserted his right to be identified as the author of this work in accordance with the Copyright, Designs and Patents Act 1988.

This book is printed on paper suitable for recycling and made from fully managed and sustained forest sources.

10 9 8 7 6 5 4 3 2 1
08 07 06 05 04 03 02 01 00 99

Printed and bound in Great Britain by
Antony Rowe Ltd, Chippenham, Wiltshire

Contents

Acknowledgements	vi
List of Abbreviations	viii
Introduction	1
1 'Enough is not enough': Consumption and Depression	16
2 Gertrude Stein's Great Depression	52
'Distribution and equilibration'	52
'Money is not give but sell'	65
'There is always this thing, what is it'	78
'There is no detection'	91
3 Value from Obligation	100
'The Capital and Capitals of the United States'	100
'Dois-je le dire'	112
Gertrude's Stain	127
4 'New Deal or Steal'	142
Introduction: 'To administer the public trust'	142
'If the common man get together'	150
'The people's issue of nothing'	161
'Nothing of value'	181
5 Animated Things	198
'Licit consumption impeded'	198
'The worker's image'	214
'Let him be consumed..!'	232
Notes	252
Index	282

Acknowledgements

I am grateful to a number of people for their contributions, whether direct or indirect, to the writing of this book. Vincent Pecora was in on this project from a very early date, inspiring me to go in a number of directions, for none of which he is to blame. Kenneth Reinhard introduced me to possible ways into and out of this project I had for some reason refused to entertain. Samuel Weber was very generous in providing the conditions under which these possibilities became somewhat manageable. Lucia Re intervened at a critical point with a perceptiveness that set me on the right path. Timothy Murphy has endured many questions, offered many challenges, and accompanied me with some sympathy down some rather winding paths. In my graduate class in 1995 I was fortunate enough to work with dedicated students whose intelligence continues to inspire me: V. Angela Bowcott, Michael Conlon, and Rachel Taylor.

I am grateful also to Susan McCabe, though I'm not entirely certain why. Despite these accumulating debts, however, this book is dedicated to Wendy Welch – for many years.

Quotations from the following works of Ezra Pound are used by permission of New Directions Publishing Corporation and Faber & Faber Ltd: *The Cantos* (© 1934, 1937, 1940, 1948, 1956, 1959, 1962, 1963, 1966, and 1968 by Ezra Pound); *Literary Essays* (© 1918, 1920, 1935 by Ezra Pound); *Selected Prose 1909–1965* (© 1960, 1962 by Ezra Pound, © 1973 by the Estate of Ezra Pound); *Pound/Zukofsky* (© 1981, 1987 by the Trustees of the Ezra Pound Literary Property Trust). Quotations from the following works of Gertrude Stein are used with permission of the Estate of Gertrude Stein: 'What Are Master-Pieces?'; 'Before the Flowers of Friendship Faded Friendship Faded'; 'Money'; 'All About Money'; 'More About Money'; 'Still More About Money'; 'My Last about Money', in *Look at Me Now and Here I Am*, ed. Patricia Meyerowitz (New York and Harmondsworth: Penguin Books, 1971); 'And Now'; 'I Came and Here I Am'; 'The Capital and Capitals of the United

States of America'; 'Why I Like Detective Stories'; and 'How Writing is Written,' from *How Writing Is Written* (Santa Barbara: Black Sparrow, 1974); 'Identity. A Tale' and 'Political Series', from *Painted Lace*, vol. 5 of *The Yale Edition of the Unpublished Writings of Gertrude Stein* (New Haven: Yale University Press, 1955); *Four in America* (New Haven: Yale University Press, 1947); *The Geographical History of America* (New York: Vintage, 1973); *Everybody's Autobiography* (New York: Vintage, 1973). Acknowledgement is also made to the Estate of Gertrude Stein for permission to quote from the following unpublished works from the Gertrude Stein Collection at the Beinecke Rare Book and Manuscript Library, Yale University: 'Introduction' to Gertrude Stein's translation of Marshal Pétain's *Paroles aux Français*; and a manuscript entitled 'All Of It'. Acknowledgement is also made to the Johns Hopkins University Press for permission to quote from selected lines from Louis Zukofsky, *A* (© 1978 the Johns Hopkins University Press) sections 8, 9 and 12 (pp. 43–111, 202–3).

List of Abbreviations

Ezra Pound
C   *The Cantos of Ezra Pound* (New York: New Directions, 1986)
LE   *The Literary Essays of Ezra Pound*, ed. and with an introduction by T.S. Eliot (London: Faber, 1954)
SP   *Selected Prose*, ed. William Cookson (New York: New Directions, 1973)
PZ   *Pound/Zukofsky: Selected Letters of Ezra Pound and Louis Zukofsky*, ed. Barry Ahearn (New York: New Directions, 1987)

Gertrude Stein
EA   *Everybody's Autobiography* (New York: Vintage, 1973)
GHA   *The Geographical History of America* (New York: Vintage, 1973)
HWW   *How Writing is Written* (Los Angeles: Black Sparrow Press, 1974)
LMN   *Look at Me Now and Here I Am: Writings and Lectures 1909–1945*, ed. Patricia Meyerowitz (New York: Penguin, 1971)
PL   *Painted Lace: Vol. 7 of the Yale Collected Unpublished Writings of Gertrude Stein* (New Haven: Yale University Press, 1959).

Louis Zukofsky
A   *A* (Berkeley: University of California Press, 1978)
P   *Prepositions: the Collected Critical Essays of Louis Zukofsky* (Berkeley: University of California Press, 1981)

The reciprocal and all-sided dependence of individuals who are indifferent to one another forms their social connection. This social bond is expressed in *exchange value*, by means of which alone each individual's own activity or his product becomes an activity and a product for him; he must produce a general product – *exchange value*, or, the latter isolated for itself and individualized, *money*. On the other side, the power which each individual exercises over the activity of others or over social wealth exists in him as the owner of *exchange values*, of *money*. The individual carries his social power, as well as his bond with society, in his pocket. Activity, regardless of its individual manifestation, and the product of activity, regardless of its particular make-up, are always *exchange value*, and exchange value is a generality, in which all individuality and peculiarity are negated and extinguished.... The general exchange of activities and products, which has become a vital condition for each individual – their mutual interconnection – here appears as something alien to them, autonomous, as a thing. In exchange value, the social connection between persons is transformed into a social relation between things; personal capacity into objective wealth. The less social power the medium of exchange possesses ... the greater must be the power of the community which binds the individuals together, the patriarchal relation, the community of antiquity, feudalism and the guild system. Each individual possesses social power in the form of a thing. Rob the thing of this social power and you must give it to persons to exercise over persons.

Karl Marx, *Grundrisse* (New York: Vintage, 1973), pp. 157–8

Introduction

ENLIGHTENMENT MODERNITY AND UTOPIAN MODERNISM

Faced with the demise of the nineteenth-century marketplace and with the challenge posed to the ideology of classical liberalism by monopoly capitalism and widespread labour unrest, the political desires of the modernists seemed unable to transcend the alternatives of an obsolete liberalism and an often authoritarian corporatism. In this book, I attempt to demonstrate that the modernist project was inseparable from a utopian impulse that could not be answered by the political categories and ideologies inherited from the Enlightenment. The reason for this, I argue, is that modernity and modernism are characterized by a melancholic division in the social subject. This division assumes its dominant ideological form in the contradiction, which has characterized modern political discourse, between contractual and corporatist models of the social. This is the historical and ideological field of contestation Gertrude Stein, Louis Zukofsky and Ezra Pound would enter in the thirties.

Briefly, the argument of my book is that, by way of the aesthetic displacement of political discourse, these three writers arrive at the limit-point of the political economy not only of modernism but of modernity, where it becomes apparent that the object of their reflection is a hybrid and total object that is not fully accounted for in any of the discursive or even practical registers made available by the Enlightenment. This total object does not in any proper sense exist as an object of representation (such as 'society', 'economy', 'the political') for any of the disciplinary distinctions inherited from the Enlightenment division of knowledge. Writing in the early fifties, Wallace Stevens suggested that such hybridity extended to the national economy which could therefore be considered a 'poetico-economy'.[1] I follow Stevens' cue by conceiving the hybrid object of my study as the poetico-'political economy' of modernity and modernism. The very divisions instituted by the Enlightenment promise a totality and a universality that they cannot deliver; this utopian promise motivates both the most regressive and the most progressive political activities of modernity. From the divisions and fragmentations of subjectivity and experience that it institutes, modernity gives rise to a phantasm of the lost differentiated totality of a community, or what Ferdinand Tönnies famously theorized as *Gemeinschaft*. For some modernists, of course, this differentiated totality was expressed in a longing for archaic forms of social relations prior to the Enlightenment and modernity.[2] For those (like Stein and Zukofsky, of my examples) who refused such phantasms, the utopian impulse to totality or universality was not itself considered the source of illusion. Instead, their critical insistence on recalling the promise of universality provided them with a way of realizing how the universality promised was immanent to the institutions of Enlightenment, and embodied in historical forms of economic and social exchange.

The most important objection that could be raised at this point is that my insistence on the utopian impulse to universality or totality in the texts of these modernists is unwarranted. In the context of contemporary criticism, what is above all important are the moments of difference and singularity to be found in these texts. From such a perspective, a critical study of the politics and economics of modernism should focus on the implicit critique of universality that these texts make available. This is particularly true in the case of Stein, recent criticism of whom has focused on gender, sexuality and to a lesser extent ethnicity, as providing her with a subject position resistant to universalizing and abstracting discourses; this is also true of Zukofsky, who, born in 1904, was the youngest son of a working-class Yiddish-speaking Russian Jewish family that had emigrated to New York in 1900 and who, moreover, was sympathetic to the 1917 revolution. The first reason I offer for my claim that the impulse to universality operates in these minoritized writers is quite simply the limited focus of my study. The object of this book is above all economic discourse, and the political discourse that emerges largely from the failure of the former adequately to represent the hybrid object that it purportedly analyses. Because these two discourses historically claim (either in concert or competition) to forward the promise of universality, the particular subject position of the speaker of the discourse tends to be effaced. By this I mean that the critical perspective on the discourse of political economy does not come from particularity as much as it comes from an immanent critique of the discourse itself.

I would like to make two points clear, however. First of all, I do not want to claim that critical attention to difference and particularity has to take a back seat to an analysis of the recalcitrant 'modernity' of these writers. Second, my purpose in focusing on the Enlightenment legacy in modernism is not intended to support any claims that Stein, despite the minoritized position of a lesbian Jew, was in the reactionary camp that at one extreme includes Pound. Nor, similarly, do I want to redeem Pound's disastrous political choices by allying him with Stein's more forgivable contradictions. My purpose is instead to provide a framework for understanding the historical and ideological limits that the utopian impulse of modernism encounters. Having said this, I would add that contemporary critical attention to moments of difference and singularity or particularity tends too quickly to ignore what I argue are the discursive resources historically available to the subjects inhabiting the complex objects to be represented in those discourses. The modernist political impulse confronts the promise of universality at the point at which, arguably, the category exhausts itself and makes way for what we have come to call postmodern ways of reflecting on the legacy of the Enlightenment;[3] it would be historically inaccurate, I think, to claim that Stein and Zukofsky criticized the promise of universality as repressive or violent without recognizing their investment in the possibility of its being realized.

If the particularity of their positions does not provide them with a substantive point from which to critique claims to universality, the effacement of particularity demonstrates the impossibility of universality without sacrifice or loss and, consequently, the economies of restitution and reappropriation that predominate in the post-Enlightenment period.[4] This impossibility is in fact the very theme of this book. In the first chapter, devoted in large part to Stein, I will analyse what I call the ethic of sacrifice that Stein advocates throughout the Depression. What is to be sacrificed in response to this ethic, this imperative, is not the self in any psychological sense or any of its qualities as much as it is particularity as such, including the singularities of the body and the psyche to which the self cannot lay claim. Stein's commitment to the value of universality is demonstrated by her most reactionary political gesture, when she abandons her classical liberalism in order to side with the archaic and repressive universalism of Marshal Pétain in 1941. The potential for this reaction lies with her commitment to the Enlightenment promise of universality. Stein's notion of 'the human mind', as we will see in the second chapter, is a category that deliberately retains associations with particularity, even as it results from an obliteration of particularity in a universal category that Stein approvingly affiliates with the abstraction of money. At the same time, Stein's texts demonstrate the experience of suffering that comes from such sacrifice. In the conclusion of Chapter 3 I focus on Stein's identification with a sacrificed particularity in the form of a 'thing', calling itself 'Gertrude Stein', that haunts the universalizing and abstracting language of the father – a 'stain' on the paternal name of 'Stein'.

Though the sacrifice of particularity is the major theme of this book, I would like to argue finally that the insistence on universality by these writers sustains the utopian impulse in ways with which postmodernity has yet to come to terms. It appears from these texts that what emerges from the immanent contradictions of Enlightenment universality is the survival of a promise that cannot be answered by the insistence on difference or particularity. This insistence plays itself out against the background of the utter failure of the promise of the Enlightenment to be fulfilled in anything other than the nightmarish form to which Pound notoriously gave his consent. Stein and Zukofsky experienced this failure in their particularities, but did not give up on whatever the collective thing or substance is that since the Enlightenment has gone by the name of 'universality'. This is because they were attentive to the limits they encountered: particularity assumes its value within the economy of sacrifice effected by universality.[5] Their attention was focused on that which is of most value to the utopian impulse, which is adequately conceptualized neither in terms of particularity or universality, since that opposition depends in advance upon the loss of that which is of most value. As will become apparent in my first chapter, this thing can be identified neither as particularity nor in universality, but is sustained or presented only in the dialectic of both, which threatens with the nightmare of domination even as it holds out the promise of democratic community.[6]

The utopian impulse is melancholic in that it attempts to inhabit those forms of sociality and exchange to which it is historically bound in such a way as to repair the loss that is immanent to them. For this reason, and others that I hope will become clear throughout the chapters that follow, I refer to the division in the social subject as melancholic. Suffice it to say for now that melancholia is the consequence of a constitutive sacrifice of particularity. Freud claims that melancholia is caused by an 'unknown loss', the loss of something that in the final instance cannot be represented as an 'object', that is to say, as a person or as an ideal. While an ego in mourning can identify that which has been lost, the loss at the origin of melancholia lacks a proper name and the narrative form that would provide it with a history through which the ego could establish a normative relation to it. As Freud says, melancholia requires the loss of what is of most value to the ego. This loss cannot be overcome through mourning because 'the unconscious (thing-) presentation of the object... is made up of innumerable single impressions (or unconscious traces of them)'.[7] Reading against Freud's assumption that a proper and finally identifiable object has been lost, I argue (following contemporary interpretations of melancholia)[8] that the lost object was not an object as such, available to representation. For melancholia to overcome itself, an identifiable object must be 'made up', as Stein says, in order to be either recuperated or abandoned. The various strategies of concealing the constitutive melancholia therefore must always fail; melancholia is an endless process because of this inevitable failure to represent, and so abstract, the particular moments and ways in which loss is experienced in the very 'thing presentations' that attest to the survival of the lost thing.

By encountering the limits of Enlightenment discourse, these writers present the moment where the deepest investments of utopian desire remain embedded, awaiting their fulfilment. For Stein, the market embodied this promise; for Zukofsky, following Marx, the structure of industrial labour, culminating in a thoroughgoing commodity fetishism, retained traces of this desire. Pound's powerful utopian impulse led him to encounter these limits as the real form of any possible universality, and therefore as a form calling for adjustment and transformation on the part of errant egos. Pound ultimately thought that Enlightenment differentiations among institutions should be erased; specifically, by the late thirties he thought the most powerful relation of which an ego is capable, the relation of selfless, sacrificial love, should be generalized to the political relation to the state and the leader as well. In a similar vein, when Stein committed herself briefly to the authoritarianism of Marshal Pétain in 1941, the relation of citizen or subject to state that she thought ought to be institutionalized was that of children to their strict but loving father. Their critiques remain immanent to their historical object; the utopian impulse responds to the unfulfilled promise of universality within the institutional, social and psychic divisions of modernity, rather than projecting an ideal outside of them. But the utopian impulse thereby also remains within the pathology of modernity, exacerbating its melancholia by finding substitutes in order to conceal the originary loss of the unnamed thing that haunts it as its promise of fulfilment. My argument focuses on two ways by which modern melancholia attempts to heal itself, both of which are forms of what Freud calls 'fetishism'. The first is the fetishism of the market, which projects the 'general equivalent' as a guarantee of abstract value; the second is the fetishism that puts the paternal leader in the place of the lost thing.[9] These two moments, I argue, are the parodic forms of universality characteristic of modernity. Despite the political and ideological differences of Stein, Zukofsky and Pound, they responded in common to a third parodic form of universality which also, though it advertises itself otherwise, is founded upon the sacrifice or loss of particularity. The universality that the modernists resisted or critiqued in common is the emerging universal subject of mass consumption.

The subject of mass consumption can be seen as an effect of the melancholic form of identification characteristic of modernity. In psychoanalytic terms, we could say that melancholic identification is a constitutive failure of identification. According to Freud, the melancholic identifies with the lost object in order to deny its loss. The identification takes place through a narcissistic regression to the archaic form of identification by way of incorporation. The result is a split ego (not unlike the split ego characteristic of fetishism) which is subject to an internal agency of potentially abusive domination, which Freud calls the ego-ideal. At the same time, the subject is haunted by an ideal ego, which is ambiguously and tenuously identified with the authoritative and potentially authoritarian ego-ideal. The ideal ego is a narcissistic image of what the ego most wishes to be; the ego-ideal can alternatively forbid or require the ego to become this imaginary figure. In either case, the impoverished ego will fall short, whether it rebels against or submits to the authority exercised upon it by the ego-ideal. The ego-ideal represents the community of which the ego is to become a member; the ideal ego can therefore be seen as the ego's private fantasy of autonomy and omnipotence.[10] The psychoanalytic terminology therefore provides some insight into the more ideological language of 'public' and 'private' spheres and selves. From the failure to measure up to the demands of the ego-ideal emerges the subject of mass consumption, dominated by a conflated ego-ideal and ideal ego, which together occupy the position of the universality against which particularity weighs its own abjection.[11] Measured against the ideal ego, the subject can never be what it fundamentally *is* – that is, it can never occupy the place of its being, become what it wants to be; measured against the demands of the ego-ideal, the subject cannot become what it *ought* to be. Moreover, this means that the subject has neither a determinable private nor a determinable public space – a fact which does not reduce the conflict between the two. The gap or antagonism between private and public also gives rise to the discourse of alienation, and therefore also to economic and political discourses of the restitution and reappropriation of that which has been alienated, appropriated or stolen from the ego. When these writers encounter the limit of Enlightenment discourse, it is the limit primarily of a discourse that would economize upon the constitutive, melancholic loss – which is the very discourse of economy. Such economization is maximized in the economy of mass consumption.

MODERNISM, MELANCHOLIA, AND MASS CONSUMPTION

In the twenties it became apparent to Henry Ford, among others, that in order for the development of mass production in America to be sustained, a concomitant development of mass consumption was necessary. Where the development of mass production required an extensive transformation of the system of production, mass consumption required an equally extensive transformation of the social, psychological and cultural values that permeate and support any given historical economic form. Where the ideology and rhetoric of nineteenth-century American capitalism organized its moral justification and authority about the spectre of scarcity, mass consumption required that scarcity be displaced by the value of 'material abundance'. I argue that, despite their apparent differences, Pound and Stein share a profound ambivalence towards the substitution of scarcity by its opposite; this ambivalence is also at the root of the anxiety and the hope they held for the various political possibilities presented by the economic and political upheavals of the thirties. Their anxiety towards any regime of value based on material abundance seemed to them justified by the return, in the Great Depression, of the spectre of scarcity in the midst of a promised abundance.

Stein and Pound respond to the lived crisis of the Depression by reflecting on the economic and political forms available to modernity. However, they do not respond to the crisis from within the discipline of economics or of political theory, but from the aesthetic and ethical space that takes as its object what I referred to, after Stevens, as the poetico-political economy. This means that their economic categories are informed by social, cultural and psychological values, and that their economic reflections reveal what is invested in (for example) the classical liberal economic categories of exchange. For example, the institution and ideology of consumer credit that developed during the twenties as one of the conditions of the emergence of mass consumption is reinterpreted morally and psychologically by Stein and Pound during the Depression as obligation and guilt. For both, I argue, the remedy for the guilt associated with the value of material abundance is finally expiation through sacrifice – the political institution and enforcement of scarcity.

Stein, like Herbert Hoover, did not feel that the Depression challenged the fundamental beliefs and values of her classical liberalism, and she therefore continued throughout the thirties to defend the principle of the autonomy of the market. However, though she resembled Hoover in this respect, when aesthetic and cultural autonomy came under threat by market values, she once again became the aesthetic modernist she fundamentally was, and betrayed a profound ambivalence to the market. During the Depression, Stein continued to defend money and the market, but her ambivalence deepened; as she continued to claim that one should 'believe in money', it became apparent that the only reason to do so was because there were so few options available. The only other alternative was submission to one of the 'depressing fathers' of the thirties, among whom Stein included Hitler, Mussolini and Roosevelt.

Stein's liberalism is constructed in opposition and reaction to what she calls the 'organization' of modern social and economic life. It acknowledges that the threat of domination does not come from without, but from within the economic sphere. In particular, the centralization of economic power evident in monopolies and corporations at the end of the nineteenth century – which Stein calls 'organization' – predicts a new feudalism, a new form of submission to the father. For this reason, Hitler's fascism and Roosevelt's New Deal were both instituted by 'depressing fathers' on the basis of possible 'corporate' political forms that inhere within the economy, which is therefore only apparently autonomous in relation to other regimes of value.

Stein hoped that the Depression might dismantle the corporate subjective structures that threaten the private life of (for example) the labourer – by returning labour to its status as the worker's private property. Stein's Great Depression does not therefore simply threaten from without the contractual freedom of the private sector and the individual worker; such freedom was already under siege from within the economy. Stein implicitly recognizes that a paternal instance is immanent to the economy, and cannot be effaced. Even if individualist contractual relationships were once again to predominate over emerging corporate identities – or, in Stein's terms, if 'employees' are once again to become 'hired men' – the subjective structure of dependency that the market otherwise conceals would persist in another form. The political decisions Stein makes throughout the thirties and forties come down to a choice among forms of domination. The market, which Stein is so concerned to defend against Roosevelt's state, is in the end not simply opposed to 'government' – as it is in classical liberal discourse. Stein's resistance to 'depressing fathers' can therefore turn into its opposite, as is evinced most powerfully by her consent to Pétain's paternalism. Even when Stein affirms the liberal marketplace, it is not in defence of the individualism or freedom it might make possible, but because of the scarcity it institutes and perpetuates. For this reason, Stein's defence of the market during the Depression assumes the form of an ethic of sacrifice, which, I argue, is a historically new version of the traditional American ethics of thrift, restraint and work.

My analysis of Stein's 'depressing fathers' in the first three chapters serves to develop the three concepts discussed above, namely, melancholia, sacrifice and fetishism, which are the foundation of the entire argument. The most important is melancholia – one meaning of the 'Depression' of my title. Melancholia brings together a cluster of concepts that will be deployed throughout the argument of the book, providing the link between economic and apparently non-economic spheres of value. I have mentioned the example of consumer credit, the social and psychological dimension of which appears as guilt and obligation. The notion of debt is situated between two regimes: the political-economic regime of contract and right, and the moral regime of obligation and guilt, which I argue are the two sides of a modern and modernist melancholia. In social rather than economic and legal terms, the first regime is expressed in the value of 'individualism', which classical liberalism claims to protect; in social rather than psychological and moral terms, the second regime is expressed in 'corporatism', which Pound and others advocated during the Depression as a corrective to the extensive destruction of society, culture and community caused by the liberal marketplace. One can see the conflict of these regimes at work in Pound's obsessive concern (which I discuss at length in Chapter 4) with distinguishing between public and private debt, which involves regulating the borders between the private, economic sphere and the public, political sphere, borders which are blurred beyond recognition in modernity.

The second important concept to emerge from the reading of Stein is sacrifice. For Stein, like George Simmel, the constitution of any economy of values is based on sacrifice. In Simmel's interpretation, borrowed in large part from classical economics, sacrifice is framed in an economy of balanced exchange. For Stein, however, that which is of most value, which she would in the thirties call 'the human mind' or 'entity', is the result of a sacrifice that does not repay in kind.[12] I argue that this aligns her to some extent with Marx, who pointed out that with the exchange of labour for wages, which is foundational for the capitalist economy, the worker gave more than was received in turn. Though she was no Marxist, Stein was aware of Henry George's theory of 'value from obligation', according to which obligation is the 'power to command labor without the return of labor'. This unequal exchange, I argue, refers back to the originary debt of the subject to the ego-ideal. However, in contrast to Marx's economy of reappropriation, Stein's melancholic economy of loss presupposes that exchange is always off-balance; for this reason she did not advocate any attempt to reappropriate the alienated social substance. Instead, for Stein, any economy must preserve the moment of sacrifice or loss that constitutes the possibility of exchange. In practical terms, this means that not everybody can eat. The concept of sacrifice operates for Pound and Stein within the opposition of scarcity and material abundance. What both fear in the emerging consumer economy and its phantasm of material abundance is the imaginary and melancholic concealment of this constitutive sacrifice or loss. For Stein, that promise of abundance leads to Depression; any demand for 'just distribution', that is, any demand on the part of an individual or a class or other group for the return of an equivalent of what was sacrificed in the originary exchange forecloses the constitutive lack of the economy. This leads, according to Stein's political economy, to the very domination to which Pound turned when the reform of money seemed to him no longer enough to transform the political order.

Stein's political economy demands that this original, melancholic debt, which is incurred at a site of sacrifice and suffering, be both maintained and concealed by commodity exchange. The term I use for this double gesture is disavowal, which refers to fetishism, the third concept to emerge from the analysis of Stein's political economy. Disavowal is the fetishist's form of negation, which preserves in secret that which is negated. The fetish erected upon the site of sacrifice simultaneously forgets and remembers what is sacrificed. It is because of the double gesture of fetishism that, when Stein confronts the phantasm of material abundance, she begins to reinterpret the concepts and values of her liberal capitalism in light of the disavowed acknowledgement of the paternal will as expressed in castration.[13] Her liberal capitalism therefore reveals its complicity with its apparent opposite, an authoritarian paternalism. At this point, money announces what had always been its fundamental form for Stein: it becomes apparent that her defence of the market was to guarantee a means of discipline against emerging mass consumption. Like the Freudian fetish, money materializes lack; it is above all intended to make up for, to memorialize, and to conceal a fundamental, melancholic guilt. The domination built into it allows Stein, at least during the Depression, to forgo appealing directly to a paternal leader who will curtail the inflation of consumer demand.

The final two chapters take the argument beyond Stein's classical liberalism to Zukofsky's Marxism. During the thirties, Zukofsky's poetics develops in a direction similar to Pound's in the use of citation and montage; also similar to Pound, Zukofsky's poetry at the time was 'econ / conscious', in Pound's phrase, and it was above all attentive to the fascist corporatism that was becoming prominent in Pound's thought during the early to mid-thirties, when the two poets, though living on different continents, were in contact on a regular basis (PZ 162). In Chapter 4 I argue that Pound was for Zukofsky an example of the larger crisis of liberalism, which I examined in the case of Stein. In Zukofsky's view, Pound's insistence on monetary reform implicitly acknowledged the failure of Enlightenment political discourse to theorize a collectivity not reducible to contractual reciprocity. As is well known, the reform of money was to play for Pound a significant role in the restoration of 'the public good' (rather than 'material abundance', for example) as a determining value of political, economic and social life; it would do so by providing the material conditions of a paradoxical corporate individualism. In order to determine what is at issue between the two poets, I examine the various group theories and institutions that emerged in America after the demise of the market and the exhaustion of its ideology. Zukofsky recognized that the emerging ideological redefinition of the boundaries between the private and an attenuated 'public' sphere in effect took as its model of the social the corporate institutions of monopoly capitalism. His response is not to provide a more adequate theoretical account of any possible collectivity or universality; he is far too aware of the authoritarian potential of such concepts, even such an apparently democratic one as 'the public good' or 'the public interest'.

Zukofsky's Marxist suspicion of the claims of certain groups to define the 'public interest' extends so far as to include the identification of Labour as the universal class. Zukofsky was aware of the profound ideological transformation that was to rebuild the collapsed economy by interpellating labour into the sphere of consumption. While in Chapter 4 I develop Zukofsky's conceptual translation and apparent fetishization of Labour into 'Energy', in Chapter 5 I demonstrate that Zukofsky's metaphorical apparatus is governed by the second law of thermodynamics: Labour is lost in its translation into Energy, which is subject to decay, to entropy; it becomes 'unusable', and thereby takes itself outside of any revolutionary-utopian reinstitution of 'natural use'. What is thereby lost or appropriated is not, as Marxist discourse would claim, surplus labour; it is instead what Zukofsky calls a 'constant', which in its various historical transformations and identities has no proper name. Citing Charles F. Adams, Zukofsky sees the new corporate structure of the economy and of society as dominated by 'a power for which our language has no name'. Though Zukofsky would clearly like to name this power 'Labor', and thereby demystify social-symbolic value, the historical subject to which Marxists ascribed the name 'Labor' is, in Zukofsky's analysis of the American imaginary, susceptible to a corporatist ideology derived from the legacy of contractual notions of the individual and the social.

His Marxism is therefore highly critical of itself, and in the end can only be called Marxist in a highly qualified way. Though there can be little doubt of the radical impulse motivating Zukofsky's poem, the name 'Labor' should be understood through Zukofsky's text as an ideological figure that serves to organize desire. In A-8, Zukofsky tracks the libidinal network of debt and guilt that will allow an economy of consumption to emerge from an industrial economy of production. Insisting on the continuity between the earlier economy of production and the new economy of consumption as much as he insists on the rupture between them, Zukofsky preserves what is most crucial in Marx, namely the concepts of surplus value and of commodity fetishism.[14] Since he retains these traces of Marx, his reading demands that we ask what takes the place of 'labor' in a revolutionary politics, or what name will restore to the economy the thing that has been sacrificed.

However, even as he preserves the key concepts of Marx, he rejects the economy of reappropriation to which they give rise, recognizing that economies of reappropriation are founded on the subjective structure of domination that I have characterized as melancholic. Though his critique of the Marxist universality of labour does not lead Zukofsky to affirm the universality of capital or the Poundian universality of the paternal leader, it does not leave much room for the revolutionary impulse to articulate any alternatives to domination. Zukofsky's critique of economic discourse pursues it to the furthest moment of commodity fetishism, where labour has been interpellated entirely into the sphere of consumption; Zukofsky's perspective is entirely absorbed by the fetishism he analyses. This becomes apparent when, in order to recapture what can no longer be symbolized under the name of labour, he follows Pound and turns to two other names for the missing cause of commodities: love and light. With these two names, Zukofsky begins to articulate the political possibilities that remain in the post-industrial consumer economy. Love provides Zukofsky with a metaphor to mark the historical transition from the primacy of production to that of consumption. In *A-9*, Zukofsky (borrowing from Pound) encodes the suffering of the labourer under industrial 'terror' in terms of courtly love, which valorizes and eroticizes suffering or sacrifice. Deploying this image of the labourer-lover, I argue that the burgeoning sphere of consumption is founded on, but not reducible to, the corporate subjectivities established by industrial production. Zukofsky's labourer-lover combines feudalism and capitalism in a way that announces the form of domination upon which the new economy of consumption will rely. Tying courtly love into melancholia, I argue that in Zukofsky's analysis the contractual and individualist utopia of consumption paradoxically realizes the corporate subjectivity Pound thought only the fascist State could provide.

Such is the politics of love; but what of light? Film, the technology of 'light', provides Zukofsky with a metaphor for the libidinal economy which enables the historical transmission of desire from the sphere of production (where it appears under the name of labour) to that of consumption. Zukofsky's film metaphors link together two uses of the technology: on the side of production film is used for the analytic surveillance of workers in the rationalization of the production line; on the side of consumption film is a mass medium, the representative of which is for Zukofsky the ambivalent figure of Mickey Mouse. Zukofsky's political aesthetic appears to culminate in a vision of universal and total fetishism in which the redemptive social substance is 'camouflaged', to use Zukofsky's term (in his interpretation of the aesthetic techniques of Charlie Chaplin), but not available for representation and, therefore, reappropriation.

Zukofsky's dead-end vision of 'animated things' – things and subjects animated with a missing social substance, without any capacity for resistance or revolutionary action – is to a certain extent a result of his critical deployment of the Enlightenment discourse of economy. However, though Zukofsky's utopian impulse requires something other than what his predominantly Marxist vocabulary allows him to articulate, a change of vocabulary would not suffice to provide a critical perspective with some redemptive or revolutionary possibility. The competing (aesthetic, romantic, philosophical) discourses that he sets to work in A-8 and 9 only, in the end, reveal their own complicity with the discourse of economy and economization. The limits he encounters are historical and ideological, but not in any sense that would imply that they could be transcended by critique. From this I draw some conclusions concerning the need to reconsider both the politics and the aesthetics of modernism without emphasizing either the political or the aesthetic alone. Though Zukofsky and the modernists approached the hybrid object of my analysis through an aesthetic politics, I suggest that in doing so they presented within Enlightenment discourse and ideology not political or economic objects, but what must perhaps be called ethical modes of relation and determination that cannot be absorbed by the various mutations of Enlightenment ideology or its historical conditions.

1
'Enough is not enough': Consumption and Depression

> The survey has proved conclusively what has long been held theoretically to be true, that wants are almost insatiable; that one want makes way for another. The conclusion is that economically we have a boundless field before us; that there are new wants which will make way endlessly for newer wants, as fast as they are satisfied.
>
> Hoover Committee Report on Recent Economic Changes in the United States (1929)
>
> The consumer's dollar has been discovered.
>
> Edward A. Filene (1931)
>
> Remember the depression, dont be afraid to look it in the face and find out the reason why, dont be afraid of the reason why, if you dont find out the reason why you'll go poor....
>
> Gertrude Stein (1945)[15]

Ezra Pound, like many radicals in the thirties, thought the Depression would be the final crisis of capitalism; however, though he thought Marx's analysis of the self-destruction of capitalism to be substantially correct, he could not accept or advocate for Europe or America the revolutionary step taken by Russia in 1917. Instead, Pound recommended C.H. Douglas's proposal to increase consumption by increasing the purchasing power of producers with the issue of state-controlled currency. This was a nonrevolutionary strategy to resist the logic that Marx saw as essential to the self-destruction of capitalism, namely, the falling rate of profit and the subsequent decrease of wages, leading to a steady decline in living standards.[16] According to Marx's analysis, of course, the dialectical logic of capitalist crisis could not be resisted by the means Pound advocated. But Marx was generally seen to have been superseded by the development of capitalism and the second industrial revolution, which made mass production possible. According to its defenders, capitalism in the thirties was simply going through another stage, but the advent of mass production meant that the stage would conclude the cycle of depressions that had plagued American capitalism over the past hundred years. Mass production, the argument went, need not require an intensification of the contradiction of labour and capital; in fact, capitalism could not survive without its producers becoming consumers of the wealth they, in cooperation with capital, help to produce. As Henry Ford put it: 'Our buying class is our working class, and our working class must also become our "leisure class" if our immense production is to be balanced by consumption. Besides it is only just and human and progressive and educational that the people should use what they produce.'[17]

Economists recognized that the Depression was not a crisis of overproduction; in fact, the concept of overproduction was considered meaningless in light of the fact that increased growth was the goal of capitalist production. Instead, the problem was underconsumption and the urgent task at hand for writers like Edward A. Filene was the production of the consumer in order to increase consumption. In terms of labour history, the hegemony of the quantitative claim for higher wages resulted in part from the discovery by industrialists like Ford that the only way out of the Depression was by such an increase in consumption, which was perceived by businessmen and political leaders even before Ford not only to be necessary but also desirable.[18] Filene, like Ford a homespun prophet of mass production, while arguing the case for a shorter working day, summarized the means of recovering from Depression:

> Mass production, which is the most effective form of production, can not live unless the masses can and do buy in adequate quantities. The masses can not buy adequately unless they are provided with adequate buying power, and will not buy unless they have adequate leisure in which to play the part of consumers. Mass production, therefore, for necessary business reasons, constantly puts wages up, puts prices down and provides more and more leisure for its employees.[19]

It has only been in this century that leisure has become available for the mass of workers, and the 'private life' that has come to be identified with free or leisure time has become predominantly the product of the expenditure of wages. Thus, in a comment that only became possible when the labour movement narrowed its focus to demands for increased wages, Pound defines a bourgeois as 'What the working man becomes the moment he has the least opportunity' (SP 354). It should be clear from this scornful comment that Pound and Ford would hardly agree on the question of consumption. For Pound, who always theorized about labour on the basis of an artisanal or even artistic model of production, consumption was primarily productive of further *things* that could themselves be *used* productively. A 'consumer', in Pound's vocabulary, could only be a consumer of use values – that is, there is no such thing as a 'consumer' as such, for consumption should serve production at all levels of the economy.[20] The money that serves as a medium of circulation is a dangerous link in the cycle of consumption–production, because it is a moment at which the individual can migrate, as it were, from the sphere of production to that of consumption; it is the moment at which the 'market' can be constituted – unless, of course, patterns of consumption are regulated by the state by means of encoding ethical value at the level of production.[21]

Pound claimed that '[i]n politics *the* problem of our time is to find out the border between public and private affairs' (SP 240). For Pound, the historical figure of the usurer, whose activity derives from that of the merchant, is the cause of the blurred borders of private and public; the usurer or merchant perverts private 'appropriation', which should properly serve the management of the *oikos*, or household, by crossing it with the public, political life, the *polis*, where the collective and sovereign Good is to be posited.[22] The usurer also transforms these categories as he blurs their difference – the private interest of the *oikos* becomes private interest in the mercantile sense, which has come to dominate in modernity; the collective or public dimension of the Good disappears in what Pound, among others, saw as the frenzy of private appropriation.[23] Pound's normative concept of the private life is based on the individual artisanal mode of production, that is to say production not for the market but for barter or for personal consumption. For this reason, Pound's desire for a more democratic and efficient redistribution of wealth through the reform of money and credit should not be confused with union demands for higher wages. It is not noticed often enough that Pound tries to demonetarize money, to bring it as close as possible to a good to be bartered.[24] The modern form of private appropriation is always potentially 'bourgeois', and so the material abundance it promises cannot be made the basis of a radical politics. For many reasons, wages pose a difficult problem in Pound's economic thinking; one of the more significant reasons is that he is resistant to the determination of production and value by the market: he does not want the consumer to be alone responsible, by means of market mechanisms, for determining not only what is available for consumption, but also for what is privately consumed. The 'volition' of his 'volitionist economics' is not the popular will as expressed in the supposedly democratic mechanism of the market, but is the will of a leader, or a father, who should be at the centre not only of public life, but also of private appropriation. Money is not a condition of the individual freedom to consume, but binds one to the system of the state.[25] The borders of the private life are determined by the public Good.

Though his model of the private life relies more on Aristotle than on an analysis of the bourgeoisie, Pound did realize that the rationalization of production for mass output and the reduction of skilled labour to abstract industrial labour meant that the artisanal unity of hand and head could not find expression in the workplace. According to Pound, the industrial age has lost the collective dimension of the Good in labour, and has thereby reduced manual labour to an appendage to the machine. His normative figure, the artisan, precedes the radical division of intellectual and manual labour that mass production requires; but Pound, who was so self-consciously modern, never advocated a return to older modes of production. Nonetheless, he never clearly sorted out normative from descriptive concepts. His political and economic discourse is dominated by moral, cultural and spiritual causes of historical degeneration. Though he thought 'usury' answered to the methodological demand that political analysis must attend first and above all to material conditions, the term only served finally to obfuscate historical causation by clustering too many distinct objects under one concept. Therefore, normative concepts always dominate his rhetoric, and provide it with its often unfocused outrage. For example, though his economics attempts to address the damage done by industrialization, there is a powerful element of moral blame in his attitude towards labour. This is reflected in his aphoristic description of the bourgeois as a labourer who got lucky. This class-based normative and moralistic attitude puts Pound in the unlikely company of conservative reformers. The increasing rationalization of industrial production meant that traditional modes of leisure, which were not always so radically divided from the workplace, were rendered obsolete, and Pound feared that what might take their place, namely mass consumption, would contribute to the decay of value that he identified with bourgeois culture. One of the many significant effects of the industrial division of labour was a more intense opposition between work and the time allotted for the reproduction of labour power – the time which, as Filene and Ford pointed out, good business demanded be reorganized into leisure. To echo both the conservative and the radical critics of industrial labour: the body in the workplace was an adjunct to the machine, and the mind had very little role to play. Durkheim's account of the anomic division of labour, which was for him an abnormal development of what should have been a healthy 'organic solidarity' in the modern capitalist division of labour, indicates, with some scorn, one of the routes certain social critics proposed to overcome its debilitating effects:

> As a remedy, it has sometimes been proposed that, in addition to their technical and special instruction, workers be given a general education. But, suppose that we can thus relieve some of the bad effects attributed to the division of labor; that is not a means of preventing them. The division does not change its nature because it has been preceded by a general culture. No doubt, it is good for the worker to be interested in art, literature, etc., but it is nonetheless bad that he should be treated as a machine all day long. Who cannot see, moreover, that two such existences are too opposed to be reconciled, and cannot be led by the same man![26]

As Durkheim points out, the reformers of the nineteenth century who proposed 'general education' as a corrective to the effects of industrial labour on the worker sought to reconcile modern production techniques with their concept of the good life. Though some were strong advocates of the work ethic, most of the American social critics realized that industrial labour made it difficult to argue according to the traditional ethic of the nobility of work, and therefore generally agreed that the one basic requirement to reconcile industrial production with the need for the good life was to reduce the working day, and thereby provide more time for productive leisure, for 'culture'; industrial work, unlike traditional modes of work, left no time for the Good (whatever one understood this term to mean) which was a requirement for the production of a good citizen who would not be subject to the agitations of revolutionaries. Rather than renounce the value of efficiency and rationalization and attempt to transform the workplace, such critics attempted to resolve the division while preserving the structure of labour, which was after all remarkably efficient and productive. The failure of the conservative critics, such as those to whom Durkheim refers, to question industrial modes of production with an eye to their transformation leads to the moralization of the modes of consumption of the working class.

Much attention has been paid to Pound's anti-semitism and his hatred of the capitalist as financier and usurer, but little is said of his attitude to the working class. His commitment to traditional modes of production and consumption runs very deep, of course; the guardian of such traditions is the artist, the fundamental source of values in a society. Yet Pound's attitude towards the working class is extremely ambivalent. He clearly believes that industrial modes of production are inferior to more traditional modes, but is certainly not simply given to a romantic anti-capitalism. His commitment to the machinic forces of modern culture are revealed in his Vorticist and Futurist sympathies. But there can be little doubt that for Pound modern modes of production have lost sight of the Good in labour, and resulted in what Durkheim called anomie. At times, Pound, in the tradition of nineteenth-century moralists, indirectly blames the labourer for the state of production in an industrial society, by identifying the labourer with the mass consumption to which such mass production gives rise. As in the aristocratic branch of the Platonic tradition of social thought, the working classes are identified with the lower appetitive functions. With the hegemony of the demand on the one hand for fewer working hours, which originated at least in part with conservative reformers, and on the other for higher wages, which was not necessary for the cultural plans of the reformers, the 'private life' of the labourer became the product of the expenditure of wages.[27] The result, the 'culture' of mass consumption, is not of course what the reformers had in mind. Mass consumption became, for people like Pound, an extension of the bourgeois domination of the cultural sphere.

Pound's view of economic crises is that they are conspiratorial attempts to 'impede' 'licit' or 'legitimate consumption'. The notion of illicit consumption can be illustrated by Pound's use of the Circe episode of the Odyssey in the first Canto, where questions of labour and leisure come together in what might be taken as a cautionary tale. First of all, the very choice by Pound of Odysseus as a hero for his long poem is significant. Pound's Odysseus can obviously serve as a figure for the heroic leader, later to be imitated by Mussolini; but whatever Pound's intentions, Odysseus is also a figure for the Poundian capitalist or entrepreneur. Odysseus, for Pound, is at the place of *sacrifice*, but the end for which he makes sacrifice is capable of endless substitution; it may function as a public Good or as the private good of the capitalist (which is itself, according to the doctrine of enlightened self-interest, in the service of the public Good). As Adorno and Horkheimer argued, Odysseus anticipates the bourgeois capitalist, who is able to forgo immediate pleasures in favour of calculated future gain.[28] For Pound, on the other hand, the noble sacrifice or expenditure implied by Odysseus' heroic status serves the Good, and if we adopt Pound's view, the Circe episode becomes an authoritarian political fable; Odysseus' sailors, indulging in the pleasures which Circe offers, are figures of what he might call 'illicit consumption', the consumer's version of usury.[29] The sailors are like labourers, unable to live up to the standard of the heroic Odysseus. But this is not to say that labour does not perform effectively when called upon to do so. Odysseus' sailors in the Circe episode are labourers taking time off for consumption. It is significant that the Cantos begin with the departure from Circe's island, with a return to the heroic undertaking of culture under the direction of a powerful leader.

Given his early medievalism and his occasional anti-modern nostalgia for an agrarian past, one might expect Pound to have some sympathy for traditional modes of leisure. Yet just as he requires economy without waste in poetry, he is also sympathetic to the demands of efficiency that were simultaneously being made by the proponents of scientific engineering. In Canto 43, Pound recounts the preparations for a parade following upon the founding of the Monte de Paschi, and the description is exemplary in

'Enough is not enough' 23

revealing his ambivalence towards consumption. It would seem, of course, given Pound's high evaluation of this state institution as a model for all banks, that the parade is seen positively as a traditional mode of the consumption of leisure to celebrate and reaffirm the public Good. This is not borne out by an ambiguous statement Pound makes at the conclusion of the recording of the details of the parade:

> four fat oxen
> having their arses wiped
> and in general being tidied up to serve god under
>   my window
> with stoles of Imperial purple
> with tassels, and grooms before the caroccio
> [...]
> One box marked '200 LIRE'
>   'laudate pueri'
> alias serve God with candles
> with the palio and 17 banners
> and when the six men had hoisted up the big candle
> a bit askew in the carroch and the fore ox had
> been finally arse-wiped
> they set off toward the Duomo, time
> consumed 1 hour and 17 minutes.

The concluding statement, noting down the time consumed, may be a parody of American efficiency of the Benjamin Franklin variety – but is the time noted down because it was consumed efficiently, or inefficiently? Pound's comment or quotation may be a bureaucratic notation of time wasted, an accounting with which Pound might be quite sympathetic. The repetition of 'serve god' in connection with the 'arse wiping' and selling of candles certainly suggests an ironic gap between the speaker and the consumers of time.[30] The speaker does not include himself among those who would serve the particular public Good that the 'god' implies. Instead, this rather patronizing attitude to such a consumption of time reflects the conservative American moralists' attitude not to traditional modes of consumption among immigrants and the working class, but to emerging 'inefficient' kinds of consumption.

Pound's ideal subject was the *good citizen*. He had no particular admiration for aristocrats or for labourers, and certainly no respect for the bourgeoisie; he located the source of that possible citizen in no recognizable class, but in an élite that was not class-identified. If we leave out the artisan, the closest Pound came to a model of the good citizen was in the entrepreneur and the agricultural worker, but it was evident to him that not everybody could serve the public Good in the same function. The question that arises is, on what historical basis could the good citizen emerge from the amorphous public of a mass society? On what ground could such a subject be formed? For someone who was so vocal when it came to social reform, Pound lacked a real reference-point for the production of the good citizen. This is one reason why the *leader* became essential in the realization of the Good. As I will argue in more detail in the second half of this chapter, the leader occupies the centre of a structure of belief. Rather than higher wages for an increased share in the products of their labour, workers would be required to submit to a Good that was conceived to be in their interests, and which justified their place in the productive process. The division of labour peculiar to industrial production need not give up its momentum in order for the interpellation of the producer as its subject to succeed. According to Durkheim, the only remedy for the anomic division of labour is not 'to temper it with its opposite...'; rather,

> it is necessary and it is sufficient for it to be itself, for nothing to come from without to denature it. For, normally, the role of each special function does not require that the individual close himself in, but that he keep himself in constant relations with neighboring functions, take conscience of their needs.... He is, then, not a machine who repeats his movements without knowing their meaning, but he knows that they tend, in some way, towards an end that he conceives more or less distinctly. He feels that he is serving something. For that, he need not embrace vast portions of the social horizon; it is sufficient that he perceive enough of it to understand that his actions have an aim beyond themselves. From that time, as special and uniform as his activity may be, it is that of an intelligent being, for it has direction, and he knows it.[31]

The descriptive, prescriptive and normative are almost as ambiguously indistinct in Durkheim as they are in Pound. Pound's 'volitionist economics' reveals that the 'ought' will have the final say, and that the economy requires a leader for its proper regulation. Workers must be made 'to understand that [their] actions have an aim beyond themselves'.

Durkheim, like Pound, was concerned to resist the culture of consumption emerging in the industrially developed capitalist countries. According to Durkheim, the separation of the economic from the social sphere effected by industrial capitalism meant that the economy of goods (or commodities) lacked the traditional ethical dimension of the Good; in the place of *le bien*, there is *bien être*, well-being or satisfaction. Witnessing the birth of the modern consumer, Durkheim argued that mass production and the destruction of traditional forms of the Good lead to an increase in *imaginary* needs and desires beyond their natural form. Desires without limits, which are demanded by the emerging consumer economy, 'constantly and infinitely surpass the means at their command; they cannot be quenched. Inextinguishable thirst is constantly renewed torture.'[32] The very notion of 'purely material or economic motives', a notion fundamental to all spiritual, 'cultural', or traditional critiques of the emerging culture of consumption – that is, all critiques that posit a traditional form of the value of the 'Good' – involves a number of contradictory representations determined by class perspectives. The purely material or economic motive, the so-called 'private interest', can be seen as determining *both* the capitalist accumulation of capital *and* the immediate consumption of pleasure. Traditional critiques of consumption must locate the 'origin' of generalized consumption; a variety of social mobility, a crossing of class boundaries, a democratization of certain patterns of consumption can always be found at the root. As the brief discussion of Pound's sailors was intended to demonstrate, consumption is at times seen as 'materialist' in the popular sense of the word, an immediate indulgence of the gratification provided by material things – a less noble form of what Bataille calls 'expenditure without reserve'.[33] Pound among others feared the degeneration of 'culture' as the work of history and civilization. Such a notion of culture always implies a hierarchy of values, beginning on the lower level of both base and basic material needs and rising into the spiritual, 'sublimated' forms of 'culture'. Such a concept of culture became what we would now call *high* culture, no longer organically or hierarchically related to what thereby comes to be considered a separate *mass* culture. This historical and ideological opposition makes it possible for such critics to see the origins of generalized consumption as the infection of the upper classes by the pleasures of those without culture – the collapse of 'culture' as the product of sublimation into a kind of compulsive pleasure principle, embodied in the working class and, above all, in immigrants. Representations of the working classes in terms of such immediate consumption of pleasure are legion, of course; Pound's own sense that 'values' are perverted in modernity can at times assume this form of contempt for the working classes as well as the more apparent contempt for the bourgeois consumption of value. But the contradiction between 'material' or 'economic' motives as the immediate gratification of the proletarian and as the deferred consumption of the usurer or capitalist continues to operate. Pound's Jew in fact unites both of these apparently irreconcilable motives: he is at once a usurer, denying the healthy pleasure of immediate gratification, and the base consumer, indulging, like Odysseus' sailors, in the immediate pleasures of the flesh. As we will see in the fifth chapter, just as Bataille attempted to reconcile these contradictions in his concept of 'expenditure without reserve', Pound attempts to reconcile them in his ideal model of 'licit consumption', the courtly love of the troubadours.

Consumption is also often seen, by Pound and Bataille among others, as a generalization not only of proletarian pleasures, but also of the bourgeois mode of 'conspicuous consumption', as Veblen called it, the consumption of symbolic value, a debased imitation by the bourgeoisie of older aristocratic modes of consumption. We may not want to adopt Veblen's account of consumption uncritically,[34] but his position in the debate over the development of the culture of consumption is central. Daniel Horowitz has argued that Veblen distinguished himself from earlier American moralists, economists and sociologists in embracing industrial mass production, and 'machine' culture in general. Yet Veblen also condemned the wasteful modes of consumption such mass production depended upon. Mass production, in his view, would only generalize the bourgeois patterns of conspicuous consumption, and thereby lead to further distinctions and systems of valuation in the procedures of 'invidious comparison'. The most likely way to reconcile such an embrace of mass production with the possibilities of mass consumption would be to do as the technocratic interpreters of Veblen did in the thirties, and recommend a reorganization of industry with the goal of a more efficient production of goods to satisfy needs and create conditions in which productive leisure could be pursued. Veblen, however, provided no image of what Good was available as an end for mass production; his cynicism and misanthropy prevented him from forming any positive concept of the good society, including one based on the democratic distribution of goods to satisfy need. His high estimate of machine culture was not based, as it was for the technocrats, on the idea that it could establish the conditions for the full realization of human potential, or any other such Good. Veblen's concept of the 'instinct of workmanship' was not an anthropological concept on the basis of which the good life or the Good could be theorized; also, though he welcomed the world-view based on machinic production, which was to supersede the animistic world-view of the era of workmanship, his anti-bourgeois stance could not affirm the culture or the leisure that mass production seemed to promise. Veblen's uniqueness in the tradition of the critique of consumption can be attributed to the fact that he proposes no ethical model for reform, neither a work ethic nor an ethic of restraint. Veblen was not, again unlike his technocratic followers during the Depression, a reformer; he offered no positive concept of justice.[35] But we should not follow Horowitz' conclusion that Veblen was a 'transitional' figure who could not extricate himself entirely from the bourgeois morality of restraint.[36] Something more instructive is at issue in Veblen's refusal of the Good.

Why could Veblen, unlike so many of his contemporaries, affirm as a Good neither an ethic of 'workmanship' nor a consumer's paradise of material abundance, with the subject emancipated from work by the machine? Hannah Arendt, whose norm of *homo faber* shares a number of characteristics with what might seem to be Veblen's norm of workmanship, provides a perspective on the unspoken limit beyond which Veblen could not see the Good. According to Arendt the emancipation of labour, made possible less by automation than by the production of the consumer, could never be 'progress in the direction of freedom'. Instead, since it is founded on the presupposition that labour is the source of value, such an emancipation affirms the world (which is ultimately 'worldless' in a Heideggerian sense) that the ideology of labour implies. While 'work', in Arendt's definition, is very much like Pound's notion of work as the production of durable things for use, 'labour' is not so much the productive as it is the *destructive* appropriation of things: 'the ideals of *homo faber*, the fabricator of the world, which are permanence, stability, and durability, have been sacrificed to abundance, the ideal of the *animal laborans*. We live in a laborer's society because only laboring, with its inherent fertility, is likely to bring about abundance; and we have changed work into laboring. . . '.[37] For Arendt (like Simmel, as we will see shortly), labour is a species of consumption. The determining condition of this structure is survival, or subsistence, and, since it presumes scarcity, its highest good is material abundance. Therefore, the valorization of labour affirms a world based on scarcity and necessity, and so subjects the emancipated to another form of necessity which is 'the life process' itself, namely 'the necessity inherent in the laboring metabolism with nature'.[38] Scarcity and necessity are not escaped even in an economy of abundance; 'the spare time of the *animal laborans* is never spent in anything but consumption'.[39] Imagining the full realization of the utopian consumer society, which, by virtue of automation, would exist in such a way that the site of labour would remain invisible, Arendt sees only the fulfilment of what is already implied by the structure of labour, which is natural process itself: 'eventually only the effort of consumption will be left of "the toil and trouble" inherent in the biological cycle to whose motor human life is bound':

> However, not even this utopia could change the essential worldly futility of the life process. The two stages through which the ever-recurrent cycle of biological life must pass, the stages of labor and consumption, may change their proportion even to the point where nearly all human 'labor power' is spent in consuming, with the concomitant serious social problem of leisure, that is, essentially the problem of how to provide enough opportunity for daily exhaustion to keep the capacity for consumption intact. Painless and effortless consumption would not change but would only increase the devouring character of biological life until a mankind altogether 'liberated' from the shackles of pain and effort would be free to 'consume' the whole world and to reproduce daily all things it wished to consume.[40]

Animal laborans can never be anything other than *animal laborans*; its full realization would lead only to a 'reckless dynamism', and 'the grave danger that eventually no object of the world will be safe from consumption and annihilation through consumption'.[41] Arendt allows us to see that Veblen's cynicism acknowledges the impossibility of realizing the ideal promised not only by classical political economy but by the emancipation of labour: 'growing wealth, abundance, and the "happiness of the greatest number"', an ideal whose roots Arendt locates in 'the age-old dream of the poor and destitute'. *Animal laborans* can never transcend its conditions.

Modernity, in the vision of Veblen and Arendt, is thoroughly economic. Whereas the private life of appropriation in Greek thought complemented the public life, the vision of modernity held by Veblen and Arendt, among others, claims that there is no possibility of sustaining or opening a properly 'public' space. Gertrude Stein's own anxieties about the mass or collectivist public of 'human nature' is not so much the traditional American suspicion of groups as such, but is rather a recognition of the historical consequences of capitalism's erosion of the conditions of a public sphere. It would be wrong to criticize these three thinkers from a class perspective, to claim that their refusal of a Good results from an anxiety over the enfranchisement of the working class. Historical Marxisms have been implicated in the very logic that has provoked these thinkers into foreclosing the Good. When I say the Good, I mean also an instance of universality as the condition of community or of the *polis*. For both Veblen and Arendt, the Good is foreclosed from the economy of modernity. As Arendt argues, modernity *is* economy, and for this reason its politics precludes a *polis*.

The Good is inadequately represented in the forms of political economy, and in modernity it has been absorbed by them entirely – as just another 'good'. The symptomatic response to this foreclosure was to invent a sphere of value that was separate from the enclosure of political economy. This sphere of value was theorized under various names, but could be summarized as 'culture'. Stein's defence of 'the human mind' is an excellent example of this tendency, though we will see in the two chapters that follow that her notion of the human mind involves Stein in a number of contradictions productive of insights into the economy of modernity. Pound was among the modernists who recognized the historical limitations to conceiving the Good outside of political economy, but unlike Stein, Veblen, and Arendt, he refused to accept the limitations it imposed upon thought and practice.

Like others who attempted to resist the economy of modernity, Pound tried to articulate a concept of value that exceeded the framework allowed by *animal laborans*; like the most significant political and economic theorists of modernity, he also attempted to mediate between cultural (or 'kulchural') and economic value. Only such a total system of value could both serve political-economic rationality and at the same time further the Enlightenment promise of community and universality. As we will see in the fourth and fifth chapters, Pound's attempts to develop an alternative notion of value inclusive of economic value leads once again to the limit of the political economy of modernity. Pound is resisting one form of universality, the 'abstract' universality of exchange value, in order to further another; but it becomes apparent that his alternative and inclusive form of universality does as much violence as does the abstract universality of exchange value to that with or from which it intends to form a community. Frustrated by the resistance of the object of his critique, Pound runs up against the limit of modernity by requiring that a powerful, paternal leader embody and enforce the universality refused by political economy. This universality is no less false than that of exchange value.

The notion of culture, as I mentioned, serves to present a form of universality. This notion held particular sway in the debates that led up to the ideology of German and other European fascisms. Rarely, however, did such notions of culture attempt to mediate cultural and economic forms of value as Pound's did. Oswald Spengler is an interesting exception. Spengler argues, in what amounts to a parody of Marxist Hegelianism, that the concentration of power effected by capitalism lays the groundwork for the emergence of a true culture that is productive of values undreamed of by either capitalism or communism. According to Spengler's historical dialectic, as presented in *The Decline of the West*, which had wide currency in the English-speaking world after its translation in 1928, the concentration of capital in the hands of a few corporations set the conditions for the emergence of the universality promised by the Enlightenment: 'money is the form of intellectual energy in which the ruler-will, the political and social, technical and mental, creative power, the craving for a full-sized life, are concentrated'. The post-war economic crises culminating in the Depression indicate that money will soon be overpowered and displaced by the true form of the utopian impulse of the Enlightenment, the political will of the powerful leader: as Spengler says, 'there now sets in the final battle between Democracy and Caesarism, between the leading forces of dictatorial money-economics and the *purely political* will-to-order of the Caesars'.[42]

As Spengler's dialectic suggests, the false abstraction might be conceived to be the historical form in which the promised universality presents itself. As we will see above all in the fourth and fifth chapters, Marx encountered this difficulty when analysing the abstraction or 'real subsumption' of labour into the system of capital. But the conclusion to draw from this is not that we should have faith that history will work out universality in some Hegelian fashion, but that the false abstraction of exchange value has a further condition, which it is the concern of this book to explore, focusing on a particular historical moment when the utopian impulse of the Enlightenment was both frustrated and provoked by the collapse of the system of exchange. I have suggested, more or less in line with Marx, that exchange value is the dominant false form of universality in modernity. When it comes to the ideological organization of a society of producers and consumers, the form of universality by which utopian social desires are interpellated requires a more complex form for the presentation of value than the universality of exchange. However, not all universality is merely a mystification of capital. The complex form of value and universality provides some insight into the further conditions of the historically dominant abstraction of exchange value.

The ideological notion of 'culture' served well the purpose of presenting universal value for a number of reactionary, particularly fascist political organizations. But the Spenglerian rhetoric of plenitude is not the rhetoric of American authoritarianism, nor even of American fascism. The 'craving' that American fascism and Pound's economics appealed to was more material, relying less on images of spiritual and cultural depth. Unlike German or Italian fascism, which tended to bring into view the Good that the capitalist economy of goods had forgone, American versions of fascism tended to predicate themselves on the material abundance of goods that capitalism seemed to promise but never deliver. Despite all the emphasis placed by critics on Pound's adulation of Mussolini, Pound wanted nothing more than an efficient means for the distribution of the abundance that modern forms of production had made possible. However, for Pound, the increase of purchasing power required a total reorganization of the state according to a 'volitionist economics'. To achieve this, a ruler-will was necessary. In *The Coming American Fascism* (1934), Lawrence Dennis argues that fascists like himself should be grateful to the radicals responsible 'for the familiarization of the American public with the ideal of greater material abundance', since this will also make the public responsive to the fascist desire for 'realizing the ideal of maximum production' through industrial and social rationalization. Such rationalization of course requires an all-powerful state and 'an adequate leader'; as is the case with Pound, the consumer should by no means be 'sovereign'.

Dennis's radically pragmatic version of fascism does not require the ideological notions of 'culture' that the European fascist and Spenglerian images of historical depth or racial purity serve to justify. For Pound, on the other hand, 'Kulchur' was such an ultimate value. Being a radically anti-bourgeois artist, Pound could not value material abundance as an end in itself. Yet he considered it a necessary condition for the good society. For Pound, the Depression, like all other economic crises, was an impeding of 'licit consumption' by the usurious practitioners of illicit consumption (C 213, 216). Mussolini's economic reforms and curtailment of consumption was an attempt to impose what Pound in Cantos 42 and 43 called 'licit' or 'legitimate consumption' by imposing a hierarchy of values corresponding to the needs of society (C 213, 216). But, despite the appeal to material abundance, what supports these efforts is an ethic of sacrifice and suffering, opposed to the liberal, reformist and revolutionary attempts to create a society on purely economic motives, a society without a *polis*. Dennis too demonstrates an awareness of the resources made available to the fascist leader by the fact that material abundance is not enough:

> To be successfully adjusted, an individual does not have to have two cars or even a full stomach. He merely needs to have a place, or, to belong.... People don't mind suffering. On the contrary, some of them love to suffer all of the time, and all of them love to suffer some of the time. What people cannot endure is not belonging. The tragedy of capitalism – unemployment – does not inhere in the phenomena of want and privation, but in the spiritual disintegration of large numbers of people from

the group culture. Hitler can feed millions of his people acorns, and, yet, if he integrates them in a spiritual union with their community, they will be happier than they were while receiving generous doles from a régime which gave them no such spiritual integration with the herd.[43]

In light of Dennis's remarks, Pound's prediction of a mental depression consequent upon the economic Depression makes perfect sense: on the one hand, economic depression maximizes material privation, but the ensuing 'mental depression' is a complex of cultural and psychological factors which, though triggered by the collapse of the economy, cannot be attributed only to a fear of such privation. In October of 1931, Walter Lippmann addressed the 'anxiety which has gripped the American spirit'. This anxiety, wrote Lippmann,

> is not due primarily to the actual losses which almost everyone has suffered. Apart from those who are unemployed and destitute – a large number absolutely but a small number relative to the whole population – the problem is not yet one of actual privation or even of a serious reduction in the standard of life. The problem is one of fear of what is to come: the fear of the wage-earner that his wages will be cut or even that he will lose his job entirely, the fear of the employer that he will not be able to meet his obligations, the fear of men that they will not be able to pay their taxes, or the interest and instalments on mortgages, the fear that savings will be lost, and so forth. These individual fears spread like an hysteria in a crowd which is trapped in an inclosure and cannot find the exits, and the hysteria itself accelerates the very evils which men fear.[44]

The fear of becoming poor is perhaps not surprising in the context of an economic Depression. Yet one shouldn't too quickly presume that the object of fear is material deprivation. A comment made by Freud in 'Mourning and Melancholia' provides a useful corrective: Freud points out that one of the puzzling symptoms of melancholia is 'the prominence of the fear of becoming poor'. He suggests that 'the complex of melancholia behaves like an open wound, drawing to itself cathectic energies ... from all directions, and emptying the ego until it is totally impoverished'.[45] Even in Lippmann's analysis one can see that the fear also concerns questions of personal character and responsibility: will I be able to pay my taxes? Will I be able to repay my debts? The fear of poverty, however reasonable or universal, always involves intimately the moral and psychological life of the frightened. Moreover, the fear always has some historical specificity.

What can we make of the specificity of a fear of becoming poor in the Great Depression? To imagine it, it is necessary briefly to reconstruct the ideologemes of the American worker, which notoriously share a permeable border with those of the middle classes. Inculcated in the rhetoric of individualism and the market, itself rooted in agrarian property ownership and artisanal production, workers found unpalatable the socialist notion that their revolutionary self-recognition should give priority to a collective identity. Instead, nineteenth-century labour movements tended to employ the rhetoric that Marxists and socialists had identified as the ideological tools of capital. As Daniel Rodgers points out, American labour platforms tended to have a 'peculiarly individualistic cast'; 'communistic ideas of economic justice made far less headway in America than those that promised to link a man's reward directly with his work'.[46] Richard Sennett argues that workers and the middle classes tended to form their political beliefs and identities from such classical liberal concepts as individual freedom. Though it was not 'humiliating to be dependent' in more traditional societies

> [i]n industrial society it became so. The market made positions of dependence unstable. You could rise, you could fall. The most powerful impact ideologically of this instability was that people began to feel personally responsible for their place in the world; they viewed their success or failure in struggling for existence as a matter of personal strength or weakness....[47]

This fear of personal failure and culpability, though rooted in the work ethic derived from the Puritan heritage, extends deeply into American social and cultural values. However, the work ethic is not enough to account for the range of interpretations that could be applied to the Depression. The work ethic was rooted in conditions of scarcity; therefore, it underwent a transformation as America increased production. 'As industrialization shook the idea of the permanence of scarcity', writes Daniel Rodgers, 'the ascetic legacies of the Protestant ethic slowly and steadily eroded, [and] it became harder and harder to insist that compulsive activity, work, and usefulness were the highest goals of life.'[48] What became of the moral life when abundance made 'the fear of becoming poor' less immediate? One response, the moralization of the consumption of leisure time as 'recreation', was rooted in the paternalism of the nineteenth century workplace; another, later response, was the imperative to consume, which, with the advent of the demand for mass consumption could function more efficiently without regard to moral considerations. Yet within this imperative, according to Gertrude Stein, there still lies a certain relation to the father.

In the era of abundance and increasing wages, the emerging prospect of mass leisure might in fact seem like a liberation from the paternalism of the nineteenth century. While this challenged moralists who were concerned to preserve certain cultural values from an emerging mass culture, it also laid the groundwork for a new kind of freedom, and a new definition of democracy in terms of consumption. By the twenties, Ford was not comfortable with what seemed to be the paternalism of his home-inspection programme. He makes it clear that it was not morality or sentimental humanitarian considerations that made him supervise the lives of his workers, but a concern for efficiency. The same concern for efficiency made him approach the question of increased leisure as simply 'a cold business fact'. When discussing 'the value of leisure', Ford considered it best not to dwell on the humanitarian side, 'for then leisure may be put before work instead of after work – where it belongs'.[49] Despite his concern for the morality of workers, an efficient and cold businessman like Ford would not moralize the increased consumption good business requires: 'We are not of those who claim to be able to tell people how to use their time out of the shops. We have faith that the average man will find his own best way – even though that way may not actually fit into the programmes of the social reformers.' The democratization of consumption and free time lays the groundwork for a new conception of democracy as the freedom to consume.[50]

But this ideology reflected an era of abundance and the pressures of the demand for the higher consumption that went along with higher wages. Freedom from the paternalism so strongly rooted in the work ethic was possible only once scarcity had been overcome. With the Depression, scarcity returned, and so, therefore, did 'the fear of becoming poor'. It is important to keep in mind the historical newness of the Depression's conditions of scarcity, and therefore the challenge it presents to the various systems of interpretation historically available to Americans. As Albert Romasco points out, Americans during the Depression 'were a people perplexed by plenty. They saw the nation's productive plant intact, its ability to produce unimpaired. And yet, in a land celebrated for its abundance, the people were plagued by scarcity.'[51] From the various ideologemes available to them, American workers and the middle class would fashion a number of responses. Yet if one draws upon one strand, one begins to discover a knot binding these ideologemes together, which I call the ethic of sacrifice. It begins, as Gertrude Stein detected, with the return of a form of paternalism. According to Richard Sennett, the ideologeme of the freedom and individualism of the worker contended with another, which also served the interests of capital, namely the ideology of paternalism. As workers experienced the contradiction between their economic dependency and the ideology of their freedom and dignity, capital required for its moral legitimation an image not simply of authority, which would openly conflict with the apparent freedom of the worker, but of benevolent authority. Paternalism, according to Sennett the dominant image of benevolent authority in nineteenth-century America, coexisted uneasily with the idea of freedom. During the Depression, therefore, 'people who were caught up in the economic turmoil knew in the abstract that they were in the grip of impersonal forces they could not control; still, they took their misfortunes as signs that they had not been strong enough to cope'.[52]

Nonetheless, the dominant theme of Depression-era political consciousness hardly emphasized the personal failure of Americans. Instead, the central political focus was on the 'impersonal forces' of the capitalist system. Rather than emphasizing that one has failed in one's person, this political or proto-political strategy of interpretation emphasizes that something or someone has failed oneself. The perplexity at scarcity in the midst of abundance in fact generated a frenzy of political activity and analysis on a scale arguably unprecedented in American history. Yet even this emphasis on the impersonal system relies on the political and legal concept that is essential to the contractual basis of the market society, which is the concept of right. This is especially important in the midst of economic collapse. Having become poor in the midst of abundance, one may make the much more political claim that a social contract has been violated, or in a more mythical or spiritual vein, that the idea of 'America' has been betrayed, usually by a certain moneyed class. This does not, however, imply that proto-political discourse or practice always assumed that the problem could be resolved only by new systems or institutions, or a new form of the social contract. Beneath much of the discourse was a strong ethical tendency, of the sort that is evidenced in Europe above all by Spengler's work, which sees the crises of modernity as variations upon what is at root a spiritual, and therefore moral, crisis. Moreover, the proto-political perspective rediscovers in itself what it would seem to have overcome: if the institutions, the beliefs and values by which one lives have been proven false, then one is implicated in the failure, especially if one has recently enjoyed the fruits of prosperity. The fear of becoming poor that Lippmann and Freud refer to pertains to this moral perspective, which is embedded even within the political claim of individual rights.

The return of scarcity after an era of relative prosperity establishes the conditions for the moralization of abundance as excess;[53] outdated ideologemes are pressed into the service of interpreting the economic collapse. Since Ford's 'cold business fact', and not an autonomous value, determines the function of leisure in the period of rising mass consumption, the work ethic remains a viable ideologeme to employ when conditions change. Yet during a period of high unemployment even more functional would be the concomitant ethic of restraint. This may seem an odd claim; how can one practise restraint when there is no possibility of excessive consumption? The traditional ethic of restraint, which has priority over an ethic of work in an economy with high unemployment, cannot return in the same form. It returns not as a guide to conduct, but in a disciplinary form, as the ethic of sacrifice, in order to exploit, even as it provokes, a collective guilt; it demands repentance and sacrifice.

Freud's thesis about melancholia is useful in arguing for the unity of the moral and the political moments in the cultural interpretation of Depression. In melancholia personal guilt and the attribution of blame coexist dynamically, and one of the consequences can be, as Dennis knew, a love of suffering. As I suggested above, Freud sees melancholia as a disturbance of the subjective world provoked by a crisis in the psychic economy:

an object of love, which had been at the centre of the ego's world, suddenly disappears. Yet it need not disappear; in fact, the melancholic need not even know that something has been lost. What does occur, however, is a devaluation of the object that is simultaneously felt to be the abandonment of the ego or a failure of love. The instigating cause of melancholia is complex, and cannot be reduced to a narrative; narratives, rather, explain the felt loss, and the various narrative possibilities conflict with each other, attesting thereby to the ego's ambivalence to the object. Melancholia is the bitter loss of faith or credit in the very possibility of restoring a world; it refuses the investment that the return to economic health would require. However, even as the object is devalued, so is the ego, which continues to believe surreptitiously in the value of what has been discredited. Despite the bitterness and even hatred for the object that has abandoned the ego, or has failed it, melancholia secretly keeps the faith in the missing object, developing strategies to maintain its presence. Though the ego seems to have given up the love-object, it attempts to conceal the 'open wound' by 'setting up . . . the object inside the ego'.

The strategy to preserve what is lost and so restore the world has political consequences. In its demand for love, the ego transforms object-libido into narcissistic libido, 'forcing itself, so to speak, upon the id as a love-object and . . . trying to make good the id's loss by saying: "Look, you can love me too – I am so like the object."' One of the crucial mechanisms for resolving the tension and reconciling the contradictory demands of the ego is, in effect, to look to a leader. When a melancholic comes into analysis, Freud says, the analyst runs the risk of being 'put in the place of the analysand's ego ideal'; 'this involves a temptation for the analyst to play the part of a prophet, savior and redeemer to the patient' – in short, to answer to the demand of the analysand. The impoverished ego subjects itself to its ego ideal, which may go so far as to exercise sadistic control. Returning to the primal, 'direct and immediate identification' at the origin of the ego-ideal (which does not originate in object-cathexis) allows the ego to 'give up' the lost object, but not without a cost in melancholic subjection. By identifying with the lost object, the ego preserves it; thus, the abandoned portion of the ego, in order to assuage its guilt, must suffer for the aggressive feelings it harboured for the lost object, which now, occupying the place of the ego-ideal, takes its revenge. In melancholia, 'we find that the excessively strong super-ego which has obtained a hold upon consciousness rages against the ego with merciless violence, as if it had taken possession of the whole of the sadism available in the person concerned'.⁵⁴

Freud suggests that melancholia differs from mourning in that, for the melancholic, *what* is lost is more important than *who* is lost.⁵⁵ The question of faith or belief ties melancholia into the symbolic structure of the cultural and the social; the ego's identification with the lost object allows it to preserve the ideal, which is embodied in the object, upon which it has constructed a world. Disappointment more than loss or death provokes the regression that allows the ego to derive pleasure in its suffering, its self-sacrifice. This is why economic Depression, as Pound said, is merely the prelude to 'mental depression'. Economic collapse, as I argued above, implicates the entire symbolic structure within which the social and cultural articulations of the ego are founded. Moreover, Depression exposes the collective dimension that makes possible the economic and political individualism of an era of abundance. The collapse of the economy exposes the 'wound' upon which democratic independence is founded, and uncovers archaic social bonds of indebtedness. The economic condition is debt: as Freud says, the ego 'borrowed [the] strength' for repression 'from the father, and this loan was an extraordinarily momentous act', an act that can be crippling even to the mature ego, which, despite its illusion of maturity and independence, 'remains subject to [the father's] domination' by way of the super-ego.⁵⁶ This 'borrowing' puts the ego in debt to the father; the persisting social bond for Stein (as we will see in Chapter 2) is the unconscious subjection of a group of brothers to the ego-ideal, and the result is an 'unconscious sense of guilt' that takes advantage of the economic disaster in order to reinterpret the world of material abundance in moral terms.

In her political and economic ruminations, Gertrude Stein perceived even as she deployed the range of melancholic responses to the Depression, concluding in effect that melancholic guilt exploits economic Depression to revive a latent ethic of sacrifice. Yet for Stein, the roots of the economic and political crisis were to be found in prosperity itself. The demand for and promise of material abundance, along with the emerging democracy based on individual rights, frightened Stein in the 1930s. Dennis's American brand of fascism makes evident that an ethic of sacrifice finds support even in the promise of material abundance – which, as Stein well knew, can serve as much as paternal love to answer to the 'open wound' at the heart of the social. Stein's fear of the new economies of abundance that seemed to be emerging before the Depression seem at first to resemble Durkheim's fear of the increased desires attendant upon the new economic conditions of late industrialism. The similarities between Durkheim and Stein end here, however. While according to Durkheim, the increased emphasis upon and isolation of the private life of economic interests requires regulation by social institutions, for Stein, the private life made possible by money is the condition of a welcome release from paternal authority. Stein proposes a 'barbaric' individualism, rooted in what she calls 'the human mind', as a corrective to what she sees as the emerging individualism rooted in mere 'human nature'. However, Stein's 'private life' is not quite identical with the realm of what Durkheim called *bien être*, or satisfaction. Stein in fact reverses Durkheim's view, and sees the paternal form of social authority as 'filling everything', satisfying consumers rather than limiting consumption and regulating the production of needs and desires by means of social institutions. Unlike the paternal economy of the Spenglerian Political, which 'fill[s] everything', the economy of privacy is, according to Stein, based on *privation*: 'a private life is when not everybody is being fed' (PL 76). Stein clearly differs from Pound considerably in her understanding of the private life, seeing it negatively as the life of privation, rather than as the site for the production and consumption of use values. Stein's ethic of the private life is founded on privation, on the limitation of consumption – and the subsequent rejection, which she shares with Durkheim, of the Good of *bien être*.

Stein is at times a bourgeois conservative, often a libertarian, and at other times she demonstrates an aristocratic nostalgia for a peasant and artisanal tradition. Particularly conspicuous is the American strain of bourgeois moralism that Stein reflects in the form of an ethic of restraint, as seen in the advice offered by one of the father-figures with whom she is in complete agreement: 'As Robinson Crusoe's father said to him the pleasantest state of man is to be neither rich nor poor and to remain in enjoyment of a private life' (PL 76). This bourgeois moralism, animated by what Weber called 'the spirit of capitalism', is best expressed by Benjamin Franklin's values of frugality and accumulation, the stricture that all investment should be productive.⁵⁷ This modest notion of the 'private life' motivates her evident anti-fascism. Stein sees fascist and paternal leaders as promising a plenitudinous satisfaction of consumer demands; historically, therefore, Stein's apparent anti-fascism is best understood as a glimpse of and a fear of the new consumer society and its awakened demands or desires. Her ethic of restraint, which is opposed to liberal, reformist or revolutionary attempts to create a society on what Durkheim considered to be purely economic motives, can go as far as to demand sacrifice and suffering.

Though Stein at times seems to be anti-paternal and anti-patriarchal, the privation demanded by the private life can find political expression in the subjection to the paternal Leader who demands renunciation or sacrifice.⁵⁸ Stein's anti-fascism is thus based on a misunderstanding of fascism, and actually participates in the authoritarian reaction characteristic of so many of the modernists: the bad fascist father, whom she significantly calls 'depressing', is not to be overcome by forces resistant to patriarchy, but by an appeal to a good father. Though it cannot be denied that Stein assumes various stances, at times parodic, and occasionally oppositional, to various patriarchal instances, she is often quite respectful. One of the more puzzling and disturbing moments of respect for a paternal figure is Stein's enthusiasm, in 1941, for Marshal Pétain, the leader of Occupied France. This enthusiasm led her to undertake a translation of *Paroles aux Français*, a collection of Pétain's speeches and radio broadcasts from the thirties through to 1941. Pétain, without calling it by the name we now use, saw a proliferating consumerism as the cause of cultural and spiritual decay, and in his *Paroles* demands sacrifice, duty and discipline from the French. Stein's introduction displays all the fervour of a convert: 'I want to present to my compatriots the words the Maréchal Pétain has spoken directly to the French people, Maréchal Pétain who in the last war saved France by a great victory and in the war has saved them throughout their great defeat.' The anti-liberal, paternal rhetoric of the Marshal's *paroles* infects Stein's introduction: 'We in the United States until just now [after the Japanese attack on Pearl Harbor] have been spoiled children'; as her introduction suggests, Stein thinks this particular patriarch may have some words of wisdom for these 'spoiled children', who are like the decadent liberals who have 'ruined France'.⁵⁹

Stein's critique of fathers remains entirely within the institutions of state and family. Her characteristic attitude towards father-figures is ambivalence of the variety that Freud thought to be a condition of melancholia. In particular, her critique of the paternal leaders of the twenties and thirties (the time of 'Hitlerism and Fascism and Rooseveltism') simply measures them, to their detriment, against a paternal ideal. This ideal is 'the father of a family', who regulates the expenditures and consumption of his spouse and offspring:

> When you spend money that you earn every day you naturally think several times before you spend more than you have, and you mostly do not.... [I]f there was any way to make a government handle money the way a father of a family has to handle money if there only was. The natural feeling of a father of a family is that when anybody asks him for money he says no.[60]

The implication is that the father is a wage-earner, and his family, which is an analogy for the entirety of civil society, is composed of consumers, not producers. Stein's prohibiting father remembers the expenditure of labour, or the *sacrifice*, required for the acquisition of the quantity of money called the wage. His liminal position as a producer at that particular point of the exchange of goods (labour for money) distinguishes him from the mass of consumers whose demands he needs to regulate.[61]

The production of the consumer in the twenties and thirties requires that contesting ultimate values, versions of the Good, be subordinated to *bien être*, which advertises itself as the diminishment of sacrifice and suffering. For Stein, this promise of *bien être*, the promise to end privation, prepared the ground for another form of domination which needed to be resisted with an ethic of sacrifice and suffering. In its weaker form, the ethic of sacrifice is an ethic of work for the sake of work, and the subject of this ethic is a producer. At the end of the war, Stein reveals her enduring commitment to the old conservative, anti-labour union view of work when she calls upon America to 'fight a spiritual pioneer fight' and 'to learn to produce without exhausting [the] country's wealth'.[62] There can be little doubt that she had never learned Henry Ford's lesson that mass production generated the concomitant imperative to consume. In her conservative defence of the private life, Stein follows Spengler's dialectic right up to the transformation of the economics of money into the politics of the will; but the *polis* that returns in the heart of the private life is not the Father as the Spenglerian or fascist Leader. It is something that for her is perhaps worse, namely, the domination of capital in the production of the consumer. But as soon as Stein imagines a politics that might resist this domination, she is required to formulate another kind of domination, that of a prohibitive paternal authority. Yet this too is dangerous, since a powerful leader, such as Roosevelt, may serve the same psychological investments of the subject. Considering Roosevelt's threatened destruction of money, Stein wonders if he has 'an other meaning' inside of him to take the place of money's meaning; the promise of 'an other meaning' points to the material abundance crucial to American reformist or revolutionary politics. Roosevelt's 'other meaning' is not the non-economic end or Good that Durkheim and other critics of the emerging consumer society would want to recall to the economy of goods, but is the Good as a mere intensification of goods. The 'other meaning' appears out of the destruction of money, on the horizon beyond the mediation of the symbolic structure of money that Stein thought protected the ego from domination. But the promise of wealth and enjoyment does not require the delivery of material goods. 'Enough is not enough', Stein writes. Lawrence Dennis proves a useful guide to her meaning: 'enough' in material terms 'is not enough' to heal what Freud called 'the open wound'. The promise of 'an other meaning', a sign of love, is enough to replace what has been discredited. The 'other meaning' may just as well be the paternal domination that melancholic America desires. Nonetheless, though Stein ends up advocating paternal authority and an ethic of production, her perspective can occasion a critique of the very economy her logic exemplified: in opposing fascism *and* the consumer economy, Stein affirms that neither will return the Good that is fundamentally lost; just as the father still experiences in his body the pain that was translated into the wage, so the members of his family must not allow themselves to move too far from the site of suffering.

Therefore, Stein is not simply negating the values of material abundance and happiness; the ethic of suffering is rather more complex. The psychological investment of belief that she recommends (first in money, or failing that, in the prohibitive father) must be justified in some terms that acknowledge what America has become historically. The question remains: what will America get in exchange for submitting to sacrifice? The father who says 'no' to the family, rather than the consuming family members themselves, provides a model for happiness. According to Hannah Arendt, 'happiness' originally designates the moment of relief from the pain of labour, and is therefore a moment implicit in the labour process itself. Without the pain of labour, there could be no happiness; therefore the emancipation of labour and the creation of a society of consumption cannot achieve the happiness that is its highest value. According to Arendt,

> The rather uncomfortable truth of the matter is that the triumph the modern world has achieved over necessity is due to the emancipation of labor, that is, to the fact that the *animal laborans* was permitted to occupy the public realm; and yet, as long as the *animal laborans* remains in possession of it, there can be no true public realm, but only private activities displayed in the open. The outcome is what is euphemistically called mass culture, and its deep-rooted trouble is a universal unhappiness, due on one side to the troubled balance between laboring and consumption and, on the other, to the persistent demands of the *animal laborans* to obtain a happiness which can be achieved only where life's processes of exhaustion and regeneration, of pain and release from pain, strike a perfect balance. The universal demand for happiness and the wide-spread unhappiness in our society (and these are but two sides of the same coin) are among the most persuasive signs that we have begun to live in a labor society which lacks enough labouring to keep it contented. For only the *animal laborans*, and neither the craftsman nor the man of action, has ever demanded to be 'happy' or thought that mortal men could be happy.[63]

As Spengler said, America can have no true *polis*; in a culture founded on the values of *animal laborans*, 'Economics' dominates by symbolizing the Good as material abundance. The value of happiness has a meaning only as relief from pain. In a culture that forecloses the site of pain (production) from the sphere of happiness or satisfaction (consumption), suffering persists as anomie. According to Arendt, the division signals a dangerous disruption in the economy of the human body. The culture of consumption presumes that emancipation from suffering is possible through consumption, which is to say by placing ultimate value on the high point of the cycle of production, and neglecting the role of suffering or pain as a condition of emancipation. Stein poses a similar problem: what Good will occupy the place left vacant once Roosevelt has destroyed money? For money, in Stein's imagination, unlike the material abundance it can be exchanged for, embodies the scarcity and suffering that is the condition of abundance. Roosevelt's 'other meaning' may conceal the site of suffering, just as consumption conceals the sphere of production. The concealment of suffering, for Stein, merely intensifies a constitutive sacrifice.

The experience of suffering persists in the weak form of anomie, or what Arendt calls 'unhappiness'. Stein too would have agreed with Durkheim's conclusion that anomie remains latent even in the regime of achieved satisfaction or *bien être*. Arendt points out that the emancipatory possibility of free time 'rests on the illusion of a mechanistic philosophy which assumes that labor power, like any other energy, can never be lost, so that if it is not spent and exhausted in the drudgery of life it will automatically nourish other, "higher," activities', and so give rise to higher values. The emancipation of labour made possible by the production of the consumer, however, has revealed that 'the spare time of the *animal laborans* is never spent in anything but consumption, and the more time left to him, the greedier and more craving his appetites'.[64] The value of things consumed does not translate into the material plenitude that will gratify need or desire, but paradoxically heightens the experience of scarcity. Yet this constitutive scarcity does not appear as such.

The concealment of suffering can be characterized as melancholic in that it centres on the crisis of 'an unknown loss', a state of emergency requiring all the ideological resources of the symbolic structures of the social and economic, which piece themselves together into a new discourse. The Good of Stein's world is primarily money, and only secondarily or in cases of emergency the father who earns the money, because money is a paradoxically enduring monument to scarcity and depletion. In a consumer society, Arendt suggests, money, or abstract value itself, is the only durable thing (which Stein calls 'a thing non-existing'). Like the labourer who only makes enough to reproduce the labour power expended during the working day, Stein was aware that the moment money is translated into a material good, value begins to be depleted. She knew this despite her simultaneous identification with the merchant, who gambles on an increase of value through expenditure and exchange. But Stein shares the merchant's fear that even money will be destroyed in an economic crisis, provoking a flight to goods. When the economy functions properly, everything but money haemorrhages, and its permanence guarantees that what is of value will not disappear. If money is destroyed, value must be embodied in less permanent goods, which gives rise to the illusion that the 'open wound' of want can be filled with the consumption of material objects. But for Stein, whatever is consumed does not replenish or fill, but deprives; it constitutes a loss not only for the producers from whom a surplus is extracted, but for the consumer. Stein's perspective is melancholic: all goods, but above all money as the Good of goods, embody suffering or deprivation; but only money can guarantee that what is lost will remain.

Stein would, I believe, concur with George Simmel's claim that the constitution of any economy of values is based on *sacrifice*. According to Simmel, 'sacrifice does not in the least belong in the category of what ought not to be, as superficiality and avarice would have us believe. Sacrifice is not only the condition of specific values, but the condition of value as such; with reference to economic behaviour . . . it is not only the price to be paid for particular established values, but the price through which alone values can be established.' Sacrifice, according to Simmel, in what amounts to another critique of the consumerist ideology of *bien être*, permeates all levels of culture and society: 'from the lowest level of satisfaction of wants to the attainment of the highest intellectual and religious goods, every value has to be acquired by the sacrifice of some other value'. Rather than making it a unique and exceptional category, Simmel includes labour within the category of consumption. Simmel does not deny that labour is or can be exploited. Instead, he attributes the extraction of a surplus of labour, much as Veblen would, to the archaic roots of contractual exchange in robbery and violence. The exploitation of labour increases the sacrifice attendant upon the exchange of one's labour in order to extract the maximum amount of profit, which means that the exploitation of labour is simply one in a series of exchanges that constitutes culture as a whole. From behind Simmel's labourer appears the spectre of the consumer: 'the isolated individual who sacrifices something in order to produce certain products, acts in exactly the same way as the subject who exchanges.... The valuations that determine his actions are generally those involved in exchange. It is of no concern to the economic subject whether he invests his property or labour power in the land or transfers them to another person, if the result for him is the same.'[65]

The conclusion to draw from this is that Marx's insight into the exceptional nature of the exchange of labour for the wage should be extended to consumption. Consumption itself implies a sacrifice and a loss, or the extraction of a surplus, that is the condition of value as such, including cultural value. I say this despite the fact that Simmel's concept of exchange as sacrifice, having become current after much neglect, would seem to be opposed to Marx's labour theory of value, which is thus assigned by its critics to an obsolete metaphysics. For example, Arjun Appadurai retrieves from Simmel an interpretation of 'value' which would not separate 'cultural' from 'economic' value, but resituate their interrelation in *regimes* of value, a concept based on the 'formal truth' 'that things have no meanings apart from those that human transactions, attributions, and motivations endow them with'. Christopher Herbert returns to Simmel's concept of exchange as well, in conjunction with Adam Smith's notion of the sacrifice involved specifically in labour, in order to arrive at a concept of value similar to Appadurai's: Smith's and Simmel's account of sacrifice and exchange mean that 'value can never again be conceptualized and fetishized as a positive term, but only taken as a contingent and indeterminate one, subject to potentially endless interpretation.... Value always depends on one's point of vantage and is impossible to grasp except as a conventionalized fiction of a particular social system – which is to say that *it becomes identical after all to its price in money*.'[66] What should be retained of Marx's analysis of surplus value, and what cannot be retained if one insists on an exclusively textual or systemic model of culture, are the division between price and real value. Instead, Marx's crucial category of real value should be understood in the light of the Lacanian notion of the 'symbolic system' of value, which is disjunct from the 'real value' of a phantasmatic 'substance' that is not only a mirage effect of the price system of value, or meaning, but is in the position of the *real* at the limits of the differential symbolic inscription of value – it functions as what Stein calls 'an other meaning' beyond the mediation of the differential symbolic structure, which is in this case represented by money.

In this Lacanian interpretation, 'real value', or the *value of the real*, is not 'merely' posited by the system, but is the most important term to which analysis of the symbolic and the imaginary cultural forms can have reference. Lacan, after anthropologists like Marcel Mauss, would make explicit the idea that a kind of 'sacrifice' is the condition of exchange.[67] Sacrifice makes the normative, historically specific cultural-symbolic mediation of the real and the imaginary possible; but a crucial role is thereby given to what is given up. In the normative accession to the symbolic, with which any one who has encountered Lacan's work would be familiar, there is an ultimate term about which the symbolic is ordered. In his seminar of 1959–60, Lacan calls the real *das Ding*, or the Thing, and what I will call the thing of value.[68] This thing is the *real* of value, just as for Marx labour is the value that is falsely represented by the market price system. The expulsion of the thing is, as it were, the originating moment of economic exchange, upon which future exchanges are founded.

The original sacrifice is an unequal exchange. According to Freud, the ego 'borrowed strength . . . from the father, and this loan was an extraordinarily momentous act'. But the borrowing of funds implies a debt upon which exchange or consumption is based; the act of borrowing is simultaneously the transference or deposit of a certain quantity elsewhere, in exchange for the very possibility of economic and social relationship, that is to say, of the symbolic structure. The ego had to *give up* something for the quantity required for its founding repression. This thing is held in reserve by the father-figure, to whom the ego is indebted. But the melancholic ambivalence to the father is never resolved; a sense of injustice, that one has given up more than one acquired in exchange, persists on the part of the ego.

In economic rather than political terms, the sacrifice of the thing is the condition of the melancholic's paradoxical attempt to preserve it in the congealed form of value. In Stein's version of history, America transferred the thing from the father to the signifier 'money'; however, in the midst of monetary crisis, she would have it transferred back to the father as to a more durable good. This mercantile ethic of sacrifice-as-exchange might be stated in the same terms that give us the speculative economy of melancholia: 'Give up what little you have; only in this way will you get all you want. Sacrifice the thing in order to keep it in reserve elsewhere.' This ethic, which is also fundamentally contractual, does not rely exclusively on the representation of the Good as material abundance; instead, it functions by suspending in ambiguity the representation of the Good between material abundance and another kind of value, as yet unnamed, but which can be appropriated by what Stein calls a 'depressing father'. For this reason, Stein insists that everyone must 'believe in money', since money, an abstract thing, provides the necessary distance from both material goods and paternal authority. However, the structure of 'belief' demonstrates that the ethic of sacrifice shares its ground with the fascism Stein seemed at times to deplore; it attempts to return to the 'politics' that is prior to 'economics', therefore to maintain the foundations of the symbolic structure of the social in belief in the father, or the credit implied by what Freud calls the 'loan'.

Stein disavows the submission to paternal authority implicit even in mercantile exchange. I mean this in the strict Freudian sense of disavowal, which refers to the unshakable belief, on the part of the fetishist, in the persistence and universality of what he or she consciously knows is lacking. To say that Stein disavows the relation to paternal authority means that she both knows it and refuses to know it. But both Pound and Stein require that the site of sacrifice not be effaced. The mass-production of commodities creates a surplus of material culture that, it would seem, compensates for the sacrifice at its origin. Yet, under the specific conditions of industrial capitalism, the material culture thereby produced cannot efface the suffering of the initiating sacrifice, but serves to intensify it. In a discussion that bears significantly on the suffering implicit in Simmel's notion of sacrifice, Elaine Scarry has argued that material culture provides the objectification of the body that is required to relieve suffering, or 'the burden of sentience'; the scene of pain or suffering is the site of the creation of a material artifact. Historically, according to Scarry, the question of suffering in ancient Jewish culture was answered by structures of belief; a material resolution of the problem was forbidden. The Christian resolution to the problem recognized '[t]he advantage of material culture over a culture of belief'. Yet 'the material solution to the problem of belief itself becomes the problem in nineteenth-century industrialism, and so that site comes to require a new form of repair, as in the multiple strategies of distribution that have, since that time, begun to arise from both capitalist and socialist sources'.[69] The solution to this constitutive suffering, for Stein and Pound, is not material abundance but belief in an ideal, or a father – in short, 'an other meaning' that allows for relief through belief. Belief can relieve melancholic guilt through suffering; simultaneously, belief can relieve suffering through melancholic guilt.

The Depression was above all a crisis in the structure of belief upon which capital depends. The pain to be relieved is not the pressure of material want alone, as Dennis perceived, but is a pain on the horizon where the symbolic structure not only of the economy, but of America itself, appears to be haemorrhaging. One of Pound's economic slogans demonstrates that the ideologeme of 'relief', though it seems to concentrate on material needs, could serve to answer the crisis in belief in the symbolic structures of America. 'Relief' can paradoxically be obtained by deprivation, by submission to conditions of scarcity. In Canto 37, Pound states that 'Relief is not got by increase but by diminution of debt' (C 183). The slogan is clear in terms of Pound's economic system: 'relief' from want demands relief from debt by means of a diminution, or better yet cancellation of both public and private debts to the usurious private banks.[70] However, the word 'relief' extends beyond its material economic meaning to signify a complex of concerns. First of all, the demand for relief implies that there is pain and suffering; the word 'relief' itself begins the process of obtaining it, the process of rendering relief material. Yet material relief is only the necessary condition, for Pound, of work of higher value. Moreover, for Pound as for conservative moralists, material relief is dangerous in that it could also lead to a moral turpitude. There is nothing to prevent the suffering worker from becoming bourgeois once relief is provided (SP 354). As we saw in Dennis's claim for fascism, the demand for material relief must therefore be predicated on a further condition, which is at bottom ethical and political. Prior to *relief*, there must be *belief*; there must be 'credit'. This is not peculiar to Pound; there can be little doubt that the mechanism of belief has been crucial to all modern attempts at economic recovery – the modern political rhetoric of crisis always tries to increase confidence, to persuade voters or consumers that the institutions by which they have been living remain worthy of credit. Economic crisis, especially during the Depression, implicates structures of belief as much as it does material concerns.

If the possibility of material abundance and satisfaction always evokes ambivalence, we can exploit the ambiguity of the grammar of Pound's slogan by focusing on the first part of the statement: 'Relief is not got by increase' – not increase of debt, but increase as such, which may add up to a threatening abundance. While Roosevelt's own deficit spending programme supposed that 'increase' of debt was necessary to 'increase' in the sense of economic growth, Pound's own demands for the diminution of debts to the private banks required that consumption be curtailed, that the demand created by a liberal market economy remain unsatisfied for disciplinary reasons. Only then could illicit consumption be corrected by the new economic system founded on the true hierarchy of value, rather than on a system that values the Good of *bien être*. 'Relief' from the pain that takes the form of want is not got by 'increase' (of availability of goods, and thus increase of debt): consumer demand must be limited; an ethic of sacrifice must be imposed. Relief, paradoxically, is got by diminution and privation, an increase of suffering. The very strategy of obtaining relief is melancholic, and therefore doomed to failure. The ambivalence at the foundation of the social in belief or credit maintains the 'open wound' that feeds cultural systems of value.

2
Gertrude Stein's Great Depression

> Quantity is one of the things to think about and how much do you use.
>
> She complains that some who do not live on flat lands do not know how much of anything they use.
>
> What has this to do with money. Nothing at all really and now I will explain all about money.
>
> How do you do all about money.
>
> Money is what they know that they give and take.
>
> Oh yes yes....
>
> Money is very important because anybody can think about that and it has nothing to do with the human mind....
>
> Human nature can mix itself up with it but that is another matter. Really money really has to do with the human mind. (GHA 169)

'DISTRIBUTION AND EQUILIBRATION'

The New Deal challenged American proponents of free-market capitalism by attempting to penetrate what had traditionally, or at least since the nineteenth-century advent of industrial capitalism, been the sphere of 'private life'. For these classical liberals, among whom I will provisionally include Gertrude Stein, what Pound calls the determination of 'the border between public and private affairs' was exclusively an economic, not a political matter. For Pound, on the other hand, the most dangerous threat to justice was the invasion of the public sphere by private interests. The modern form of the 'political', according to Pound, was more often than not a disguise for private, more properly 'economic', interests. In his effort to distinguish the truly 'political' from these economic interests, Pound looked to various historical sources, assured as he was that a model for their proper relation was not, until the glaring exception of Mussolini's politics, to be found in the twentieth century. The articulation of the economic and the political in Pound's case is clearly not the one current in twentieth-century American political discourse, but alludes to a Jeffersonian and, finally, Greek opposition of the private as economic and the public as political. Like Spengler, Pound thought the properly political to have been effectively excluded from the modern world, the determinations of which are thereby thoroughly economic. This is nowhere more true, according to Spengler, than in America. For Stein, in her more traditionally classical liberal moments, this was the way things should be in order to prevent the return of the 'purely political will-to-order' of the ruler who will come to answer the 'craving for a full-size life'.

At her most classically liberal, Stein considered that money serves as the condition of the individual's freedom from the system of the state, or rather from the more total system of what she called 'human nature'. Her notion of 'human nature' was developed during her visit to the United States in 1934, after 31 years of living in France. After returning to the Continent, she worried that America during the Depression was beginning to resemble the emerging European dictatorships. Stein was startled that an intelligent young man could say to her that 'after all we are all glad to have Roosevelt do our thinking for us'. In *Everybody's Autobiography* (1937) she argued that 'There is too much fathering going on now and there is no doubt about it fathers are depressing':

> Everybody nowadays is a father, there is father Mussolini and father Hitler and father Roosevelt and father Stalin and father Lewis and father Blum and father Franco is just commencing now and there are ever so many more ready to be one. Fathers are depressing.
> ... I say fathers are depressing any father who is a father and there are far too many fathers now existing. The periods of the world's history that have always been most dismal ones are the ones where fathers were looming and filling up everything. (EA 133)

'Human nature' attaches itself to the father in order to assure its 'natural' identity. A paternalistic military organization, which Stein calls 'Hitlerism and Fascism and Rooseveltism', lingers on after the First World War, which got everyone into the habit of submitting to 'the comfort of being in uniform and receiving orders'. Human nature is not, however, only a form of behaviour that can be corrected by knowledge: 'everybody knows' that this leftover military structure persists, 'and yet everybody does this'.

For Stein, unlike Spengler, the possibility of such authoritarianism was not a healthy sign of the modern, but a dangerous regression from the advances of American capitalism, chief among which was for Stein the 'human mind' made possible by the universalizing abstraction of money. Stein therefore shared Spengler's insight that (in Adorno's words) 'money and mind go together'.[71] She did not, however, share his enthusiasm for the necessary outcome of the historical dialectic of economics and politics: the overcoming of both money and mind in the 'coming Caesarism' of the properly political order. According to Stein, the noble and invaluable value that she calls 'the human mind' can only be preserved within the market economy that other modernists saw as compromising value.

The private life depends on having money in the hand, and on 'not everybody . . . being fed' (PL 76). In other words, privacy requires someone's privation. 'Depressing fathers' like Roosevelt and Mussolini seemed in Stein's eyes to be taking the 'little piece of money' out of the people's hands, and in doing this they threaten to destroy 'the private life'. By attempting to feed everybody, Mussolini, Stein believes, inevitably draws what Stein calls 'the barbarians' into Rome. The food he gives to satisfy hunger or need weakens his people. The 'depressing' fathers who give their names to 'Hitlerism and Fascism and Rooseveltism' destroy the private life by 'fill[ing] up everything', thereby putting an end to the privation that money implies. As Stein argues, using the example of the French, what the Italians really require is a 'little piece of money' to attract their interest. This 'interest', a sign of the human mind, keeps the French safe from the barbarian invasion. But the piece of money returns with the barbarians of the marketplace, firm believers in money who come to 'enslave everybody' (PL 76): 'Are there any barbarians left to come. Well I suppose there always are, since somebody is sure to be living a private life and anybody living a private life is a believer in money and therefore a barbarian and the barbarians are always strong and those who are fed are always weak. You cannot be strong if you do not lead a private life' (PL 76–7).

On the horizon of the economy governed by the 'depressing' paternal figure, a barbaric monetary or market economy operates, producing a strong people who, unlike 'those who are fed [and who] are always weak', are able to renounce food and defer consumption. The barbarians do not *need* anything; they simply *are*: 'Now do you begin to see the difference between need and is, between human nature and the human mind and of course you do see why it is not interesting to any one who has *need to be* that is who finds human nature interesting' (GHA 172; my italics). The barbarians believe in money, but are far from being hedonists since they are apparently beyond need. They do not indulge their needs or desires, but have managed to sublimate them into a single desire for money.

Thus, Stein's claim that 'fathers are depressing', written when the Depression was well under way, has both a psychological and an economic significance: Depression is caused by the return of the father to an economy that is based on his absence. Stein fears that if Franklin Roosevelt destroys money, he will also destroy private life in a collectivist or a mass psychology. In this moment of Stein's monetary and political theory, as I have said, money is the figure that guarantees the place of the human mind, while fathers take advantage of human nature's identity, even found that identity, at the expense of the human mind. However, though 'human nature' prefers 'identity', or habit and security, it has an ambivalent relation to the paternal remnants of the war: 'They like it to be like war and they hate it to be like war', and this 'makes after war be so foolish'. This ambivalence is fundamental to the structure of identification that is the condition of human nature, but as we shall see, it is also the condition of the autonomy of the human mind. Whereas in Roosevelt's America, everybody does what they are told, the French manage to resist the foolishness of 'after war' because 'they are so interested in any little piece of money that they have in their hand that they do not have to hear what anybody tells them to do' (PL 75). The French know the value of what Stein calls 'the private life', the life not of human nature but of the human mind, which despite Stein's apparent uncertainty (as seen in the epigraph to this chapter) appears to have something 'to do with' money (GHA 169). But as I attempted to demonstrate in the first chapter, money requires an ambivalent identification with the father as its foundation. According to Stein's historical dialectic, periods of belief in money give way to periods of belief in fathers. In *Everybody's*

Autobiography, Stein expresses this dialectical view: 'The Jews and once more we have the orientalizing of Europe being always certain that money is money finally decide and that makes a Marxian state that money is not money. That is the way it is if you believe in anything deeply enough it turns into something else and so money turns into not money' (EA 41). As Stein points out in her characterization of Jews, 'not-money' is the father: 'The Jews and they come into this because they are very much given to having a father and to being one and they are very much given not to want a father and not to have one, and they are an epitome of all this that is happening the concentration of fathering to the perhaps there not being one' (EA 142).

Though she tends to present the conflict within modernity as an opposition between fathers and money, Stein also indicates that these two terms are not exclusive. According to Stein, everybody must believe in money. What protects the barbarians from the father is their 'interest' and *belief* in, 'any little piece of money'. But at the same time, as we have seen, Stein recommends that credit in the father could be the cure for America's economic ills: 'government' should 'handle money the way a father of a family has to handle money'; that is, it must say no (LMN 332). In her monetary theory, Stein is a 'gold-bug' for whom money is essentially scarce. Since money is scarce, the father must say no to the desire for money: not all needs and desires are to be satisfied. Stein's insistence that the private life depends on the belief in money means that the deferral of consumption, that is to say, privation, must be maintained; such a deferral is constitutive of money. It is therefore not quite correct to say that for Stein money is essentially scarce; rather, money *embodies* a certain scarcity, no matter how abundant it might be. Stein sees money as a fascinating or 'interesting' auratic object embodying or materializing a certain lack. Money has an authority built into it that prevents the need for a depressing father to curtail the inflation of consumer demand. Thus, despite Stein's resistance to paternal authority, her notion of the private life, which is founded on the possession of money for private consumption, coexists with a demand for authority. Though the barbarians may seem to have no need of a father to regulate their economy, this is only because they have internalized his authority: what they have learned from him is to curtail their consumption, to limit their needs, to accept privation or castration. Stein's investment in money is fetishistic, in a Freudian sense: it serves to sustain a paradoxical relation to the paternal will as it is expressed in the threat of castration. Money is a fetish in that it is a *disavowal* of castration, both an affirmation and an unconscious denial of paternal authority.

'The human mind' is therefore actually the split mind of a fetishist: both affirming and denying lack, or castration, it simultaneously submits to and rejects the authority of the father. Therefore, in the crisis of Depression, it is to the advice of symbolic fathers, such as Robinson Crusoe's father, that one should attend. The human mind thrives in a barbaric economy that permits it to 'remain in [the] enjoyment' (PL 76) that the father has allotted. The fetishism of the human mind also means that, even though Stein's barbaric monetary economy is regulated by the symbolic father who says 'no', it is permeated also by the refusal to acknowledge the loss of the thing that it has foreclosed. As I argued in the introduction, this refusal points to the melancholic, or 'depressing', condition of fetishism. Fetishism shares with melancholia a refusal to give up the thing of value. While fetishism disavows the loss, thereby retaining the thing in a secret reserve of the split ego, melancholia preserves the lost thing in the very act of giving it up, by identifying with it. Stein claims that 'the human mind is always yes' (GHA 138); but this affirmation is founded on a melancholic refusal to mourn. As we shall see, Stein claims that 'only in America are the dead really dead', so that no one has to 'pay respect' to them (GHA 94–5). The refusal to mourn would seem to Stein to guarantee the autonomy of the human mind, which is made possible by the abstraction of the monetary economy; instead it is a fetishistic disavowal of loss, the prior condition of which is the melancholic relation to the lost thing.

The barbaric economy of the fetish is therefore extremely fragile, and rests only on the 'belief in money'. In order to protect it, Stein has to abandon all of her more aristocratic-conservative social and economic values (to which so many modernists, including Pound but above all Eliot, were committed) and affirm not only the cultural modernism of which she was such a well-known proponent, but also the economic and social modernity of which she was not always so unambiguously supportive. When the Depression forces her to make some fundamental decisions, she finds herself on the side of 'the barbarians' of the market, and not on the sidelines with either the defenders of high culture or the populists of traditional 'popular' culture. As we will see in the rest of this chapter, Stein's aesthetic, cultural, social and economic systems of value resonate with each other because each is determined by the unstable structure of the fetish; each is connected to the other in the system of value that gives rise to the human mind. As we will see, money is the pinnacle of the expression of the thing of value.

Whereas anti-capitalist proponents of culture denounced the false universality of exchange value, for Stein money and universality seem to be identical. This does not mean, as we will see in more detail at the end of this chapter, that Stein anticipates contemporary affirmations of the 'popular' culture of democratic equivalence and exchange. Just as her simultaneous defence of the human mind and of the market cannot presuppose their simple opposition, it cannot presuppose their identity. Instead, Stein foregrounds their conflictual, asymmetrical relation. Though the human mind is like money, this does not seem to imply for Stein any imbrication of the human mind in the monetary economy. In fact, Stein's theorization of 'the relation of human nature to the human mind' was prompted by her discovery that she and her work were put at risk by market forces. Stein always said that she wrote 'for herself and for strangers', not for a coterie of friends or familiars (HWW 71): the distance between herself and her audience is essential to maintaining her autonomy, her 'private life'. In economic terms, Stein values the separation of producer and consumer that is made possible by monetary abstraction: this distance allows the artisan-producer to work without reference to any immediate external control. But these market relations also provide channels for the consumer's demand to return upon the producer in order to influence her production. With the success of *The Autobiography of Alice B. Toklas* (1933), Stein found her autonomy, what she would only then begin to call the private life of her 'human mind', compromised by her celebrity and by the overwhelming presence of an inquisitive audience:

> What happened to me was this. When the success began and it was a success I got lost completely lost. You know the nursery rhyme I am I because my little dog knows me. Well you see I did not know myself, I lost my personality.... So many people knowing me I was I no longer and for the first time since I had begun to write I could not write and what was worse I could not worry about not writing and what was also worse

> I began to think about how my writing would sound to others, how I could make them understand, I who had always lived within myself and my writing. (HWW, p. 63)

In 'What Are Master-Pieces?' (1936), Stein argues that when one is writing, or creating, there is no such thing as succeeding or failing: such evaluative criteria are only possible when an audience is present:

> When you are writing before there is an audience anything written is as important as any other thing and you cherish anything and everything that you have written. After the audience begins, naturally *they create something* that is they create you, and so not everything is so important, something is more important than another thing, which was not true *when you were you that is when you were not you* as your little dog knows you. (LMN 156; my italics)

The artist's or producer's prerogative of 'creation' is usurped by the 'work' performed by the audience of consumers: the consumption of the master-piece 'creates' the scale of values reflected in the resulting work. The general equivalent in relation to which the audience measures the value of the product to be consumed is what Stein in the mid-thirties began to call the 'identity' of the writer, which is opposed to 'entity'. The 'you' of entity, of originary artistic production or creation, the 'you' that is called 'the human mind', is not the same as the 'you' created and recognized by the audience, which demands the familiar identity of human nature. One 'you' is distinguished from the other as essence is from appearance. Stein repeats this distinction in terms of a divided 'value': when 'my success did begin', she writes, 'suddenly it was all different, what I did had a value that made people ready to pay, up to that time everything I did had a value because nobody was ready to pay' (EA 44).

> The thing is like this, it is all the question of identity. It is all a question of the outside being outside and the inside being inside. As long as the outside does not put a value on you it remains outside but when it does put a value on you then it gets inside or rather if the outside puts a value on you then all your inside gets to be outside. (EA 47)

Like the 'you', 'value' is divided into what is beyond the measure of an audience of consumers, that is to say the *real value* that is inside, and the inessential quantity determined by the outside, which is the *price*. The risk involved in success is revealed in the chiastic confusion of inside and outside that results from the circulation of the commodity on the market. But the distinction of real value and price is not absolute: as Stein says, 'all your inside gets to be outside', which implies that there is an actual transfer of quantity from the inside to the outside. Pure interiority does not remain in place, simply concealed by market relations: it is actually there, outside, on the market. Because of this crossing of inside and outside, Stein must defend the market and the money that maintains it: money and commodities preserve the interiority of the human mind – not in the sense that they create the conditions in which it can live *separately* from the market, but because they actually embody traces of the human mind.

It was not always this way, Stein suggests. The time of the 'creation' of a master-piece, according to Stein, is the pure present of entity, of the human mind. Yet the trouble with composition 'now', she writes in 'Composition as Explanation' (1926) is that this model of time as the 'continuous present' is no longer valid after the historical rupture in and of time. (As Stein sees it, the historical break that is indicated in the 'now', and which is one of the central topics of this lecture, is the First World War.) It is important to read the following passage not only in terms of Stein's own aesthetic career, but in a historical sense:

> In the beginning there was the time in the composition that naturally was in the composition but time in the composition comes now and this is what is now troubling every one the time in the composition is now a part of distribution and equilibration. In the beginning there was confusion there was a continuous present and later there was romanticism which was not a confusion but an extrication and now there is either succeeding or failing there must be distribution and equilibration there must be time that is distributed and equilibrated. This is the thing that is at present the most troubling and if there is the time that is at present the most troublesome the time-sense that is at present the most troubling is the thing that makes the present the most troubling. There is at present there is distribution, by this I mean expression and time, and in this way at present composition is time.... (LMN 30)

Notice how the language of the market appears in this passage, with the Jamesian sense that 'now there is either succeeding or failing' on the market for the American. In 1926, then, Stein was aware that the market had come to dominate even the perception or experience of time. The trouble 'now' is that 'the continuous present' has given way to 'time that is distributed and equilibrated' according to an economy that places the human mind or entity at risk. The 'distribution' is related economically to the confusion of inside and outside, as Stein suggests in the term 'expression'. The expression of what is inside places it in the economy of distribution, which disrupts the proper places and identities of values and things by putting them in circulation, or placing them on the market. There is a risk that value will not return; though time is necessary for the return of value, it is no guarantee.

Artistic success and failure depend on the audience's measuring the work or product against an implicit standard or general equivalent – which we have seen in the 'you' of identity, created by the audience. The 'interest' of the human mind is potentially in conflict with the 'interest' of the audience; the work put into circulation in the economy of distribution and equilibration might return to entity as something not recognizable, bearing another value, just as the 'you' created by the audience returns to trouble the 'you' of entity. The market has a certain kind of disciplinary 'governing' built into it, which Stein resists even as she defends the system of private property as necessary to the survival of the human mind. This disciplinary mechanism threatens the autonomy of the entity of creation, obliging one to be who one is, according to the rule of what is in effect a printed and published enforceable contract that one has signed involuntarily. This contract circulates on the market as property that is no longer one's own; yet it returns upon one, bearing one's name, holding one to an obligation to be that identity or commodity. This contract-property, impersonal yet bearing one's name, has the force to enforce, but it does not serve one's best interest, the interest of entity. Stein is ambivalent towards the market because it serves 'interests' that are at odds with each other – it supports the human mind, yet identifies it.

How, Stein asks, can the human mind separate itself from the time of distribution and equilibration without becoming unmodern, European and feudal, without rejecting money and falling prey to a depressing father? Continuing her discussion of the success of *The Autobiography*, which also marked the first time she had made any money of her own, through her own labour, Stein says that she now understands why so many of the young writers whom she admired, 'once they had made a success... became sterile' (HWW 63). Of her own experience of 'succeeding', she writes:

> It did not frighten me, I was enjoying myself. I was spending my money as they had spent their money all the other painters and writers that I had blamed and condemned and here I was doing the same thing. And then the dollar fell and somehow I got frightened, really frightened just as all of them had gotten frightened really frightened these last years, but luckily for me being older the fright has made me write. I say luckily for me because I like to write. It is what I like best. I like it even better than spending money although there is no pleasure so sweet as the pleasure of spending money but the pleasure of writing is longer. There is no denying that. (HWW 64)

Writing and spending money, or consuming, as the audience consumes Stein and her works, differ only quantitatively, in the length of pleasure involved. Writing is a kind of consumption, but a higher form than the immediate and temporary gratification of spending money. While her friends spend their money and become 'sterile', Stein manages to hold on to her reserve, like a miser, thereby remaining creative and fertile. But she still spends, or consumes, and derives pleasure from it, since writing is like spending money and 'there is no pleasure like spending money'. This is because the value of the human mind is only realized in its circulation. Stein qualifies this statement, however, when she says that there is nothing like spending money

> unless you can really have the pleasure of being a miser... and it is hard to be a miser, a real miser they are as rare as geniuses it takes the same kind of thing to make one, that is time must not exist for them. There must be a reality that has nothing to do with the passage of time and it is very hard for any one to have that in them, and not hard almost impossible, but there is no way of having it unless you have it, I have it and so had Hetty Green, oh yes. (EA 154)

Stein has this reality, like the famous miser Hetty Green, but her reality coincides with the pleasure of expenditure rather than reserve alone. However, Stein's ability to spend assumes an at least equal return on the dollar: as a consumer and writer, she spends freely only because consumption serves a miserliness, a hoarding of a certain quantity that 'has nothing to do with the passage of time'. Stein's miser emerges from a long tradition of hoarders; her conjunction of the miser and the liberal spender is perfectly Hegelian in that the expenditure is in the service of the reserve.[72] The question then becomes, what guarantees the return? In other terms, what guarantees that entity will survive its externalization and commodification in the master-piece?

A dropping dollar may seem like a strange parallel or cause for the fright of realizing that one is the creation of one's audience. Entity is what is most proper to oneself, what is 'one' about oneself, as Stein will say; it is what is least subject to the determinations of value by others. Why then should fluctuations in the market affect it? Stein's fear indicates the extent to which the notion of 'entity' and the private act of writing, the creative articulation of entity or mind, is modelled on the possession of property – which is, in a market economy of success and failure, fundamentally alienable. Stein never made this connection explicit, but it becomes evident in the frightening crisis of the autobiography and permeates the notions of entity and mind, which she develops in response to the crisis in order to preserve the value of the elusive quantity of entity. For example, Stein says at the beginning of 'What Are Master-pieces?' that she was tempted to 'talk this lecture' rather than write and read it,

> because all the lectures that I have written and read in America have been printed and although possibly for you they might even being read as if they had not been printed still there is something about what has been written having been printed which makes it no longer the property of the one who wrote it and therefore there is no more reason why the writer would say it out loud than anybody else and therefore one does not. (LMN 148)

She chooses not to because talking, unlike writing, 'has nothing to do with creation'. But writing itself is dangerous because, like material property, it is alienable; writing makes the creation available for mass printing and thus for distribution; inevitably, its original value – indeterminate, undetermined, measureless and invaluable – will be displaced by its exchange value. Though Stein attempts to separate entity, mind and master-piece from the market, her paradoxical celebration of the market expresses the ambivalence Stein feels for it. In this case, Stein rejects the market in favour of the private act of creation. But why does writing have more to do with creation than talking does? If 'talking' is understood as presence with minimal or no mediation, it would seem to appeal more to Stein's apparent desire to maintain self-presence. Similarly, the private manuscript, the schoolgirl 'copybooks' that Stein used to write in, is distinguished from publication or printing in that it is unique like the signature: 'writing' is the craftsman-like or artisanal proximity of intention and product. Though entity appears at times in the Poundian guise of artisanal property, it bears more resemblance to private property in a money economy. Like private property, it is characterized by a material exteriority that makes it alienable; both writing and the possession of private property figure the necessary proximity in distance that is the only means of sustaining the presence and the present of entity. The private manuscript is not valued as the immediate inscription of the human mind, but already participates in the larger economy to which publication would definitively introduce it.

The private 'you' of entity without relation can without difficulty be seen, in its resemblance to private property, as an effect of the market. However, Stein would reject this equation of property and entity. For her, property belongs to the system of human *nature* and *identity* rather than the human mind and entity. She suggests that the self-interest that motivates and justifies the possession of private property can easily be exploited by the state to the detriment of the traditional value of aristocratic autonomy. In the paragraph preceding the one quoted, she argues that the identity of human nature is what makes 'governing' possible: 'If there was no identity [and thus no private property] no one could be governed, but everybody is governed by everybody and that is why they make no master-pieces, and also why governing has nothing to do with master-pieces' (LMN 156). Stein's values at this point are best seen, perhaps, in relation to the tradition of conservative, aristocratic, agricultural attacks on *bourgeois* private property, together with a conservative opposition to the institution of the state in favour of traditional forms of privilege and private property. But of course in other ideological circles, private property is the sole defence against the incursions of the state into the private life. Stein, as we will see, invests in the market as a means of preserving a realm of freedom against 'governing', but private property is an ambivalent thing. It is at the border dividing entity and identity. As we shall see, property is only the *relative* expression of the value of entity; Stein's defence of the human mind against the dangerous and crucial 'now' of the historical present, or the 'present' of the historical now, the present of the market, ultimately requires a defence of money, which, as I will argue in the next two sections of this chapter, is the *absolute* expression of value.

Private property acquired on the market is no guarantee against loss, and Stein finds it necessary to invest in something more stable, something that embodies value itself and guarantees her investment. Private property, which is alien and alienable, is not abstract enough to entify the human mind. Entity or mind are not property as much as they are money, which as pure quantity is the pinnacle of the expression of value.[73] Stein preserves entity and mind in money, *and not in use value*, not in artisanal or even bourgeois private property. Money is both material, like private property and human nature, and at the same time is immaterial or abstract, like the human mind; it is an exteriority that embodies pure, empty, interiority. Stein's human mind is not opposed to things, but must be *entified*, must be presented as a thing *outside of the person*. That exteriority is the domain of the authentic quality of the human mind, which paradoxically is pure interiority.[74] But as soon as this entification takes place, the threat of identification persists. Stein's economy of mind and nature is thus structured about this ambivalence: the mind requires things in order to present itself, yet things in a market economy can only serve to relativize and commodify the human mind.

'MONEY IS NOT GIVE BUT SELL'

As the last section attempted to make clear, economic discourse provides Stein with a system of analogies for her aesthetic theory and practice, but the two regimes are often at odds with each other. As she reflects on the new market temporality of 'equilibration and distribution', she betrays a longing for an older economy 'when you were you', that is to say, 'when you were not you as your little dog knows you' (LMN 156) – the economy of 'the continuous present'. The gift of the present is embodied in the aesthetic 'master-piece', 'something that is an end in itself and in that respect... is opposed to the *business of living* which is relation and necessity' (LMN 151; my italics). The 'business of living' neatly sums up the familiar modernist perspective that Stein's economics and politics often assume, opposing the aesthetic to 'business', and to the 'life' such business sustains: the life served by the instinct of self-preservation and survival, operating according to the principle of utility and the retentive instincts of the miser – 'human nature' as a system designed to function in the realm of scarcity and 'necessity', as Marx would point out. Yet as the economic analogies discussed in the last chapter make clear, the traditional aristocratic and anti-utilitarian values of nobility – values inherited by the modernist aesthetic – coexist uneasily in Stein with an unrepentantly 'American' affirmation of the practice of 'business'. Though Stein's ambivalence towards the market makes her lean occasionally towards the economy of an archaic nobility, she is far too self-consciously modern (among other reasons) to embrace it.

Traces of the older economy remain in the moment of creation, the time 'when you were you'; in spite of the market economy, this moment persists as a gift, a 'continuous present'. Stein describes the creative act, indicating the manner in which the aesthetic intuition of the master-piece appears: 'I was just thinking about anything and in thinking about anything I saw something. In seeing that thing shall we see it without it turning into identity, the moment is not a moment and the sight is not the thing seen and yet it is' (LMN 154). The thinking concerns a particular 'anything', but the intuition is double: the 'thing seen' is a 'sight' that both is and is not the thing seen. It would seem that 'the thing seen', the intuition, is part of the phenomenal series of 'human nature', while 'the sight', the negation of 'the thing seen', connects with the series of the 'human mind'. However, the terms 'sight' and 'thing seen', are interchangeable; neither one goes beyond the visual reference of the other. How can the sight not be the thing seen, and the thing seen not be the sight? The intuition is single but divided, or double. The two terms are bound by and despite the negation, 'not', which returns the eye from the sight to the thing seen. Stein's 'not' returns to the 'sight', distinguishing it from itself, presenting a 'thing seen' that cannot be seen or presented apart from the 'sight' that it negates.

This 'sight' provides the clue to what kind of a thing a master-piece is: aesthetic intuition is a form of fetishism. This becomes particularly evident when Stein is at pains to distinguish the aesthetic experience of the master-piece from the pathological affect of fear to which human nature is prone when it is threatened, as Stein's human nature was threatened by the collapse of the dollar. In 'What Are Master-pieces?', Stein says that the human mind, unlike human nature, is not frightened at what the master-piece presents, namely the fact that 'time and identity do not exist'.

> We live in time and identity but as we are we do not know time and identity everybody knows that quite simply. It is so simple that anybody does know that. But to know what one knows is frightening to live what one lives is soothing and though everybody likes to be frightened what they really have is soothing and so the master-pieces are few not that the master-pieces themselves are frightening no of course not because if the creator of the master-piece is frightened then he does not exist without the memory of time and identity, and insofar as he is that then he is frightened and insofar as he is frightened the master-piece does not exist, it looks like it and it feels like it, but the memory of the fright destroys it as a master-piece. (LMN 154–5)

In Stein's view, this knowledge may have nothing to do with the 'memory' that constitutes human nature, but it does have something to do with another kind of memory, which Stein describes as 'the memory of the fright'. Though Stein claims that the master-piece has no fright in it, a traumatic fright is its constitutive condition. We could schematize this in Stein's terms as follows: when the master-piece presents itself, human nature is frightened to learn that time and identity do not exist; human nature dies at this moment, and from this death emerges the human mind. The human mind therefore is founded on this constitutive fright, and yet is independent of it: it is 'without the memory of time and identity'. Yet a certain form of memory is required, even if it cannot be called the 'memory of the fright'. The master-piece, as a fetish, is not a memory of the fright, but a memorial to what it allows one to forget; it marks a rift in the ego between 'the human mind' and a sacrificed and encrypted 'human nature', where 'the memory of the fright' lays buried. The Steinian 'master-piece' is in fact aptly described by Freud's analysis of the fetish as 'a memorial' to 'the horror of castration'.[75] According to Freud, it is precisely the terrifying 'knowledge' of castration – as the exercise of the paternal will – that the fetishist unconsciously disavows. He or she *knows* that there is castration, that the mother has no phallus; but in order to reduce the terror of that knowledge, he or she *believes* nonetheless that there is no castration.[76] Freud says that 'when the fetish is instituted some process occurs which reminds one of the stopping of memory in traumatic amnesia'. The fright must be *disavowed* in order for the human mind and its master-piece to present themselves. The fetishistic glance stops the glance at an intuition just prior to the traumatic perception, allowing the fetishist not to know what it has already perceived; in Stein's terms, 'the human mind believes in a glance' that the thing of most value is still there (GHA 171).

Stein's analysis of the master-piece in relation to the fright it causes has a direct connection to her own experiences of fear. As we have seen, one of her most important meditations on fright was instigated by the collapse of the dollar at the beginning of the Depression. Stein emphasizes another occasion on which she was frightened, which both illuminates the fright at the drop in the dollar and brings out the implicit scopic dimension of the fright. For someone so excited about modernity, Stein had little contact with its most pronounced technological phenomena. When she had occasion on her visit to the United States to 'broadcast' over the radio, it confirmed her model of the ideal relation of the writer to his or her audience: 'In writing *The Making of Americans* I said I wrote for myself and strangers and this is what broadcasting is' (HWW 71). But one experience with new technology disturbed her; the disturbance is related to the other possible relation to the audience, which we have considered above. Stein was asked, and agreed, to make a newsreel:

> and so they proceeded to make one and I did just what they told me and it was not even astonishing and it certainly was not natural but they made one. Then they told me it was successful and they asked me to go to see it. And I did. It was a strange thing that happened to me. One never gets quite used

to seeing one's name in print no matter how often it happens to you to be that one; it always gives you a shock of a slightly mixed-up feeling, are you or are you not one. No matter how often it happens there is always this thing, but what is that, imagine what is that compared to never having heard anybody's voice speaking while a picture is doing something, and that voice and that person is yourself, if you could really and truly be that one. It upset me very much when that happened to me, there is no doubt about that, if there can really not be any doubt about anything. (HWW 68)[77]

In another, unpublished description of the same event, Stein emphasizes the 'fright' and the 'shock' of seeing her speaking body on the screen:

> It was awful. That is awful to me. I do not suppose anybody who hears all about it can understand, but it was like a second Saint Therese in the opera, I realise now it might have been a shock to the first Saint Therese to have a second Saint Therese. It was a shock to me. It is a shock to one much as one is used to it to see one's name unexpectedly in print in a book or in a newspaper, it happens often but even so every time you see it it is a little a startle to you. But to see the whole of yourself and your voice it was more than a fright and a startle the same thing but so much more.[78]

This should be read in conjunction with the 'fright' Stein felt when the dollar dropped in value, which was related to the sense that her human mind or entity was threatened by her celebrity: observing the newsreel, Stein sees herself on screen as a simulacrum circulating in an ambiguous disembodied body, *like a commodity on the market*, subject to the evaluations of others and the vicissitudes of the price system. If a saint, like entity, is above the market, nothing prevents its plaster or plastic simulacra from circulating in exchange, or its image from appearing on screen; but what is worse is that the image is thus held fast on film, like what is held fast in the printed book, and is thereafter no longer one's own property. This simulacrum stands before the theater audience in place not of the real thing, but effacing the all-important gap between the writer and the audience of strangers. The value of entity thus becomes subject to the determinations of identity, to 'relation and necessity'. One's property is no longer one's own, but is circulating and being consumed by others.

In the cinematic moment in which Stein or the saint is (dis)embodied, the gift of entity becomes alienable property, which can never be truly 'private'. It circulates publicly, and returns upon one as a model of what one is, and, in its imperative dimension, what one must be, as if according to a contract. Therefore, it is *permanent*, it is the embodiment of one's value, one's general equivalent, that against which one is measured. What Stein sees on screen is her public self, the centre of a system of value constituted in the gaze of the audience. Immediately this provokes the ambivalence Stein holds towards value in general: where is the human mind in this system of value? This moment on screen puts her empirical self, in its material body, not so much in the place of human nature or the human mind as in the place of particularity, as what will not in the end survive its symbolization on film. The 'wholeness' of Gertrude Stein on screen gives the off-screen Stein a fright because she is in the position of contingency, particularity and mortality.

At the same time, the public Gertrude Stein on the screen, which embodies everything that she is and ought to be (according to the contract), is also a commodity; as the Depression made apparent, this means that its value is subject to the market. What Stein realizes when the dollar drops is that this alienation of one's entity into identity means that, if the market collapses, if inflation devalues the dollar or even if deflation causes prices to collapse, one's substance may disappear. Stein's shock and fright are thus signs of a possible collapse in the economy, the system of distribution and equilibration that serves to preserve and distance the thing that one is. The economy constituted across the poles of human nature and the human mind conceals a thing beyond its measure, but its oppositions attempt to temporize, that is, both to defer and guarantee, the presence of this thing – which always disturbs the economy while providing its impetus.[79] But it also always returns upon one as a *missing quantity*.

Stein's fright before her own image cannot be submitted to her dualistic opposition of mind and nature, or entity and identity, since the place in which the thing is held in reserve is unstable, disappearing in a chiastic relation of essence and appearance. Yet – if I may speculate beyond this example of the fright at seeing herself on film – it is not only the fear of loss that strikes

Stein; it is also the fear of the abjection implied by the melancholic debt, which is the imperative form in which the missing quantity returns as missing. We could say that the gaze of the audience is not in itself significant, except in so far as it implies another gaze. Like the fetish, this missing quantity implies and requires a certain economic relationship to the father. Stein recognizes, in the crisis of seeing herself on screen, that the system of value is pinned together by an unacknowledged guarantee. The place of what is beyond value, of what is immeasurable, requires that a third term be sustained in the chiastic dialectic of nature and mind, entity and identity, or essence and appearance. I am pushing this speculative interpretation of the cinematic crisis because this moment itself pushes the dualism of Stein's vocabulary to the point where a third term is required in Stein's 'economic' reflections on value and the market. The ghost of an abstracting and universalizing third term lurks behind the screen of Stein's anecdote, and in a parallel discourse in Stein's text it assumes the form of money. Money, like Stein's commodity-body on screen, is split between the absolute and the relative, or between the abstract universal and material particularity. It serves as a figure of what is inadequately figured by 'the human mind'. The split in money is like the split in the word 'you', between entity and identity – the essential you 'when you were you that is when you were not you as your little dog knows you' (LMN 156). Value itself is subject to unseen processes of evaluation, of inflation and deflation.

To destroy money, as Stein thought Roosevelt was trying to do, is to destroy the social bonds constituted by the deferred and disavowed debt, bonds created in the foreclosure of the thing and the constitution of fetishistic exchange. According to Stein, Roosevelt as the imaginary father threatens to repudiate the symbolic debt by destroying money and substituting it with what Stein calls an 'other meaning inside of him' (PL 72). Stein considered 'fathers' to be 'depressing' because they 'fill everything', all the gaps in the symbolic, with an imaginary completion; that is to say, they deny castration and the symbolic debt. This suits the melancholic subjects of the father, since they are concerned to conceal the fact that something is missing from its place. However, the melancholic inability to mourn means that another form of payment will take the place of the missed payments of respect to the dead; one has little choice when it comes to incurring the symbolic debt. Stein's fathers, accordingly, might also be considered to 'fill' *time* with memory, which is the condition of mere human nature. The memory the fathers keep is the records of debts and expenditures, or bonds of obligation. Stein celebrates the American freedom from mourning, but at the same time she sees America paying the cost for the refusal of the symbolic debt. In this light, Stein's version of family relations is telling. The lines of communication, or 'relation', between 'brothers', she claims, are drawn by letters. But what is of interest for the moment is the topic discussed in the letters:

> Everybody who has a grandfather has had a great grandfather and that great grandfather has had a father. This actually is true of a grandmother who was a granddaughter and her grandfather had a father.
> He had brothers and they lived on where he had come from. They always wrote to one another. At any time anybody who knows how to write to one another can write to one another. But what do they write about. They tell about the weather and sometimes what they have sold never what they have given to one another because and never forget that, they always have they always did they always can sell anything that is something to one another. You may say I think you may say that no one can really give anything to anybody but anybody can sell something to somebody.
> ... And the human mind can live does live by anybody being able to sell something to somebody. That is what money is not give but sell. Believe it or not that is what money is and what the human mind is. The human nature perhaps not but of what interest is human nature.... (GHA 102–3)

Notice that the father's brothers 'lived on where he had come from'. This 'living on' has at least three senses: first of all, the brothers survive him, 'live on' after him; secondly, they 'live on' the land; and finally, they 'live on' it in the sense of making their profit from it, the money and sales they 'live by'. But whose land is this? The father's brothers seem at the same time to be his sons; they are brothers 'that he had', that he fathered; the brothers 'live on' their ancestral land, which was passed on to them by their father. Stein leaves room for one of the brothers to occupy the place of the dead father. The brothers are not all equals; one of them has precedence over the others, as a 'father'. Their exchanges are made possible, then, by their patrimony. Stein's idyll of the letter-writing brother-merchants conceals and reveals that they are haunted by the attendant debt and guilt of this patrimony, which their system of exchange is designed to disavow.

Stein opposes the 'sale' to the usual notion of familial 'gifts' of inheritance. What Stein liked about money and sales as opposed to giving is that they depersonalize social economic relationships in a way that gift exchange cannot. The classical-liberal view of money that Stein adopts states, in the words of Marcel Mauss, that 'there has only been economic value where there has been money, and there has only been money when precious things, themselves intrinsic forms of wealth and signs of riches, have been really made into currency, namely, have been inscribed and impersonalized, and detached from any relationship with any legal entity, whether collective or individual, other than the state that mints them'.[80] Mauss proposes that prior to 'money' as an instrument of exchange is a system of credit, based on gift exchange. The exchange of gifts is fundamentally off-balance; the abstraction of 'equivalence' never enters the equation. This asymmetry keeps things circulating, and maintains social ties of debt. Money emerges from the reduction of an economy founded on such credit; it replaces credit and debt with symmetry, the equivalence of exchange: each party can leave the exchange without the ties of debt. Compared with 'money' understood in this way, even contractual relationships are a remnant of the older economy because they imply a period of indebtedness. Contracts defer the return of the equivalent of the quantity of labour expended, and therefore occupy an ambiguous realm between exchange and debt, serving to conceal their difference. Money can fulfil a contract because it embodies the quantity of value that would otherwise be deferred by the contractual promise. Even paper money serves as embodied value, or value present to itself.

According to Mauss, however, the definition of money as impersonal and abstract serves the ideology of capitalist democracy, and ignores the genealogy of money in archaic relationships of gift exchange. However, as the development of paper money makes clear, money is only a social promise for the eventual restitution of the value of labour expended or thing sacrificed. Between individuals who have effected a contract, money as means of payment (as wages, for example) fulfils the promise by providing a 'thing', money, that embodies the promised sum; but the condition of the value of this thing is a further social guarantee. As a promise and contractual guarantee of a return on what one has given up, money is the sign of something deferred, hence missing. Stein says that she 'was most awfully shocked' when she first saw '[her] father's business books' and discovered that '[t]here were so many debts it was frightening'. The lesson Stein learned seemed to have stuck with her: 'I found out that profit and loss is always loss . . .' (EA 143). Stein was shocked because they had never lacked for money; her father, who had only recently died, had always made a profit. Stein discovered upon her father's death that money as a positive quantity in the hand is 'always loss' because it is a surplus that appears in the place from where the thing is missing. The condition of the money-thing is a prior symbolic contract assuring that the thing that guarantees the value of all other things is held elsewhere in reserve. The market-economy of 'sales' and the principle of equivalence is thus based on the temporization of the thing that is beyond equivalence, beyond measure.

Therefore, money is not founded on equal exchange but on a fundamental asymmetry: on the debt to the father. The brothers 'live on' where their father 'had come from', and this dangerous paternal inheritance or vestigial gift is fundamental to every commodity, including and especially money. 'Sales' require this initial credit or debt in the origin. An infinite debt permeates the monetary economy, and the dead father is the potentially despotic creditor. The enthusiasm with which Stein embraced the capitalist marketplace only measured the anxiety with which she perceived the burden of the gift that money bears with it. Money and 'sales' are constituted by a disavowal of debt, and the private life of the bourgeois individual is constructed in relation to this other economy of credit, which haunts exchange. Stein's 'sale' is an exchange among *brothers*, but the money they use is divided between this apparent equivalence and a fundamental asymmetry; it is split, like a fetish, by an infinite debt foreign to the measure of money. Stein's affirmation of the 'sale' is a disavowal of the ambivalent 'gift' or patrimony that makes the market possible. Thus, despite her antipathy to the economy of the paternal gift, Stein recognizes that 'sale and sale and sale is not money' (GHA 110); 'not-money', as we have seen, is the father as the object of belief. Though Stein frequently insists that 'money is money', she also insists, fetishist that she is, that 'money is not money'. Stein dramatizes the fetishistic split in the subject of the monetary economy in a dialogue between two people (perhaps brothers) named 'Edgar':

> Money is not money said Edgar to Edgar. What do you mean by that said Edgar, I mean by that said Edgar that money is not money if you do not owe money to another. Oh yes yes said Edgar. But you always do you do always owe money to another, no said Edgar. No.
> ... Edgar said that money is not money if you do not have to give money to somebody else. Suppose said Edgar you owe yourself money then it is not money, oh yes it is said Edgar. Edgar did not listen to Edgar because he knew better than Edgar. (HWW 146)

Edgar decides 'that they need hours to think about that', but it should be clear by now that I am inclined to agree with Edgar, who has benefited from Stein's discovery that 'profit and loss is always loss'. We have seen how money can turn into 'not-money', and assume the figure of the depressing father. What identifies money and not-money is debt. This means that, whatever freedom comes to the brothers through their ability to sell commodities to each other, the constituting moment haunts their exchanges. The violent exclusion, one of whose moments Freud presented in the form of the murder of the primal father, has only limited success; what is excluded returns and like a vampire demands something from the living. In America, 'when anybody is dead they are dead' (GHA 70): 'Please play and pay all respect to the dead, but not in America not where a country is so big that it is divided one part from the other by ruled lines and it has to be flat, or there is no hope of it not paying respect to the dead' (GHA 94–5). America is a nation of democratic merchant-brothers, the father of whom is dead and gone. But notice the 'ruled lines' that 'divide' the nation: the communication between brothers may be radically divided by an ambivalent identification. The 'ruled lines' imply a ruler, a despot whose shadow returns in the historical figures of Teddy and Franklin Roosevelt, two of the depressing fathers who will destroy the monetary economy by 'filling everything'. The *respect* due to the dead father is payment for a debt of which the merchant brothers are not completely free, one that is inscribed in the 'lines' of their descent, as well as on the lines that map out the paternal land they live on and by – in 'the geographical history of America'.

At a certain point, with value threatened from a number of sides, Stein will no longer be able to sustain her paradoxical, fetishistic political economy. Stein's fetish is money, which disavows both moments of domination we have been considering, the 'governing' of the market on the one hand and the father on the other. Money, as I have argued, appears to Stein as value in the form of self-presence, rather than value deferred; this serves as a figure for the self-presence of the human mind or entity. At the same time, however, that value depends on a disavowed debt to the father who is in possession of the thing beyond value. The 'depression' instigated by the return of the fathers to the market economy reveals the melancholic dimension of the relation to the lost thing, and thus also the bonds to the father. Recall that, according to Stein, the belief in money can turn round once again into its apparent opposite: credit in the father. In her self-imposed role as propagandist for Marshal Pétain, Stein herself will appeal to the 'faith' she and the rest of France have in the him, even going so far as to emphasize her conversion from unbelief to belief, in what is in effect a public confession of her earlier guilt: 'We have not all of us and I too have been of that number over here in France always had faith in the Maréchal but in the end we have all come to have faith....' In her introduction to Pétain's *Paroles*, she can be judged as she herself judged the American who said 'we are glad to have Roosevelt do our thinking for us'. Her fetishism assumes a more archaic, feudal form: the father is the object of faith and belief.

The symbolic and the imaginary fathers are two forms in which the thing is guaranteed. Money, the commodity of commodities, also guarantees the survival of value in exchange. However, in all three cases, the source of credit itself, the real upon which the symbolic networks of desire draw for their meaning and value, is not implicated in exchange, the 'distribution and equilibration' that requires the lack and distance at the basis of both the symbolic and the imaginary. The real is self-identical; therefore, the real father embodies the real itself. What Stein represents as France's and her humble and repentant submission to the truth of the Marshal is submission to the symbolic father of the law, but in his moment as the real father. The symbolic promises and defers, but for Stein, Pétain himself is utterly self-identical – like money. He has no need to promise: he is. This identity is not that of the imaginary, 'filling' father, because the submission is premised on guilt, loss and sacrifice – not in exchange for anything, but as ends in themselves. The real father institutes a regime of necessity and survival, based on strict discipline. There will be no more spoiled children, only dutiful ones. Because of this sacrifice, the absolute value beyond value is preserved – in the place of the father.

But the securing of stability by submission to the authority of the father does not establish a permanent social harmony. Recall that for Stein the barbarians were at the gates put up by the non-believers in money; similarly, Stein says that people in France (though as she would later say everybody 'had so many points of view so many points of view so many points of view' going on 'inside them in each one of them')[81] want Pétain to remain in power because if France were to be without him, the English 'would insist on bringing back into France all the people who helped ruin France'. This attitude hardly reflects the 'ethics of the remainder' that has been attributed to Stein. The new order held together by Pétain must exclude liberals and spoiled children, until they are willing to acknowledge their debt and their guilt, and submit to the authority of the father, the object of belief. That Stein could at any level place a value on a community that founds itself on guilt and debt might seem rather surprising for two reasons. First, the Stein who became canonical in the seventies was interpreted primarily in terms of a more contemporary form of liberalism, whether feminist or postmodern. Stein's profoundly ambiguous politics did not receive the attention that her transgressive texts did; as was the case with most criticism of Pound, the literary work was divorced from the political commitments. The second and more important reason that my claim may be surprising is that, for those who are aware of Stein's classical liberalism, it would appear that Stein's affirmation of the market is possible by virtue of the fact that she is free of any concern for guilt and debt as founding social relationships. After all, Stein seems able to assert casually during the Depression that not everybody should be fed.

But if we accept the hypothesis that Stein's politics and economics have a fetishistic structure, none of this should in the end be too surprising. What her political and economic contradictions demonstrate is not that Stein was morally culpable in any sense, but that she like Pound was deeply committed to the utopian impulse of modernity. Her contradictions are a measure of the historical limits she encountered in attempting to articulate that which is of most value to the Enlightenment, which she calls 'the human mind'. Though, as I have pointed out, 'the human mind' assumes in Stein's political economy the form of the bourgeois individual, it actually allows her to think through that which in her utopian impulse exceeds what can be accounted for by her free-market individualism. This thing raises the questions of universality and community. This is why her concern for the human mind is addressed in terms of a group of barbarians, not in terms of individual heroes. Only believers in money constitute a group that can be valued as a community that preserves the human mind. For Stein during the Depression the free-market barbarians are the last historical reserve of the human mind, which is under siege in modernity. Given a different historical moment, Stein will locate the human mind elsewhere, not in the market or with barbarians. In 1941, as we have seen, the closest we get to the human mind is in the sacrifice of all of the values Stein affirmed throughout the thirties. The contradiction between Stein's affirmation of economics over politics in the thirties, on the one hand, and her turn to paternal politics in 1941, on the other, attest to Stein's attention to the historical vicissitudes of the promises of the Enlightenment. She perceives these vicissitudes in the destiny of the human mind in a familiar modernist fashion: as signs of disaster and loss.

'THERE IS ALWAYS THIS THING, WHAT IS IT'

Stein's 1941 appeal to Pétain as object of belief is only a last and desperate measure, which raises her enthusiasm to a level one does not often see in Stein's political statements. As we have seen, the father is only called upon when the belief in money, and therefore the human mind, fails. But this means that a relation to the father persists throughout the historical transformations of the economy of modernity; the relation to the father, which itself shifts historically, is the condition under which the human mind can exist, if it exists at all. For Stein, as I have said, this condition means that what is of most value is dependent on that which threatens it the most; in her crucial example, the value of money will be depleted by the emergence of the 'depressing father'.

Stein, unlike Pound, does not identify 'what is of most value' with culture or Kulchur. One of the reasons she is such an interesting example of the modernist utopian impulse is because of the fluidity of her notion of value. Economic value and aesthetic value clearly predominate, and even these two are frequently crossed in her discursive texts. This means that 'what is of most value' can be located in neither of these regimes exclusively, and is inadequately named in either. What is of most value slips from the symbolic systems that attempt to place it in reserve. However, it is possible to identify the manner in which value finds whatever place it occupies in Stein's text. In virtually all of her relevant theoretical and literary texts, one can see at work a fetishistic strategy to attend to the presence of what is of value while disavowing the relation to the father. Such disavowal is the very condition, in Stein, of the presence of the human mind; this also means that it is the condition under which the Enlightenment promise of universality as community will be realized. Though, as I said above, Stein's commitment to the human mind might seem to preclude the notion of community, the opposite is true. In this section I want to explore the ways in which the economic, political and aesthetic regimes of discourse interpenetrate in Stein's text, in order to trace Stein's commitment to the value of community.

In a gesture that recalls the way she places the human mind in property while holding it back from the market, Stein both preserves the human mind from and immerses it precariously within history. What allows her to sustain this contradiction is a fetishistic distinction between the being and the existence of the human mind. In *The Geographical History of America*, Stein struggles to identify the human mind without relegating it to the 'identity' of human nature. She describes human nature as 'anybody being there where they are', a tautological formulation that marks the location of some substance or presence that is or exists where it is; it is therefore identical with itself. This is why Stein insists that the human mind 'does not exist'. One must be wary, according to Stein, of the fiction that acts 'as if' the human mind is 'there', 'existing', because such a fiction would turn the human mind into time and identity, or human nature: 'Have master-pieces anything to do with what you see, no because what you see is as if it were there. And where is it. It is there. Therefore when you read about it as if it were there then it is not a master-piece' (GHA 239). The human mind *'never is* because there is no time and no identity in the human mind' (GHA 185; my italics).

But, as we have seen, the human mind is divided against itself; the internal division effected by its disavowal of the relation to the father is a necessary condition of the hypothesis of the human mind, and at the same time poses the danger that the human mind will be identified with human nature, which attains its form in submission to the father. Therefore, even as Stein insists that the human mind does not exist, she must find a way of insisting on its presence, without formulating that presence as existence: *'there is* the human mind. Oh yes *there is* a human mind. Not entirely at a glance not at all at a glance' (GHA 76; my italics). The phrase 'there is' performs a double function: it both points to something as empirically self-evident, while simultaneously asserting the existence of something that may or may not be present; since the human mind 'does not exist', these two gestures are in this case at odds with each other. The second gesture of pointing is a rhetorical appeal to the audience's faith in the speaker. And since the human mind (unlike human nature) is not immediately present as a thing, even the assertion of existence calls upon belief. Neither act requires the evidence of the thing's presence; instead, the human mind relies on credit for evidence of its own presence. Though the human mind 'is' and 'is there', it cannot be seen 'entirely at a glance not at all at a glance'. A 'glance' can only inform us that 'human nature is not the human mind'; and even this is something it knows only in pieces: the human mind is known only as what is not human nature, and that knowledge is only available '[o]nce as a piece. Twice or more as a piece'. As its name makes apparent, even a 'master-piece', Stein's favoured intuition of the human mind, is still only a piece of the whole. And of course this negative 'knowledge' of the human mind is supported by 'belief': 'The human mind believes in a glance' (GHA 171). Stein's glance of belief sees 'something', but the appearance is not a fiction of existence, an 'as if'. Such a fiction would insist on the self-identity of the human mind; instead, what Stein requires is that the paradoxical topology of the human mind take priority over the problem of its existence: *'there* is a human mind'.

Fetishistic belief maintains the symbolic *place* from which the human mind is *missing*. The thing that is the human mind must be missing from the place it occupies; this implies that it not only does not 'exist' as such, but also that it has never been present in its place. Unlike other modernists, Stein never calls upon memory as evidence of the persistence of the thing she calls the human mind. In fact, she is especially concerned to avoid thinking in terms of an economy of loss and restitution, and insists instead that what is lost is not really lost because it was never present. Stein's logic is melancholic: it is necessary to lose the human mind in order to preserve it. Then of course one must conceal its loss, just as one must not pay respect to the dead; it is necessary not to remember: 'In case of there not being any possibility of remembering and therefore no way of *not losing what is not there where you are* is there any way of enfeebling imagination. Indeed what is imagining anything. Is it done a little at a time or is it done a whole at a time and is it done all the time' (GHA 234; my italics). The negations in this passage are as usual difficult to pursue, but one reading might go as follows: if something cannot be remembered, it is necessary to lose (there is no way not to lose) what is not there, where you are. It is necessary to lose the thing that, though one never had or possessed it, was nonetheless 'there'. Not only is it necessary, it would seem that it is also preferable for the human mind to make sure that there is 'no possibility of remembering', and thus 'no way of not losing what is not there where you are'. 'You' are to occupy a position of permanent expenditure or loss, and there is no way of remembering what is being lost, since it was never there; by losing it, one cannot lose it: such is the melancholic strategy. Therefore, following the logic of fetishistic disavowal, what is 'not there' is what is 'there', what is pointed at or indicated by the thing that *is* 'there', the object of the 'glance': 'not there' and 'there' are identical for fetishistic 'belief'. More important than the thing is the topology, the 'place' that has to be both there and not there – the place of a 'thing non-existing', a missing content.

Given Stein's emphasis on the primacy of topology or place over content, it is not surprising that she was intrigued not only by money, but by number. Just as her fetishism demands that the human mind be continually presented piecemeal in the process of exchange or displacement (of selling, of circulation), so it can call upon analogous processes of measuring and counting. For Stein the human mind is always 'one'; moreover, like the number one, the human mind is always a 'beginning'. Stein repeatedly addressed the problem of beginning: 'how can anyone begin when within is not cannot be begun'. 'Within' begins beyond beginnings, which means that it does not begin; it has always begun already. 'Beginning' was always there; it is, according to Stein, 'natural': 'Any one who is one can be natural if he can. If he cannot he can be just as natural as he can that is within his human mind, and in his human mind he never did begin, he never has begun he never began' (GHA 182). Thus, since it is beyond beginnings, always 'there' in a pure origin without a past, or in a pure past, '[t]he human mind does not count'. It 'does not count' because it is not a part of the set of things that can be counted; more importantly, it 'does not count' because it has no need to count or add things up. It grasps itself at a glance, one piece at a time. Yet, as I will argue, this grasp of comprehension has a very ambiguous relation to the process of counting and measuring. Contrary to Stein's insistence, the human mind does 'count', in both senses of that word; the human mind, which is always 'one', must therefore have something 'to do with number'. It counts, but it must not be counted among the things of human nature, which simply are where they are, where they can be seen.

The human mind is a 'one', Stein asserts, that is constituted, reflected, and perceived in the acts that place it ('there is the human mind'). But it is a 'one' that is not a part of the process of counting. Like the human mind, the number one is simultaneously (for Stein, if not for mathematicians) inside and outside the numerical series that it initiates. Stein says that human nature 'never knows anything about one and one' (GHA 222); identity also therefore 'has nothing to do with one and one' (GHA 155). The human mind, 'not succeeding one thing by another' (GHA 90), reserves that method of counting to itself. 'One and one' has two meanings: it is another way of saying 'one plus one', which is characteristic of human nature and identity; but, more important, it is also the simple reiteration of the figure, not its addition or (economically speaking) its accumulation. The repetition of 'one', a repetition *without remembering*, is the sign of the human mind. What is repeated, I will argue, is an abstract sum, an indeterminate quantity that is merely named 'one'. What Stein encounters in her reflections on the human mind is the limit-point of a discourse of measure (and value) as it meets something that cannot be measured in that discourse. The human mind therefore becomes an indeterminate quantity.

The difficulties of Stein's use of the number 'one' derive from the fact that 'one' is a whole unto itself even as it is a part serving as a unit to measure other wholes. First of all, let us see how the human mind is constituted as 'one' in the determinate form of something *seen*: 'When any *one* looks and sees how what it sees looks like it it cannot not know whether it is human nature or the human mind but it can know it will know and therefore as it looks at it all it can know [sic] that human nature is not the human mind. Once as a piece. Or even twice or more as a piece' (GHA 78). The phrase, 'can*not not* know', is doubled by the echoing negation: 'any one' is both utterly certain and uncertain 'whether it is human nature or the human mind'; one cannot not know, and one cannot know. But the human mind, as I have just argued, appears in the number (and of course the pronoun) 'one', the number that 'doesn't count'. In this scene of misrecognition, the 'one' sees something that resembles it, something in which it sees itself. But all it can know for certain is 'that human nature is not the human mind'.

Given this certainty, where is human nature, where the human mind, in the unit constituted by this resemblance? Does the human mind count, or not – that is to say, is it there in the determinate quantity or phenomenon signalled by 'one'? The process of counting or measuring quantities requires that the pure algebraic symbol be bound to an (aesthetic) intuition (in Kant's terms, a *comprehensio aesthetica*); this intuition provides it with a determinate content, making it a particular quantity. Together the pure number and the intuition form a 'piece', or a unit, which can be added up to make larger units, which may, as we will see shortly, be either continuous quantities or aggregates of other units which maintain their distinctness. In the passage cited above, the intuition ('what it sees') constitutes the unit of measure in the primary act of apprehension–comprehension that makes it possible to count and measure. But if we look at the constitution of the unit of measure, it becomes apparent that the human mind and human nature are still tangled up with each other. The ambiguity of Stein's scene of the human mind's recognition of itself in 'one' reflects the ambiguity of the concept of number in its role as measure.

The other 'one' to which I referred above concerns an indeterminate quantity – that is to say, quantity as such. The algebraic symbol of 'one' is, on its own without the limiting intuition, merely abstract quantity. Stein wants to hold the number one at the threshold of its becoming a unit of measure. At the same time, there must be some evidence that 'there is the human mind'. 'One' must have some phenomenal presentation. The human mind does not count; yet it requires the temporality of a certain counting and measuring in order to be presented and intuited at all. Therefore, she wants 'one' to refer to a quantity that is prior to and the condition of 'one and one'. The number must simultaneously be a formal algebraic symbol, with no content but an abstract quantity or sum, and at the same time an intuited particular quantity or phenomenon. The number 'one' must serve in effect as a fetish, marking the presence of a particular intuition, or thing, and also simply marking the place from which the thing is missing; the thing of value must be there and yet not exist.

'One' must therefore be what in her aesthetic vocabulary Stein calls a 'master-piece'. A master-piece is a unit, or a 'piece', of a quantity of value. To echo Marx on money as 'the commodity of commodities', we could say that the master-piece is the piece of pieces. However, this presumes that we know what, for Stein, a 'piece' is. According to Stein, '[a] piece is only a little way and it must finish . . . ' (GHA 78). A piece must finish, it must have limits at which one perceives that it is indeed a piece: to see a piece 'entirely', to see it as a whole, is to comprehend its limits. Consider, for example, a piece of money. Clearly, a coin has determinate boundaries, and thus is a unit of measure. But it is an artificially composed unit of a larger unity, or continuous quantity. Though a coin is a 'whole piece', a distinct material thing of a determinate size, it is simultaneously a piece of a whole 'something' that exceeds it. Money is at once composed of many whole pieces (that is, it is an aggregate of pieces) and a continuous quantity, which is called 'value'.[82] This is why Stein can say that 'money is not money'; money as a thing is not money as continuous substance, yet both are 'money'. Stein therefore argues that money cannot be 'lost' as particular use values can:

> Anything that is or can be lost is so easy to describe because it is of no interest.
> But money.

Well money is not easy to describe. It is easy to lose but it cannot be lost, and no one can really get used to it. (GHA 207–8)

Money as abstract quantity, or 'value', is a continuous quantity that is broken up into an aggregate of pieces called 'money', which can be lost. But money as value is always 'one'. As a thing that cannot be lost, it escapes 'identity', and thereby ceases to be 'something anybody can get used to' and describe since it no longer has a use value, is no longer a 'thing existing'.

Stein's analysis of what a 'piece' is tends to blur the difference between aggregates and continuous quantity. Her notion of a 'piece', like her concepts of 'one', of property, and of money, allows her to embody a valued quantity in a particular thing while denying that it requires that thing to present itself. Therefore, even though it embodies value, that particular thing can be given up without the embodied value being lost. Another example of such a blurring occurs in her discussion of America. According to Stein, 'one piece of [America] is not separated from any other one' (GHA 93). The most remote pieces of America are in immediate contact with one another because they ultimately meet one another through each other, through the mediation of all pieces by a unifying substance called 'America'. We have seen how this is possible: the pieces of the father's land 'are not separate' because of the abstract exchange value they bear in the exchanges among brothers.

There is clearly much at stake in the connection between the human mind, America and money. What links the three terms is, as I implied above, the notion of a unifying substance. In the case of the brothers, we can call this unifying substance not only 'America' but also the paternal will. Politically, the paternal will guarantees the market, and threatens to step in and 'depress' the economy whenever the brothers step out of line; economically speaking, the exchanges take place against the backdrop of value as a continuous quantity. Thus, both value and the father provide economic guarantees. But there is more to this elusive 'unifying substance' than this. It should be clear at this point that the analogy I have drawn between Stein's monetary themes and the strategies of mourning and melancholia finds its justification in various related concerns of Stein's text. One way of articulating what identifies these various concerns is to say that the spectre of universality is haunting Stein's utopian impulse. As I mentioned above, Stein does not present this spectre in any one of its ideological guises alone, but is concerned more with the political economy that provides the condition of this missing universal term. It should not be surprising that it appears above all in the form of money, which Marx called the general equivalent – which can bring into the same sphere of identity the most disparate things, constituting and finding in them what is common, namely their exchange value. As Marx points out, the moment at which the general equivalent emerges from the sphere of commodities to represent and reflect them all occurs simultaneously with the possibility of conceiving Enlightenment universality.[83] Stein finds herself caught exactly where Marx located the Enlightenment: committed to a utopian impulse, but unable to represent (to conceptualize or embody) it adequately for historical reasons. Stein stutters, as it were, at the point of articulating universality in the Enlightenment term she adopts as hers, namely 'the human mind'; but her stuttering reveals the conditions that make the emergence of such a universal term possible. Those conditions, I will argue, are best demonstrated by an analogy to Marx's analysis of the emergence of the general equivalent from what he calls 'simple exchange'.

Simple exchange is dual: a commodity finds its expression in the body or use value of another commodity. The sold commodity only finds its value expressed after it has been replaced by the one bought.[84] At this stage of the unfolding of value, each commodity can be both the relative and the equivalent form of value: money has not yet appeared as the general equivalent form. The introduction of the third element in exchange, the general equivalent, is also the institution of a new topology, the movement from a dual to a triadic relation. The exchanges are supported by the constant term kept in view by the figure of money. While in simple exchange the value of the sacrificed object is expressed in the commodity that takes its place, monetary exchange embodies the otherwise only virtual constant term; money is, as it were, a perspective object in view of which the exchange takes place. For this reason, money is a unique commodity, excluded from the circle of commodities as their general equivalent. In simple exchange, any commodity can serve as the equivalent of another; as Marx says, 'there are only fragmentary equivalent forms, of which each excludes the other'.[85] Money is qualitatively new: it is not one of the commodities that serves as equivalent, but is value itself, without use value. It is, as Alfred Sohn-Rethel says, 'an abstract *thing*, which is, strictly speaking, a contradiction in terms'.[86]

Why does this third term emerge from the process of simple exchange? Simple exchange, the chain of relative value, constitutes the economy that for Aristotle was normative: use values are only temporarily suspended in a moment of abstraction during the act of exchange, before returning to their proper form. But once the abstraction of exchange has taken place, exchange value proper lingers with goods as 'virtual value'; a negativity haunts objects, though its ghostly presence has no proper form. Money emerges from the dead end of simple exchange in order to provide the form of the general equivalent of all commodities: it embodies and realizes virtual value, and reveals retroactively that what was desired from the exchange was not a use value, but something else, something that cannot be objectified as a use value. The unusable thing is left out of and left over from the act of exchange. Money as the general equivalent marks the place of this abstract remainder, and all exchanges deictically indicate this place. Marx said that money is the commodity of commodities, or in Stein's language the master-piece of all pieces. It is both included in and excluded from the circle of goods. The topological difference that separates simple from monetary exchange does not minimize the fact that money is still a commodity, a figure in the place of value itself. The place itself is purely ideal, yet it is only 'there' by virtue of the exchanges it makes possible.

Stein's moment of recognition, when 'one looks and sees how what it sees looks like it', in which the human mind makes itself felt in its failure to appear, has an economic analogy in the simple form of value in Marx's analysis of the genesis of the money form. Neither term in the event, neither the 'one' nor what it sees, appears as the human mind itself. However, the failure to present the human mind, to identify it with or embody it in a particular thing, indicates (to develop this economic analogy) the virtual presence of value, which has not yet found its total form of expression in the expanded form of value. The human mind appears as the virtual value expressed by the acquired commodity, the substitute. On the other hand, were the recognition scene to take place within the regime of money, rather than of simple exchange, the particular thing whose loss and substitution indicated the human mind would of course be much less effective than money, which is so like the human mind for Stein. Money bears and incarnates value more adequately: the mere commodity-thing would have been sold or 'lost' in order to present value more adequately in money as profit, or the 'interest' of the human mind.

The difference between human nature and the human mind is therefore one between two kinds of exchange. Just as exchange implies two kinds of memory, so do human nature and the human mind have two kinds of memory corresponding to their particular forms of exchange. In simple exchange the value of the sacrificed commodity is only realized and expressed in its material substitute, another use value which took on the role of its equivalent. Freud's notion of normative mourning involves such an abstraction of the thing lost, a freeing of the libidinal investment in order to direct it elsewhere, on to another object, or a use value. Ideally, mourning can locate an adequate substitute once it has given up the lost object. I compare simple exchange to mourning because its capacity for substitution (which is incapacitated in melancholia) implies a 'memory' in which the value of an equivalent commodity is expressed only when its substitute takes its place. The 'value' of the first appears in the second, and thus only emerges in the exchange, only to disappear again in the use value of the object. In Freudian terms, the substitution effected by the work of mourning returns the ego to a normative relation with the world of objects.

Monetary exchange, on the other hand, requires a different kind of forgetting: the thing acquired is replaced not by a use value but by a pure abstraction, a cipher. Yet this abstraction is haunted by the traces of a missing thing – as in melancholia. Monetary exchange is haunted by a remainder that cannot be presented except in the divided body of money. Melancholia, unlike mourning, has the advantage of preserving rather than losing the thing. By a process of abstraction, melancholia effaces the name, the identity, and the memory of the thing it gives up, but preserves it in a crypt. Haunting the circulation of commodities is an original exchange, in which something was given up, lost, or sacrificed. The third term that initially presents itself as virtual value is the ghost of that thing. The third term provides the moment of universality or generality, but one that is predicated on something missing – in reference to commodities, what is missing is the material particularity sacrificed in abstraction. In the exchanges among brothers, it is the father who is missing – or murdered, as Freud's myth would have it.

We have seen already Stein's concern with mourning, with remembering and 'paying respect to the dead'. It is necessary not to remember and to mourn, Stein suggests, if one wants to have a human mind; this means that it is necessary to lose, to give up, to sacrifice – always, however, on the melancholic assumption that such giving up will preserve the thing lost. This concern reaches a climax in her assertion that the human mind 'is like being dead'. If we place this in the context of the brothers who exchange commodities among themselves, it would appear that to have a human mind is to identify with the dead father. Yet the effacement of the proper name that takes place in melancholic exchange might suggest that the real loss was not of the father, or any such identifiable object. Though as we will see shortly, Stein's texts are often haunted by the dead, Stein does not always identify the dead. As she says of detective stories, 'the first thing is a dead man or if not a dead woman'. That man may be a brother, and may in fact be the brother of a father – that is to say an uncle: 'If every day it is necessary to have an uncle killed that is if he kills himself instead of a father that too has nothing to do with either identity or with human nature' (GHA 157–8). A number of substitutions take place here, beginning with the uncle occupying the place of the father, and committing suicide in what amounts to a melancholic identification. Moreover, the uncle, because he is acting in his capacity as uncle, might be performing this act in the name of his brother or sister. But he might also be acting on behalf of the son or daughter of his brother or sister, and killing 'a father' for them, though which one is at this point impossible to know. The uncle is also son and brother, and one cannot know in which role he was acting when he killed himself, or even who is being killed, the identification and substitutions become so complex in Stein's miniature narrative. The important factor is that the suicide brings the uncle closer to the human mind because it 'has nothing to do with either identity or with human nature'. The uncle may then be 'one'.

But a more definite example of 'one' is developed a few pages after the uncle appears. Stein returns to the question of paternity and death by way of a character named 'Lolo', who 'was one no matter that he had a father'.

> Lolo was himself romantic and he is dead not by and by but dead.
> And as I pass where he had not had a father there where he is not dead by and by but as he is then there there where he is he was not where he is. Lolo is dead and any father had a mother he had a mother but none of this is dead.
> He is dead.
> Lolo is dead.
> There where there is no other. (GHA 165)

The human mind never had a father, or any other 'relation'. Instead, it has a beginning prior to beginning, prior to relation. Yet '[t]here where there is no other' is at the same time a crypt where 'none of this is dead', where the relations, the mother and father, survive. Like the merchant-brothers it secretly 'lives on' this system of relations.

Nonetheless, it would be incorrect to locate the truth of the human mind in its genealogical origins. If one were to ascribe particular identities and a particular narrative to the human mind, one would be overlooking the fundamentally melancholic conditions of its existence. Both Stein and the melancholic efface the particularity of the relations in order to present the 'first thing' that has no proper name or identity. Though '[t]he first thing [in a detective story] is the dead man or if not a dead woman', prior to the narratives of compensation and justice provided by detective stories there is an anonymous loss. Melancholia attempts to become mourning by identifying and narrating this constitutive loss. As we will see in the next section, though Stein frames her presentation of the thing within the detective narrative, the anonymity and non-narrativity of the lost thing become apparent at the limit of the frame. The anonymity of the loss means that the Freudian narrative of fetishism cannot adequately account for Stein's fetishism; her investment in money is not simply a disavowal of the relation to the paternal will. The anonymity of the lost thing allows for a glimpse outside of the narrative that her view of 'depressing fathers' implies. Stein's anxiety over fathers may then not be of the classical Oedipal order, but rather a profound sense that something else is possible, that the father is not the originator of value and the relation to him is not inevitable. One could argue therefore that this opening in the paternal network exposes possibilities not thinkable within the patriarchal system. The abstraction or effacement of 'the first thing' lost or sacrificed in a founding exchange may actually suggest that the universal term was already there as an original missing substance. To some extent this is what I am claiming when I insist that even at her most regressive, Stein is affirming the utopian impulse of modernity and the Enlightenment. Yet at the same time I am also insisting that her perception of the conditions of such utopian promise are also the conditions that lock all articulations of value into a system of sacrifice, and its concomitant network of guilt and debt. And I would also insist that what we discover at this point is not Stein's own intellectual or moral limitations, but the historical and ideological limits of the poetico-political economy. Though we can read Freud's model of melancholia critically, and demonstrate the ways in which he responded to the exigencies of an ideological narrative by placing the father in the position of the anonymous missing thing, this does not alter the fact that historically, as Stein's own political moves demonstrate, the 'depressing father' does come to occupy that place, whether in political institutions or in the cultural form of a collective ego ideal   or, as Stein thought, in both at once.

'THERE IS NO DETECTION'

The human mind has nothing to do with remembering and forgetting. Memory implies loss, and, for Stein, '[a]nything that can be lost is something anybody can get used to and that is identity'. If something can be lost, it can be remembered and recovered, or described, and has no 'interest'. Nothing that dies, therefore, can hold any interest; to remember that something or someone has died is to turn that thing into identity. At the same time, as we have seen, the fetishistic moment of this attitude towards loss and death requires that the lost value be embodied in a material thing. We have seen the ambivalence at the root of Stein's complex, fetishistic negotiations between things (for example master-pieces) and value, and how that ambivalence divides all of her basic concepts and figures, such as the human mind, down the middle. As a strategy of presenting and sustaining the human mind, fetishism must be of two minds about everything. In this way fetishism, like melancholia, remains loyal to that which is of most value, which is fundamentally lost. To put it paradoxically and summarily: though the human mind has nothing to do with remembering and forgetting, it must remember that which is of most value by forgetting it absolutely; this is because to remember it would be to forget it absolutely, to give up on it, and so to lose it. We can see this economy at work in Stein's analysis of detective stories. Though Stein was fond of detective stories, she was uncertain of their relation to the human mind. The trouble with detection is that it is a kind of remembering – and a kind of mourning for and paying respect to the dead: 'the one that is dead has no time and no identity for him to them and yet they think that they can remember what they do not have as having it without their having it for them' (GHA 213–14). Detectives 'think that they can remember what they do not have'; they try to recover what has 'no time and no identity' in terms of time and identity, and act 'as if' something is 'there'. Therefore, what disturbs Stein in detective stories is the very fact that they presume that what is missing, what motivates detection, is someone who has died and therefore is to be mourned. As always, Stein thinks the individual death is insignificant and mourning is dangerous. In light of the discussion of melancholia above, we could say that the reason for this is that no individual death is adequate to represent the constitutive loss as such, which presupposes no proper names or identifiable objects.

Stein prefers the detective stories that get the body out of the way right at the beginning, making it into 'the first thing'. As a 'thing', the dead body marks the place of the melancholic loss, and therefore also marks the place at which the human mind frees itself of 'relation'. Detective stories allow us to detect traces of the anonymous loss or death that is the condition of the human mind (GHA 126–7). What Stein likes in what she calls 'the melodrama type' of detective story is in fact that they 'have no detection'. She therefore prefers the stories of Edgar Wallace to what she calls the classic Sherlock Holmes type of mystery: Edgar Wallace 'is so good because there is no detection'. Neither the story nor the detective needs to 'remember' in the sense of mourn. However, despite her objections, Stein is interested in 'detection'. There are two ways we can imagine a motive for detection that is not caught up in the affective entanglements of memory and mourning.

If mourning is not a worthy motive or is too dangerous a one for the human mind, then it is likely that more respectable motives for Stein might be a desire for money (as it is at times for Poe's detectives, most famously perhaps Dupin in 'The Purloined Letter') and a desire for justice (in which I will include revenge – Dupin's other motive). But what could it mean to be in it for the money? We know from 'Edgar and Edgar' that 'money is not money if you do not owe it to another', and that it is probable that 'you always owe money to another' (HWW 146). According to one Edgar, money is always credit; if it is not, it cannot be money. Money measures debt; it binds its possessor to a melancholic reserve. As in melancholia, the debt that money measures is also an originary guilt. To be in it for the money may therefore be a disavowal of a relation to the paternal instance. Prior to the monetary interest is the demand for justice, even a demand for revenge. Detection too is a kind of melancholia, inhabited by the imperative memory of something immemorable, which it may be trying to symbolize in naming the perpetrator of the deed. The detective embodies a certain imperative, attesting to his ambivalent relation to the ego ideal, to which he is subjected and with which he identifies.[87] Stein may be uncertain if the detective has or hasn't anything to do with the human mind, but her hesitation reveals more about the human mind than she may have meant: the human mind is bound by a certain obligation to a 'depressing' paternal instance, and bound to repeat the expulsion or murder of the 'first thing'.

Stein's interest in the detective is inseparable from her interest in the human mind, but also from the human mind's intrication with the community of which it is ambiguously a member. Whether the detective detects for money or for justice, he or she is involved in a public function that presupposes a universal point of reference – whether money or the ego ideal, both of which, as we have seen repeatedly, are forms of the father. For Stein, the ambiguity of the detective figure brings to the fore the constitution of a community in a violent act, or the narrative of an act which constitutes the very relationships of guilt and debt we have been discussing. She explores the political implications of her two kinds of detective stories, and locates the difference finally in an economic structure. It becomes apparent in her discussion that she is trying to work out a form of democratic distribution that is not a reduction of the human mind to human nature.

Stein's distinction between melodramatic stories and those of the Sherlock Holmes variety is made on the basis of the relative values of the hero, heroine and villain: 'in the melodrama the three are equal the villain the hero and the heroine, in this order as to importance but nevertheless they all three have the right to be but in the detective hero type the rest of it becomes too dependent and eventually the hero detective having really to exist all by himself ceases to exist at all' (HWW 149). It would seem from this that the classical 'detective hero' is the very figure of the human mind, which like 'the detective hero type' does not exist and is characterized by its autonomy or lack of relation. But Stein does not like this type of detective, as if he is the remnant of an aristocratic order and not 'equal' enough to the villain and the heroine. The detective has a gift that sets him apart, and this makes him dangerous – like Roosevelt with his 'other meaning'. The melodrama scheme on the other hand is characterized by democratic equality, by distribution and equilibration rather than the unique and concentrated quantity that characterizes the gifted detective.

But this equalization has a mysterious power of growth; it is not only a better or more just distribution of an abundance, but a means of increasing the quantity: 'the melodrama scheme' has a different economy from the 'detective hero type' because it 'gives more abundance'. In Edgar Wallace's stories, 'there is a genuine abundance and the thing that can be said is characteristic of the twentieth century is that it is lavish but niggardly'. As always for Stein, lavish expenditure is simultaneously a niggardly accumulation. Despite the 'distribution and equilibration' performed by the melodrama type of detective story, an abundance or surplus seems to accumulate itself in a particular place. If the detective doesn't appropriate it then the writer will; Edgar Wallace, according to Stein, 'has the gift of writing as Walter Scott had it and that too makes for abundance' (HWW 148). Stein has to deny the value of the detective's gift of detection, but the gift always resurfaces in another place.

Stein's discussion of the relative values of the characters in the detective story therefore reflects her ambivalence toward the postwar economy of 'distribution and equilibration'. In her analysis of the detective story, Stein is attempting to distribute and equilibrate the human mind. The detective story enables the democratization of the abundance of the gift, which returns to the place of the reader: 'the only thing you have to do in an Edgar Wallace story is to detect the villain . . .'. Every reader can be a detective. The democratic extension of suspicion prevents the attribution of mastery to any detective or leader, and allows for a just distribution of value. However, though democracy may distribute the abundance more justly, the model of the detective story suggests that it does so by providing everybody with the power of attributing guilt. 'Americans are suspicious', Stein claims (HWW 74), but she is concerned to avoid one of the consequences of generalized suspicion: that Americans may select a gifted detective hero type, or a leader like Roosevelt, to answer their suspicion by providing a scapegoat for their ills.[88] The distribution of the surplus only sets the stage for the return of the father as 'doctor', or as 'detective'; but even failing that, the democratization of the surplus already implies debt. The abundance measures an infinite debt, even if the debt is not personalized and called in, as it might be with Roosevelt.

As I have argued, fetishism disavows the bonds of debt. Stein's analysis of detective stories attests to her fetishistic efforts to overcome a fundamental melancholic subjection to the father. The economy of detection demonstrates that the attempt to distribute the abundance according to a principle of justice or equivalence necessarily fails: the gift nonetheless accumulates in a certain place that is not available even to the democratized reader, who can never be master of his or her use of the quantity for 'detection'. There is always a dangerous 'more', and one is always, like the detective and the human mind – and like the suicide – in a neo-feudal relation to a taskmaster, the ego-ideal. The narrative of detection therefore becomes most dangerous to the value of the human mind when it culminates in the attribution of guilt; this moment resolves suspicion and gives determinate form to the melancholic debt. It is to prevent the culminating moment of detection that Stein strategically dismantles the various detective stories she sets up in *The Geographical History of America*. To begin with, she will not identify the dead body in her text; 'the first thing' is a dead man or woman, but we do not know what 'relation' this person may have been. Yet at the same time, there are signs that Stein's text is concerned with mourning for particular reasons. In 1934, her friend René Crevel killed himself; his is the only proper name to be ascribed to a 'first thing' or dead body in *The Geographical History of America*. It is significant that the only identifiable body in Stein's text is a suicide, not a murder victim: this frees the 'first thing' of the need for detection. With no culprit or villain, there is no need to give a proper name to the guilty party. Everybody knew that Crevel killed himself; no detection is required.

However, this assumption assumes that the community is able to identify who Crevel was when he killed himself. We have seen in all of Stein's miniature narratives that the capacity for each person to assume different relations implies a slippage in their 'identity', and therefore in the system of relations upon which the human mind relies. In his discussion of melancholic suicide, Freud makes much the same point. Regressive, narcissistic identification with the father, according to Freud, intensifies the guilt of the impoverished ego to such an extent that, in order to expiate that guilt, the ego will kill itself. Yet when it commits suicide, the ego has become that which it ought to be: the ego-ideal. That is to say, the ego has alienated whatever there was of itself entirely into the ego-ideal, and has become its own oppressor – or has identified with its aggressor. To put this in other terms, in order to become a 'first thing', or perhaps a human mind, Crevel had to become his ego-ideal, or father, and kill off his human nature.

The particular form of the narrative is not important; what needs to be emphasized is that the melancholic moment gives rise to multiple narrative possibilities, all of which serve to conceal the constitutive and anonymous loss. These narratives may assume either a melancholic or a fetishistic form. Because fetishism assumes a perspective that suspends the question of guilt, Stein's ambivalence to detection is a further sign of her fetishistic perspective. Unlike melancholia, fetishism is based on a disavowal of the relation that would constitute the ego as guilty. Instead, fetishism constitutes an ego that is split between a guilty agency (which has submitted to castration) and one that is not guilty (which has not submitted to the paternal will). Stein's fetishism determines the selection of Crevel as 'the first thing', the corpse, precisely because there is no difficulty assigning agency and guilt. Yet were one to inquire further, one would indeed find a guilty party – the split-off part of the ego that has submitted to the paternal judgement of guilt. As always, fetishism can have it both ways.

But fetishism must always maintain its system of subtle and precarious distinctions in the midst of its melancholic conditions. The threat these conditions pose can be seen in the way Stein's critical categories and concepts, like human nature and the human mind, tend to mirror each other. This becomes most apparent when Stein demands the very subjection to the father that she had resisted throughout the Depression, seeming to collapse the human mind's power of resistance entirely into the obedience and submissiveness of human nature. Yet this collapse was already implied by the precarious distinctions Stein wanted to maintain. For Stein, the group or mass united in 'human nature' is subjected to the 'depressing father' as to a general equivalent. Stein's ideal community, on the other hand, is a community of barbaric classical liberals who believe in money. But, as I argued in the preceding section, the opposition masks an identity in the form of the general equivalent. Both forms of community demand a guarantee that the thing persists despite its loss. The community of fetishists is always threatened by Depression: the melancholic collapse of value and the threatened destruction of the guarantee (which gave Stein such a 'fright') means that another, imaginary object will be called upon to serve the function of the guarantee.

It would seem from this analysis that universality as such is imaginary and therefore sacrificial. I argued at the beginning of the last section that Stein's notion of community, when it was at its most regressive in 1941, required a universality founded in guilt and debt. Both guilt and debt could only be expiated by self-sacrifice. It would seem, therefore, that the utopian impulse can find no fissure in the economy of the fetish. But Stein's fetishism allows her to reflect critically upon some of the basic political and economic categories of the Enlightenment in order to think through what promise they might still hold. The most important example for our consideration is the way in which Stein thinks through the notions of community and universality. Stein's commodity fetishism attempts to democratize the human mind, and Stein's own democratic sympathies tend towards an affirmation of popular culture as a culture of the people, particularly those whom she calls 'Americans'. At the same time it coincides with the reactionary defence of the human mind that will appeal to the father. In the tradition of the older aristocracy and the more recent bourgeoisie, Stein is a committed modernist in distinguishing 'the human mind' from the 'popular' culture of 'human nature'. In this case, Stein's defence of 'the human mind' or 'entity' reflects the bourgeois attitude to the rise of mass consumption – and the defence of the bourgeois liberal individual.

But it is also an attack on such bourgeois categories, which are merely the categories of human nature.

Stein needs simultaneously to democratize the human mind in order to prevent a threatened collectivism of human nature, and to isolate the human mind as a vanishing point in order to prevent its diffusion in mass culture. This isolation takes place paradoxically by the investment of the human mind into the invisible and democratic hand of the market as a guarantee of its preservation and its eventual restitution. As a result, the human mind is both everywhere and nowhere at once. As was the case with a number of modernists, for Stein the work of art, or the 'master-piece', is the last hold-out of the thing of value. But Stein's notion of the master-piece is also founded in very precarious distinctions. The 'master-piece', like the human mind, is without any consistency or thingness: it is the autonomous aesthetic object reduced to a vanishing point. Though Stein's modernism holds on to the diminishing quantity of the master-piece, its evanescence means that Stein does not affirm the autonomy of culture or the work of art as such. The master-piece is killed, according to Stein, by the very embodiment which makes it available for reception or consumption; the master-piece will not survive in the bourgeois museum. This does not mean, however, that Stein's ambiguous conceptual assault on the autonomous work of art should be interpreted as an anticipation of the postmodern affirmation of popular culture; this avant-gardist moment of her work, like her apparent attacks on the autonomy of the aesthetic, are resolutely in the service of the 'human mind'.[89] Her attacks on high culture are in the name of the emancipatory values that high culture was to preserve and promulgate.

Throughout her career, Stein affiliated herself as much with popular, 'democratic' American culture as with European high culture. It is important therefore to isolate neither Stein's bourgeois nor her 'popular' perspective.[90] Stein's notion of the human mind exposes the contradictions of the defence of the bourgeois individual; her politics and economics reveal the bourgeoisie against itself, in what will prove historically – and for a brief moment also in the case of Stein's enthusiasm for Pétain – to be a simultaneously regressive and progressive defence of its values. Her anti-authoritarianism is supported by her popular, democratic Americanism and her affirmation of the market, but contradicted by her distinction of the human mind from 'human nature', the public or popular mind. What is 'popular', what is of the 'people', both threatens to destroy value and holds out the promise of the renewal of value by means of a popular, authentic culture. Stein must approach human nature and popular culture with ambivalence. Stein's exemplary ambivalence towards popular culture would be exploited both by authoritarian politics and the culture of consumption, which make rival claims to be authentically democratic. Human nature, according to Stein, can revert to neo-feudal subjection because it is permeated by the disavowed economy of the gift – because it is already 'neo-feudal'. During her visit to America, Stein was startled to find that Americans in their daily life were both natural and unreal: 'it was all strange and it was all natural, as natural as strange and as strange as natural' (HWW 67). This uncanny sense of the natural coinciding with what she also calls the 'unreal' caused her to reaffirm her celebration of American culture, including the practices of everyday life, which as a whole seems in her description to become a 'master-piece'. Her perceptions of daily life implied a recognition on her part of what was most American about herself – the unreal naturalness that was a sure sign of the human mind. However, Stein's analysis of the unreal naturalness of American culture recommended itself also as evidence that America is thoroughly subjected to human nature. The 'people' of contemporary America both attracted and frightened her. After her visit, she returned to Paris to articulate her modernist opposition of nature and mind even more forcefully, in order to extricate the 'naturalness' of the human mind from its dangerous mixture with human 'nature'.

3
Value from Obligation

> Thank you for a name.
> Thank nobody for the same.
>
> (GHA 206)

'THE CAPITAL AND CAPITALS OF THE UNITED STATES'

During her visit to America in the midst of the Depression, Stein thought that the nation was demonstrating signs of becoming a mass public. Giving up on that which makes them most modern, Americans seem to have been turning towards Roosevelt and the New Deal to cure their economic and social ills. Economic crisis calls the government out of hiding, according to Stein, and alters the subjective landscape of producers: no longer do workers freely contract their labour; now they are 'employed'. In 'The Capital and Capitals of the United States', Stein says that '[t]here is nothing that makes any one know more quickly that they are employees that is that they are employed and not on their own or a hired man than when the government is where everybody always knows about it' (HWW 75). This goes against the grain of the American commitment to the values of classical liberalism. Americans, Stein claims, always keep their government out of sight where it can do as little harm as possible to the workings of the market. This is why American capital cities are never the big cities, but always unimportant ones: 'the having put the capital away, just left it where nobody would notice it unless they happened to be looking for it is a very important part of what makes the country that is the people . . .' (HWW 74). In America, the capital is 'tucked away' and forgotten 'because the country was going to be suspicious of what its capital was going to do' (HWW 73–4). According to Stein,

There is another thing about Americans. And it has to do with the way they want their capital, do Americans have they ever felt that they were employed when they were hired. They used not to feel so. All Americans perhaps they have changed now but I hope not all Americans have always felt that they were not employed but that they were hired which is an entirely different thing. Have they been slowly changing, I have been afraid these last years that is before the depression that they were changing, that they were getting to be not like a hired man but like an employee, that is someone whom some one employs. There is a difference and this difference has always been American and now that the depression has come in a funny way they seem to be going back again, back to being a hired man and not an employed one, at least I hope so. And this has also something to do with their having wanted the capital to be tucked away where they would not know that it was going on.

According to Stein's formulation the reappearance of 'government' on the subjective landscape started to take place 'before the depression'. Unlike many classical liberals at the time, Stein saw the New Deal – the reappearance of the government – more as a symptom than a cause of the collectivist tendencies that became apparent in the thirties. It is not therefore only the New Deal that threatens the freedom of the private sector and the individual worker: this freedom was already under siege. For this reason, the Depression for Stein holds the welcome possibility of a dissolution of the emergent economic and social patterns that threaten the private life of workers: 'perhaps now the depression will make them commence again to begin again forgetting that the government is something that any one of them can know is there all the time' (HWW 75). Stein opposes the New Deal because, if the market were allowed to run its course into depression, employees would become hired men again, free to wander from job to job. According to the classical liberal conception, a 'hired man' is free by virtue of the contract implied by money wages. The Depression might once again make hired men of employees by dissolving the corporate subjective structures that interpellate them, that provide them with 'identity' outside of contractual exchange. But of course the Depression also calls out the capital as government. Roosevelt makes one know where the government is, where the capital is, thereby revealing and exploiting the structure that had already instituted itself and created 'employees' 'before the depression'.

Like Pound, Stein has recognized one of the fundamental problems of modernity: the determination of the borders between public and private life. The title of Stein's essay makes punning reference to 'the Capital and Capitals of the United States' to point out the difficulty of distinguishing between what is properly public and what is properly private. Though Stein fears that the New Deal threatens private capital, the opposition masks a deeper identity: both are a matter of centralized power. Stein therefore abandons the basic differentiation upon which classical liberalism rests. Her reasons for abandoning this are historical: the market economy, as Stein well knew, had been superseded by monopoly capital. The administrative and corporate institutions of monopoly capital were already interpellating 'hired men' as 'employees' before the Depression, and before the New Deal's encroachment on the private sector – the preserve of the American values of 'rugged individualism'.[91] Robert M. MacIver, a sociologist contemporary with the New Deal, argues that the conditions that make possible the New Deal do not emerge from without or from above society or the economy; instead, 'the change in popular attitude from an individualistic to a more collectivistic philosophy was less abrupt and less complete than it seems'. It was 'less abrupt' because the collectivistic tendency was already operating in the economy, which could no longer function with individuals conceiving themselves in individualistic terms; it was 'less complete' because the forms of collectivity available to both thought and practice could not transcend their economic conditions and institute a properly 'public' identity. Stein's Great Depression implicitly recognizes what MacIver called 'the ambiguity of the New Deal':

> the so-called recovery program has in it the potentiality of two quite divergent developments. One is along the lines of a drastic control of capitalist exploitation, involving a socially planned economy in which the depersonalized pursuit of profit is subject to check at a thousand strategic points. The other is the erection of a system of industrial syndicates, somewhat analogous to the fascist conception of the corporate state but without the unifying discipline which the latter implies . . . . For example, if each inclusive industrial association is to acquire an effective

power to limit output and raise prices, the competitive struggle is merely resumed under the guidance of the individualistic motive, at a higher level of organization.[92]

The second of MacIver's options approximates what Stein sees emerging in the Depression, namely, the latent identity of a complex of 'industrial syndicates' and a 'corporate state', a convergence and confusion of private and public interests. MacIver would agree with Spengler's notion that, for lack of a truly public life, America can have no proper politics. No corporate state could exist in America because – to use Stein's terminology – its 'capital' cannot be controlled by 'the capital'. A corporate state in America could really be no more than 'a system of industrial syndicates'. America would fail to achieve a true 'capital', a true public life, but would still be guided by 'the individualistic motive'. According to my reading, Stein would say that there is not only no proper public life, but no private life either; instead, both must be referred to their common condition, itself neither private nor public: (the) capital.

Stein's normative notion of the private life is represented by 'the barbarians' of the market who manage to forget the place of (the) capital by disavowing it. However, even their belief in money, as we saw in the last chapter, will not save them from the remembering of (the) capital and the return of the 'depressing father'. Similarly, Stein's merchant brothers exchange commodities with each other, but the purpose is to forget the one to whom they are ultimately indebted. As I said earlier, this indebtedness is also related to the originary loss of the thing, a sacrifice which has two opposing forms of narrative: the form provided by mourning and that provided by melancholia. In the individualist or contractual narrative of mourning, sacrifice allows one to reclaim one's original investment and keep commodities circulating. This is Stein's normative view of the fetishistic market. When the market is operating smoothly, the sacrifice preserves that which is lost by abstracting it into the embodied form of value. Giving the thing up to the father in exchange for the abstraction of value allows one to maintain disavowed ties to the father in the form of unconscious guilt and indebtedness. The positivity of value measures an originary debt. Since money is a disavowed debt, the destruction of money or the collapse of value in economic depression coincides with the return of the 'depressing father'.

In the melancholic narrative of economic crisis or Depression, one must give up the thing in order to pay one's debt or redeem one's guilt. The cultural dominance of this narrative of debt is what Stein fears is emerging in the Depression.

For Stein, value as such is what Henry George, the nineteenth-century American economist, called 'value from obligation'. Stein was familiar with George's economic system, as she reports in *Everybody's Autobiography*:

> I was much pleased on receiving a letter from some one just yesterday about my writing in the Saturday Evening Post about money and they said it would be different if I knew about Henry George. I knew about Henry George.... I do not think I really am very interested in any of it although I can and do get excited about it. (EA 153)

Like Marx, George assumes a classical labour theory of value, but in order to account for the disparity between the value conferred by labour and the price of a commodity – that is to say, in order to account for surplus value – he appeals to another concept of value: 'there are two kinds of value, one the value from production that adds to wealth, and the other the value from obligation that does not'.

> It is because the word obligation best consorts with existing customs, and best expresses the common character of the element distinct from production that gives value, that I speak of value from obligation as distinct from value from production. For the common character of all that I am here speaking of is that their possession enables the possessor to command or compel others to render exertion without any return of exertion on his part to them. This power to command labor without the return of labor constitutes on the other side an obligation, and it is this that gives value.[93]

There are 'things' whose possession allows one to command the labour of others without exerting any labour in return. If one is in possession of, for example, 'a paper note', one has the power to demand from someone a return on its value, just as one presumably can cash in 'a verbal promise': the other is obligated to the possessor of the contractual 'thing'. Obligation is the source of surplus value, and therefore of capital, since it compels more work than that which is reimbursed by wages. But George's crucial theoretical statement is far from clear, and one can perceive in it the shadow of an originary 'power to command labor without the return of labor', a radically one-sided exchange. In terms of the narratives outlined above, 'value from obligation' narrates the originary loss or sacrifice in terms of debt: the labourer who gives up more than he is given in return is *obliged* to do so because of a social-symbolic and psychological narrative in which the subject assumes its position as radically indebted. As I read George, 'value from obligation' refers back to the originary debt of the subject to the paternal instance, which is beyond the reciprocity of contractual obligation. It is not the father who is 'obligated' but the subjects of the father – even, paradoxically, those who hold the written promise or even the materially embodied value of money.[94] Money is 'value from obligation'.

To return to Stein's vocabulary, 'value from obligation' means that there is no opposition between the economy of the gift, on the one hand, and the economy of money and sales on the other. Money and sales are not free of the structure of obligation. Let us return for a moment to the question of the 'interest in money' demonstrated by the barbarians and the Frenchmen. George's theory means that the surplus that appears to the mercantile human mind, the profit towards which its exchanges are directed, implies an obligation, a contract or pact. The pact is necessary to the surplus, yet the pact is also always a threat to the very autonomy of the human mind that it makes possible. The mercantile 'human mind' is not the capitalist who is in possession of the power to demand a surplus labour without return; that is reserved for the paternal instance, the place of which we have just seen indicated in Stein's notion of '(the) capital'. The human mind, which is not simply a merchant but primarily a consumer (and therefore also a labourer), depends on a money economy, just as the 'hired man' depends on wages; the employee, on the other hand, is involved in an obligation and an identification that are detrimental to the private life of the human mind. But as I have suggested, the human mind has another lineage, resembling the fetishistic lineage of money and capital: it is the effect of the fetishistic disavowal of the originary 'value from obligation'.

The disavowal of the bond of obligation gives rise to the fragile fetishistic structure of money and the market. The destruction of money would mean that the economy and the state would be reconstructed along the lines called for by the originary obligation to the father. In the first of her 'Political Series', in 1935, Stein examined Roosevelt's New Deal, specifically his proposals for deficit spending and inflationary measures. She thought he was 'destroying' or trying 'to get rid of money', in order to feed the people with gifts of food as Mussolini had done. But Stein is not as worried about the destruction of money – which would at least be 'interesting' – as she is worried about the possibility that he is 'only electioneering':

> Is Franklin Roosevelt trying to make money be so that it has no existence that it ceases to be a thing that anybody can count, so that nobody can any longer believe in it or is it all electioneering. It is a curious story.
>
> If he were really trying to get rid of money by using it up by making it up into such enormous sums that it ceases to have any reality and so to really discourage anybody from feeling that money is money if that is what he is doing it would be an interesting thing to do, it might even be a useful thing this that he was doing making money a thing non-existing but and that is where the trouble is I do not think that that is what he is doing. I am afraid it is only for electioneering. It is a curious story. (PL 71)

Rather than *making money*, like the father who 'earn[s] it every day' (LMN 332), Roosevelt seems to be *'making it up* into . . . enormous sums . . .' (PL 71). He acts as if the money he is spending exists. 'Making it up' in this way would be tantamount to destroying money by obviating the disciplinary mechanism built into it: money in huge sums can summon up the fantasy life of its believers, and allow them to imagine that conditions of scarcity can be overcome by a regime of material abundance. Destruction by 'electioneering' or by deficit spending – 'hav[ing] so much money to use that nobody will be able to say no to him' – therefore retains money in its appearance, but alters the way in which it represents value: not only would money cease to be a thing existing, but 'figures [would] cease to have meaning'. The phrase 'a thing non-existing' does not mean that the thing disappears; the thing remains a thing, but 'a thing non-existing'. Though money should measure the quantity of value of another object, Roosevelt 'piles up the figures' (PL 72) beyond what is known to be the available number of monetary units (measured in reference to the gold standard, for example, which was abandoned officially in 1933).[95] Roosevelt confuses counting with measuring, as if adding up the numbers beyond what is available is the same as creating or discovering new wealth. Stein sees this making-up as leading to 'a real catastrophe'. The destruction of the fetishized order of brotherly exchange would make Americans 'remember the capital'; in other words, the bonds of the debt would no longer be disavowed if the fragile mediation of fetishism were to collapse. The result would be Depression, the melancholic devaluation of the economy and the emergence of the paternal instance.

The 'depressing father' calls in the debt. But this alone is not what Stein calls the 'real catastrophe'. Paradoxically, the real threat is not that the father wants his due, but that as the father assumes his position, he proceeds to foreclose the symbolic debt, which was respected by the fetishist; he does so by putting in its place an imaginary debt, which he then claims to have 'filled'. That is to say, the 'filling' father fills in the gaps of the symbolic with his 'other meaning'. This foreclosure of the symbolic debt is implied by the other meaning of the phrase 'making it up': to pay off a debt, or in Henry George's words, to return to someone a value you are obliged to return. The imaginary, 'filling' father claims to be able to 'make up' the debt; as we saw in the last chapter, this is what makes him 'depressing'. Because he can make up the debt, his subjects are bound to him by an obligation to which they can never live up. The importance of this kind of 'making up' appears in Stein's one example of a moment when figures did 'cease to have meaning':

> During [the First World War] lots of people used to try to calculate the expense of the war by minutes by hours by days and by weeks and they finally said good-night good-night figures ceased to have any meaning. And they did cease to have any meaning because nobody has paid their war debts.
> Does Franklin Roosevelt expect just to have it get like that or has he inside him any other meaning. (PL 72)

The expense could not be calculated (and so 'made up') because 'figures ceased to have any meaning'. It would seem then that the quantity to be measured is simply too much, and the figures too high to be meaningful in terms of money. However, even if the debt were too high ever to be paid, the quantity would not be beyond the system of measure; it would not, properly speaking, be incalculable. Figures don't lose meaning as they increase; they lose meaning only in reference to that which they are called upon to measure.[96] Numbers become 'meaningless' not through their increase, but in reference to what is *innumerable*, or illimited. The numbers kept increasing because the thing measured, or the quantity, despite having certain determinate aspects, is essentially indeterminate. The meaninglessness of the war-accountants' 'figures', which leads them to 'give up', occurs at the limit of an abstract quantity that their figures cannot measure. The meaningless 'figures' gather around an indeterminate quantity, or a thing beyond the system of measure.

What justifies Roosevelt's magnificent figures? His money seems to be measuring some other thing that he has in reserve. Stein's sense that he is counting in such a way that money 'ceases to be a thing existing', 'ceases to have any reality', points out that his particular 'use' of money, his 'using it up', is a kind of use or consumption, a 'destruction', after which the means will disappear. The money is in circulation, following the usual course of economic representation, but is being destructively consumed, and thereby ultimately taken out of circulation, as it was in Germany when commodities or things took the place of devalued money. But if money is destroyed, what will be presented to 'fill' its place? Whereas the accountants of the war witnessed the point at which figures became meaningless, Stein wonders if perhaps Roosevelt 'has inside him any other meaning', and if perhaps this other meaning is what is guiding his actions and his bizarre calculations, his 'making it up'. This 'other meaning', not signified within the system of money, would authorize his destruction of the figures in order to present the thing that would finally 'fill' the people. Roosevelt's 'electioneering' is so 'uninteresting', and even dangerous, that is, opposed to the 'interest' of the human mind, because it is an attempt to elect his meaningful figure – the 'other meaning' that he may 'have in him' – to the place of money. This of course means domination: 'Of course there was Theodore Roosevelt with the big stick and Franklin Roosevelt with the *must*' (PL 72; my italics). Roosevelt's 'other meaning' is 'must'; it takes the place of money, becomes the 'thing' behind all the grammatical displacements and losses of commodity exchange, and provides it with an absolute figure, the father with his 'must', coming to fill everything, to overcome the private life of privation. He becomes the possessor of capital, and the place of investment. The imaginary function of 'electioneering' would make Roosevelt the 'general equivalent' that renders all the votes equal, or renders all of the subjects into 'voters' who will put their lot with this imaginary father.

Though Roosevelt might occupy the place of the paternal instance and act as if the symbolic debt is 'made up', no 'other meaning' provided by him can adequately reappropriate and embody the missing thing. It is because they pretend to make up the symbolic debt, or conceal constitutive scarcity with the phantasm of material abundance, that leaders like Roosevelt, Stein thinks, could 'lead the nation to a *real* catastrophe' (PL 73; my italics). Stein's example implies what the catastrophe will consist of: since after the war the 'figures became meaningless . . ., *nobody has paid their debts*'. 'Nobody' should be understood in its strict sense: these 'meaningless figures' generalize debt so that *everybody* owes the debt, and *nobody* has paid it.

As the accountants' figures become meaningless, the debtor–creditor relation becomes destabilized, betraying the fact of a generalized and infinite debt owed to a transcendent instance. But for Stein this generalized debt is already the dangerous condition of money: money *is* debt, or loan, or credit. As I argued earlier, 'money' is the paradoxical conjunction of debt and surplus, giving money an indeterminate 'meaning' in different social fantasies or narratives. 'Meaningful' figures, on the other hand, are imaginary forms that redirect the debt towards particular places, that give the debtor and creditor particular identities and narrative relations. Stein's example is the international network of debt and credit instituted after the First World War, which divided the warring nations into creditors and debtors, with Germany, the guilty party, being the source of all payments. The debate current in the early thirties concerning the war-debt raised awareness that the debt was an elaborate construction based on the 'war-guilt clauses', which placed final responsibility on the Germans. But this structure of domination is an imaginary 'figuration' of another form of debt. For Stein the fact that 'nobody has paid their debts' is a historical crisis because the narrative that historicizes an otherwise infinite generalized debt is collapsing. The crisis Stein foresees is the emergence of an ambivalently divided identity of debtor and creditor, and the ensuing indeterminacy of guilt and innocence, a situation that invites the emergence of a 'depressing father' to resolve the crisis. Roosevelt will 'make up' the debt, but this imaginary accounting will only aggravate the crisis of indebtedness. Roosevelt will face this unpaid debt if he destroys money and figures by letting them become meaningless.

This anxiety over unpaid debts may sound odd coming from a woman who thought that nobody should pay their respects to the dead. But the purpose of Stein's fetishism is to disavow the symbolic debt, not to foreclose it. That is to say, the fetishist both denies the debt and accepts its terms. Therefore, despite her attempt to erase debts and obligations from economic and social life, Stein sees the crisis of generalized debt as caused by a moral lapse: the accountants 'gave up', or surrendered, before a task that asked too much of them. But perhaps it is not entirely fair to put it this way, since their task, as I said above, is impossible. The accountants are trying to measure the loss or expenditure of the First World War in terms of money, but the memory traces (to use Freud's terms) cannot be determined according to a general equivalent. Let us step back for a moment, and recall that, though the American market economy is based on the general debt, the nation – when it is truly itself – does not pay back the debt. It cannot, because no 'figure' occupies the place of the creditor. Instead, the debt is shunted about in the symbolic exchange of master-pieces, or commodities, by the merchant-brothers who 'live on' the land of the dead father. The success of American capital is therefore evidence that Americans have escaped the condition of guilt or indebtedness to their fathers and to their dead in general. Only in America, we are told, are the dead really dead: 'Please play and pay all respect to the dead, but not in America not where a country is so big that it is divided one part from the other by ruled lines and it has to be flat, or there is no hope of it not paying respect to the dead' (GHA 95). The accountants are like merchants in that their task is to convert the quantities of war dead, for example, into monetary equivalents. Stein's accountants are a literal version of Freud's understanding of mourning as the disinvestment of the libido from one particular object in order to allow for investments in other, new objects. In this light, we can understand more exactly the way in which the accountants failed in their task: their 'giving up' is a *melancholic* abdication of the task of mourning in so far as mourning calls for translating particularity into the universality of a medium of exchange like libido.

The act of 'giving up' is fraught with the ambiguities characteristic of the fragile economy of the fetish. It not only implies the abdication of a task, such as the accountants' giving up on their task of adding up the figures, but it also means renunciation. The problem of renunciation can be seen in the passage discussed above: 'In case of there not being any possibility of remembering and therefore no way of not losing what is not there where you are is there any way of enfeebling imagination. Indeed what is imagining anything. Is it done a little at a time or is it done a whole at at time and is it done all the time' (GHA 234). This suggests that a certain amount of 'giving up' is necessary to the life of the human mind, as if to resist the 'making up' of human nature, which always acts 'as if' something is there. 'Giving up' enfeebles the imagination, and strengthens the human mind. The war-accountants' measurement of the destruction or expenditure involved in the war is a kind of remembering or mourning, like the detective-work we examined in the last chapter. It seems to me that Stein approved of the accountants' form of mourning, implying as it does a fetishistic willingness to cathect the monetary substitute, a willingness to 'give up' what is essentially lost. But something seems to have gone wrong, and the accountants have 'given up' their task instead, as if they could not deal with the necessity of loss. In the attempt to calculate the expense of the war, there was no possibility 'of not losing what is not there where you are', no way of recovering what was expended.

'Giving up' is a renunciation necessary to proper economic exchange; it is the condition of any profit, any return of money. The normal symbolic exchanges of the merchant-brothers among themselves founds itself on a renunciation that presents a substitute; their exchange is a normative mourning that conceals its melancholic moment. The symbolic exchanges among the brothers 'who lived on where he had come from' are the work of mourning and 'making up' for this original deed. Once this system of exchanges is destroyed or given up, the symbolic debt is no longer passed around in reciprocal relations, and the infinite debt makes itself felt in the melancholic subjection to the 'open wound'. Debt becomes guilt in the eyes of the 'depressing' father who 'fills everything'. But the accountants' renunciation is not of the kind that leads to the fraternal symbolic exchange of master-pieces. Instead of accepting the meaningful figures that appear as substitutes of what is renounced, they leave a gap: 'nobody has paid their debts'. An economic crisis has already set in, a sublime debt has opened beneath the meaningful figures of the historical narrative. If 'the figures become meaningless', the debt will not be paid, or will be forgotten: it will be written off. 'Giving up' as the renunciation of the task of mourning or exchange is the condition of Roosevelt's 'making it up'. Roosevelt's effort to 'make up' the debt, to fill it in, is not the disavowal of debt that we saw to be the structure of money, the fetishistic positing of what is 'there', but a foreclosure of the debt that would fill the lack with its 'other meaning'. The imaginary father takes the place of what is missing in 'after war', 'filling' in the place of the general equivalent, which was vacated when the accountants gave up their task. The renunciation Roosevelt demands is thus that America give up its relation to the thing by allowing him to destroy money. Roosevelt himself will thus take its place, will in fact be the imaginary father in possession of the lost thing, the one who has 'made up' the debt and reappropriated the missing thing mourned in economic exchange. Give up everything and you will get your thing: such is the 'interesting' promise of the 'other meaning inside of him'. Thus 'giving up' is an absolute renunciation that threatens to destroy the symbolic system of exchange. The foreclosure of the symbolic relation is in effect the destruction of the private life as the life of privation; and the result is a suicidal identification with the ego-ideal.

'DOIS-JE LE DIRE'

Paradoxically, the accountants' giving up is a sign of their 'employment', of a dangerous moral or professional earnestness detrimental to whatever they might have of a human mind. Their human minds should be occupied with converting the sacrificed particularity of the war dead into the abstract, monetary equivalent, but instead their giving up seems to suggest that money is not enough to cover what has been lost. They ask in effect for 'an other meaning', one that money cannot provide. As we have seen, Stein thought that the human mind required that the dead should simply remain dead, rather than be mourned. If they were fulfilling their task properly, the accountants could serve as representatives of the human mind. Despite their professional investment in money, however, the accountants seem incapable of proper forgetting; their project collapses when they can no longer give up the lost thing by means of its abstraction into money. The human mind 'knows everything', according to Stein, but the accountants keep coming across that which is incommensurable with the 'figures' that they know. They abdicate their task before that which they don't know. The crisis of representation they suffer brings the melancholic conditions of their exchange to the fore: figures have no meaning in relation to that which they are to measure. What is unknown or meaningless to their monetary system of significance is perceived by them as an obligation to remember properly, to mourn the thing unaccounted for in their books. The accountants are subjected to an imperative – which in Stein's vocabulary is called the 'must'. The human mind, on the other hand, is not subject to such a 'must'. Stein claims that '[i]f there is the must then there is not the knowing everything' (GHA 231).

Because of the danger involved in the fetishistic system of money, the task of accounting for and sustaining the human mind falls to the aesthetic, which would seem so distant from 'the business of living'. To avoid becoming an employed man, one had best never be employed. Stein's act of creation, though it is instantaneous – 'I was just thinking of anything and I saw something' – also allows the human mind to linger, occupying the pure, empty time of leisure, the 'continuous present' as the gift of free time. For Stein, the fact that one 'does nothing to fill time' may be a sign of the human mind:

> I have been told that I have always been nervous and *unoccupied*, that I have never cared to *fill my time* with the things that fill it and that as a result I am not likely to remember or forget and therefore have I a human mind. Is it because of this that I have a human mind. Is it because of this that any one that has a human mind does that, does nothing to fill it. (GHA 89; my italics)

Human nature occupies time, and its time is always occupied with such things as 'the business of living' (LMN 151). Just as the 'depressing fathers' who were taking over Europe were 'filling everything', so human nature demands that its time be filled.

The human mind, on the other hand, does nothing. But doing nothing is not a matter of giving anything up. During its idle time, the human mind is busy with the consumption of masterpieces. The model for Stein's empty time is the time of exchange, which is also the time of consumption: nothing 'fills' anything but the empty figure of money, or rather, the master-piece that embodies the act of disavowal.

Since exchange repeatedly makes contact with that which is lost, and the universality and abstraction of money is haunted by the particularity it sacrifices, the time of exchange can never be idle, or rather 'unoccupied'. Stein may think that in America no respect need be paid to the dead, but she is certainly not pleased that the war debts are being forgotten. This is because the war debts are a fetishistic version of a non-monetary debt or bond to the father. Because of the accountants' refusal or failure to mourn, debts remain unpaid. Though when the accountants say 'Goodnight, goodnight' (for 'figures ceased to have any meaning') they echo Ophelia's famous last words, it becomes apparent that they do not resemble Ophelia so much as they do Hamlet: like Hamlet, they too have been assigned a task, the task of taking account and demanding that *respect be paid* to the dead. In their case, the payment of respects ought to be in the form of money. In a melancholic crisis, however, they – like Hamlet – become subject to a paternal 'must'. It is this 'must' that Hamlet fails to measure up to.

For this reason, *Hamlet* – which according to Stein 'has no psychology in it', in so far as it is a master-piece (LMN 149) – concerns a crisis in which 'nobody has paid their debts'. Though Hamlet is himself a little slow in paying his respects to his dead father by acting on his imperative, he cannot accept that his mother refuses to 'pay respect to the dead'. Furthermore, while his dead father suffers in purgatory for unnamed crimes, Hamlet hesitates in killing his stepfather upon considering that Claudius may in fact have already *paid his debt* to his creator. Rather than suffering for his sins, he may therefore be sent to heaven at his death. These reflections lead Hamlet to conclude that the murder of Claudius would then not be revenge, but a service to the new king. Hamlet would then be merely a 'hired man', as Stein would say, where he would prefer what to him would be the more noble status of being the executor of his father's will – what Stein would call an 'employee':

Why, this is hire and salary, not revenge,
'A took my father grossly, full of bread,
With all his crimes broad blown, as flush as May;
And how his audit stands, who knows save heaven?

(III.iii.79–82)

But Hamlet continues to defer the execution of his task of revenge, falling short of what is expected of him. In failing to pay due respect, he is much like his mother, who has in effect followed the advice of the Player King in 'The Murder of Gonzago': when the Player Queen argues that to marry again would be to 'kill my husband dead' a 'second time', the Player King responds to this vow by recommending that she break her promise to herself not to marry again after her first husband's death: 'Most necessary 'tis that we forget / To pay ourselves what to ourselves is debt' (III.ii.198–9).

Though he seems to fill his time pursuing his father's revenge, Hamlet is really wasting time 'doing nothing'. Like his mother, Hamlet cannot live up to the promise he has made to his father. As long as Hamlet does nothing, a certain unbearable enjoyment takes place: his mother, Queen Gertrude, continues to indulge her pleasures with her new husband. However, as Freud argued, Hamlet may be hesitant to act as long as he too indulges in the secret pleasures reserved to the father. This unconscious identification and enjoyment is the one stain on his 'knowing everything'. Even as Gertrude's and his enjoyment refuses the paternal debt, the imperative to efface the stain is issued by the dead father.[97] When the human mind 'knows everything', it is liberated from any external imperatives, from any 'must': 'If there is must then there is not the knowing everything' (GHA 231). However, Hamlet's hesitation to kill his stepfather in spite of 'knowing everything', in spite of the knowledge provided by his father's ghost, means that the force of the 'must' continues to exert itself. Stein suggests that 'must' *must* be accepted as such:

Why are they inclined to leave must alone.
Because must is must.
So much for must.

(GHA 232)

'Must' must be accounted for. But to say 'so much for must' is not to be done with it; it is rather to partition a certain quantity to 'must': must gets 'so much', and only then can it be left alone, like (the) capital, to do its work. The human mind is always supervised by the 'must', even in its 'master-piece':

> And knowing everything is never left alone.
> In knowing everything never being left alone there makes a recognition of what mater-pieces [sic] are.
> Knowing everything is never left alone nor is it ever without being knowing everything. Anything else is of no account. Not in mater-pieces. (GHA 232)

To give 'so much' to 'must' is to *give up* one's thing, to place it in trust with the father as the object of belief, or credit. To echo Horatio, the human mind will always 'pay the theft' (III. ii. 90–1) – that is to say, will always be radically indebted to and dominated by the paternal 'must'.

In the midst of the 'knowing everything' is a stain that marks a task. The stain goes by the name of 'Gertrude' in the economy of *Hamlet*; the 'stain' also marks the place of the paternal name, 'Stein', that would efface it.[98] If 'Gertrude' indicates the 'ma(s)ter-piece' of an excessive pleasure – a place occupied by Hamlet's mother – 'Stein' indicates the position of the father, at which all losses are recuperated or reappropriated. This gendering of the economy of the fetish, as well as of its melancholic crisis, is explored in one of Stein's lesser-known poems, a 'translation' of the French poem 'Enfances', written by her surrealist friend, Georges Hugnet.[99] Originally entitled 'Poem Pritten on Pfances of Georges Hugnet', and first published beside Hugnet's text in the 1931 issue of *Pagany*, the translation led to a feud between the two authors, and finally to a standoff which concluded their friendship.[100] Though rarely read today, 'Before the Flowers of Friendship Faded Friendship Faded', as it was finally called, is generally considered to have surpassed Hugnet's poem to stand on its own; its status as translation seems only to be of anecdotal interest. This is fair enough, perhaps, since Stein's poem is in no strict sense a 'translation', much to Hugnet's eventual disappointment. It is, as her first subtitle says, 'written on' his poem, and is neither a translation of nor a poem about Hugnet's. Stein says of the process of translating it: 'I finished the whole thing not translating but carrying out an idea which was already existing. . . .' Yet in seeing her translation as autonomous, one misses the crucial sense in which it is dependent on the original. Stein's own description of her poem's relation to the original does not claim its autonomy:

> Hitherto I had always been writing, with a concentration of recognition of the thing that was to be existing as my writing as it was being written. And now, the recognition was prepared beforehand there it was it was already recognition a thing I could recognize because it had been recognized before I began my writing, and a very queer thing was happening.

Stein's notion of the 'carrying out of an idea', as distinct from 'translation', suggests the 'carrying over' of metaphor, but also the 'carrying out' of a work or a task. 'Carrying out an idea which was already existing' is the classic definition of labour, as found, for example, in Marx.[101] But Stein doesn't imagine herself as Marx's abstract labourer. Stein used to do her writing in the exercise or copy books intended for school-age children, and perhaps recognized herself in a figure that appears in Hugnet's poem: a schoolgirl 'sans devoir', 'without homework', or 'without duty', who is at work copying '[l]es tâches de l'écriture' (16). Stein places herself in relation to Hugnet's poem by means of this figure, and as a result generates a microcosmic political economy which analyses and challenges Hugnet's patriarchal regime. Stein's translation is a 'tâche', or task: 'copied' from or 'on' Hugnet's poem, it is a response to an assignment, to a 'tâche'. But this task, like the schoolgirl's, is 'sans devoir': it is not imperative. The work of the schoolgirl-translator, though without 'devoir' (it is not her duty, her homework, her responsibility to do this work), is a response to an imperative uttered by a paternal instance. This means that the schoolgirl, who is a figure for Stein's own divided position as writer in relation to the language of patriarchy, is both liberated from the tasks assigned by the taskmaster, and at the same time subjected to an imperative.[102]

The 'tâche de l'écriture' is also a 'stain [*tache*] of writing'; Stein's translation is spilled ink, a mistake, a failed response to the assigned task. The 'translation' is a response to an imperative, the sign of the subjection to a paternal instance, but a response that necessarily falls short of achieving its end, which is to name the thing resistant to such 'carrying out'. But the excluded thing, the ma(s)ter-piece, the missing surplus that Hugnet's economics attempts to regulate, emerges in Stein's poem through the very failure or crisis of the economy that her translation provokes. Stein translates the dialectical economics of Hugnet's poem of mourning into the melancholic sublime. The 'stain' or *tache* is the excess that is to be violently regulated and excluded by the impossible 'task' or *tâche* assigned by the ego-ideal. The task imposed is one of naming; the imperative I referred to above is concealed at the end of Stein's poem in the form of a question: 'what is my name'. Both poems translate, or name, the nameless thing that poses this question.[103] Naming is an act both of recovery and loss, just as any object in the economy of the pleasure principle is ultimately unsatisfying when measured against the originally lost object, or thing: the naming of the thing represents it as an object, and thus simultaneously repeats its loss or sacrifice.[104] The difference between the poems of Hugnet and Stein lies in the response to the constitutive failure of the melancholic task of naming.

The response of Hugnet's protagonist is borne out by Hugnet's ambivalence to Stein's translation. Hugnet would appear to insist that his poem be the 'object' of translation, that the 'by' of Stein's final lines, 'Georges Hugnet by Gertrude Stein', indicate that her poem is only a version, a rendition, of his original; he claims the right to a just translation, and demands that the version be subordinate to the original. Such a desire for self-identity leads to a melancholic (or, its obverse, maniacal) effort on the part of Hugnet's protagonist to appropriate or represent the thing to be named. However, Stein recognizes that, rather than a naming that refuses the 'tâche' of translation in the name of a justice or right claimed by the subject, the 'tâche' demands a naming that would regulate the exchanges between objects and the thing, accounting for their difference: her task is unsuccessful because it attends to what remains after the act of naming, by simultaneously unnaming it, thereby enacting what Lisa Ruddick has called Stein's 'ethics of the remainder'.[105] Where Hugnet's 'je' insists on the symbolization of the thing, which is tantamount to overcoming all mediation or symbolization and presenting what he calls a 'présence sans mémoire', Stein's schoolgirl acknowledges the gap, acknowledges that a *melancholic* relation to the lost thing is inevitable.

The doubleness of the 'tâche/tache', which is at once a task or *devoir* and a stain, reflects the doubleness of Stein's occupation as writer or translator. My analysis of the permutations of the 'stain' in Stein's work will demonstrate that it is but the other side of the paternal name, 'Stein'. What Stein calls 'an abusive stain' is the bloody 'open wound', in Freud's words, or the inscription of the paternal name on the body. The 'tâche/tache' of the schoolgirl is thus inescapably divided between enacting the violence of the paternal name, or executing the tasks it assigns, and attending to the remainder, or the thing that escapes being named. This is because the thing is itself simply the obverse side of the law, or the paternal name. Stein's translation reveals the other side of that thing to be the dominating paternal instance, which derives the force of its imperative from the 'open wound' at the basis of melancholia.

I will begin by examining Hugnet's work prior to its subjection by Stein to what she calls 'the use of passion and an abusive stain': to the 'work' or action of translation. Hugnet's is a poem of mourning and memory, an 'oeuvre de la passion' in search of the fullness of childhood. Hugnet works through various possibilities of the economy of the pleasure principle, following its law of *Wiederzufinden*, of refinding the lost object. Hugnet attempts the work of mourning to recover his lost 'enfances'. One form of such 'work' in Hugnet's poem is 'la masturbation', which 'm'habille de tes robes [he is addressing 'enfance'] / et me pousse vers toi, vers toi et le travail' (28). As the next passage reveals, the dresses worn by this cross-dressing 'onanist' may come from a 'fille en deuil':

> et toutes celles, enfances, toutes celles qui sont morts
> portes un ruban clair et la manie de la danse.
> L'onaniste se souviendra-t-il de cette fille en deuil
> drapée d'un deuil si limpide et qui l'excitait tant
> après les robes soulevées en visite, en secret
> et qu'il vit pâlir devant une image obscène.
> Chaque jour, elle pâlit davantage, chaque visite,
> jusqu'à mourir à l'ombre sur le jeune homme nu.

(24)

The 'girl in mourning' is naked, 'les robes soulevées', yet covered by a transparent veil of 'mourning'. Though in mourning, she herself becomes a corpse, 'dying in the shadow on the naked young man'. She is identified with what is mourned, and her corpse will haunt the poem as a memory, a remainder, but also as a thingly 'presence without memory' that exceeds the economic regulations of mourning. The note of melancholia in the poem indicates a dissatisfaction with the distribution that economy effects. According to Freud, 'normal' mourning serves to regulate the economy after it has suffered a crisis, a lost investment. Melancholia, on the other hand, is pathological, a dangerous malady, in which the economic crisis leads to a deep depression.[106] Between the poems of Hugnet and Stein, the melancholic relation to the lost thing will emerge as the condition of the economy of mourning.

In a preceding passage, we see where the loss implied by the girl's mourning might have occurred. As we saw with the 'fille en deuil' who herself became a corpse, someone has been lost. But someone has also been 'killed':

> J'ai perdu la plus belle en ouvrant la main,
> en changeant de pas j'ai trompé le silencieuse
> rira l'éternelle *en tuant la plus belle*,
> la morte a su garder son domaine,
> en renfermant les bras j'ai tué l'éternelle,
> l'enfance a renié, renié la souveraine ...
>
> (24; my italics)

'Tué' (killed) echoes the 'tu' addressed to 'enfance' throughout the poem. Also, a connection is made between 'tu' as pronoun and as the past tense of 'taire', 'to silence' in an earlier section, when the speaker refers to 'Tout ce que j'ai tu' (all that I have silenced) (14). These three 'tus', the pronoun, silence, and killing, are not identical, but nonetheless cannot be extricated from one another. 'Tu' stitches several passages together. Included in the list of things 'tu', silenced, are 'le partage de la conscience' and 'notre premier dialogue' (14), both of which silenced things resurface in Stein's translation. The scene of the silencing, loss or murder, the beginning of memory and 'parole', is also the scene of a 'pacte'. The symbolic pact presides over the first dialogue and the 'partage', the sharing or dividing at the basis of the symbolic community, which I will consider in more detail in my discussion of Stein.

Yet the symbolic is instituted in violence. As in the detective stories Stein was fond of, a mysterious death has occurred.[107] Opening the hand entails the loss of 'la plus belle'; but why was it opened? The rhythm of this scene needs to be carefully observed: the suspended hand opens a dialectical economy and a topology of subjectivity. 'Renfermant les bras', closing the arms again, kills 'the eternal', which the third line suggests was in turn the agent of the death of 'the most beautiful', as if 'the eternal' demanded her death, her sacrifice, for the sake of its own eternity, and perhaps its universality. The rhythm might follow such a logic: opening the hand leads to the death of 'the most beautiful', but that death occurs dialectically, in the name of 'the eternal'. Thus, opening the hand reveals 'the eternal', as if the act followed an imperative or purpose of which it was not aware. But the 'je' rebels against this law and closes his arms. 'The eternal' is itself killed as a result of this denial of the 'sovereign': 'l'enfance a renié la souveraine'. In this substitution it is impossible to know what purpose he has in mind. Is his closing of his arms an act of revenge on behalf of 'enfance', and does his 'killing' of the eternal belong to the same act as the 'renunciation' of 'la souveraine' by 'enfance'? Who is identified with whom? The verb 'renier' is also used to refer to the breaking of a promise, or of a pact; thus, a 'sovereign' pact is broken by 'enfance'. But who or what is the 'souveraine' who is 'renié[e]', and what are the positions of the 'je' and 'enfance' in relation to her? The effects of the 'partage de la conscience', or the splitting of the subject, mean that the identities of these allegorical figures are impossible to stabilize. This problem of identification will make the crucial rebellion against the 'eternal' or the 'souveraine', in spite of its apparent purpose, an action that furthers rather than resists the regulation by the imperative of the eternal revealed by the opening of the hand. The agent in this passage, divided against himself, cannot assert his own purpose, but comes into conflict with the purpose of another agent.

The division of the subject, according to Freud, provides the topological condition for melancholia: the impoverished ego of melancholia subjects itself to its ego-ideal, which can exercise a sadistic control of the ego. The origin of the ego-ideal, Freud says, is not in an object-cathexis, but is the result of 'a direct and immediate identification' which is fundamentally ambivalent. The return to this primal identification is what allows the ego to 'give up' the lost object. But this resolution has a cost in melancholic subjection. In melancholia, 'we find that the excessively strong super-ego which has obtained a hold upon consciousness rages against the ego with merciless violence, as if it had taken possession of the whole of the sadism available in the person concerned'.[108] The 'souveraine' marks the place of this ambivalent identification. The 'je' is not, in this passage, identical with the 'souveraine' who is 'renié[e]', and he can therefore act in the name of 'enfance', identifying himself with her. He thus participates in the act of renunciation or violation on behalf of 'enfance'. However, we will see shortly in another passage how the 'je' senses himself wronged, and indebted to, and so in effect identifies with the 'souveraine' who suffers from this disowning or renunciation. The pact implies obligation or indebtedness, but nothing lets us determine, in this pact between 'je' and 'tu' or 'elle', who is indebted to whom. But Hugnet's 'je' will eventually determine the debt, and call in what is due to him.

In the passage under consideration, a pact has been 'renié'. But the attempts of the 'je' to assign responsibility, to attribute guilt, to name and judge the actors in the violation of the pact, leads to contradiction. The pact is already doubled or divided beyond recuperation, however: it is justly or unjustly 'renié' by both the 'je' and 'enfance' in the same gesture, both of whom are revolting against the 'souveraine'. However, because of the concealed identification of the 'je' with that 'souveraine', an identification revealed by the later claiming of rights to which I have alluded, 'enfance' has also 'renié' a pact with, and thus wronged, the sovereign 'je'. The frustration of the 'je' at the teasing inaccessibility of 'enfances', playing its game of 'cache-cache', culminates in a new staging of the judgement of guilt, with 'enfances' having wronged the 'je' by refusing to appear in person. The position of the 'je' is ambivalently doubled between two 'names', or one name, the name of the father. (The name of the 'souveraine' will appear later as 'la fallace', the 'error' – or the phallus.) But we will also see that when the 'je' calls in the debt, it may even be in the apparently opposed name of 'enfance'. Stein's 'game of the name' will respond to this problem of identification and naming, asking, in something like a 'first dialogue', from the position of the lost thing, 'what is my name'.

In one passage the 'je' connects his writing with the closing of the arms ('renfermant mes bras') that, after the opening of the hand, killed the 'eternal'. A shadow, recalling the shadowy corpse of the 'fille en deuil', haunts the writer, and like a muse nourishes him in his sleep:

> je dors en écrivant et grandi de ton ombre
> parce que je n'ai demandé de preuves de ton amour,
> je serre dans mes bras ton épithète.

(34)

The economy of his writing depends on the repeated murder or sacrifice of this corpse. As I said above, 'tu' stitches the thread of naming, blood, and murder that is 'sewn' or 'tattooed' into the poem, as Stein will say. Hugnet connects naming and blood in referring to 'un mur plus neuf / où mon sang a nommé tes avantages' (32). It will be recalled that the book of the 'écolière sans devoir' is 'recouvert de mon sang'. The themes of naming, blood, murder and 'dois' (meaning both duty and debt) gather in the theme of the 'don', the gift, which Hugnet's poem develops. On the first page of the poem, the gifts of love at the limit of 'enfance' and 'les plaisirs adultes' are associated with blood: 'L'amour déjà et ses dons / naissaient avec le sang' (12). Love is sadistic, or masochistic, for the divided subject:

> cet amour si fragile né d'un fouet,
> cette âme surprise par les drogues,
> cette aventure où j'ai laissé
> du sang pour créer ma vie.

(30)

The cruelty of the taskmaster emerges in the persistent references to blood and flagellation in connection with both the sadistic and masochistic pleasure of the 'je'. Stein's poem will emphasize the relation of writing to such violence as is expressed in this passage:

> Recouvert de mon sang
> ces livres d'enfants fouettées?
> Et tout ce plaisir avec feu
> puis bien plus vite
> avec une écolière sans devoir

> ou les copiant sur l'ennui,
> noire des tâches de l'écriture
> et blanche de percale...
>
> (16)

Stein, as I have said, will become this 'écolière sans devoir', a female student without homework, or without 'duty', not having to give 'preuves', but instead copying the books belonging to children who are 'fouettées' (flogged), books that are 'recouvert' with the blood of the 'je'. Her copying of Hugnet's poem will focus on the 'tâches de l'écriture', exploiting between the poems the pun of 'tâche', both task, or duty, and stain. Though without 'devoir', without 'tâches', the student nonetheless produces the 'tâches' of writing: an imperative is at work in this 'plaisir sanguin', connected to the 'preuves de ton amour' of the first passage. In another passage, the flogging becomes a bloody tattooing:

> je pense à mon orgeuil
> qu'aucun regret de mes humiliations subies pour toi
> n'exerce mon enfance à redouter la nuit,
> la nuit et ses dons que tu m'as faits,
> ces dons où *se tatoua ton indifférence*
> sous la forme et la chant d'un regard particulier.
> Enfance je te nomme au centre du monde,
> au centre de mon coeur tu te nommes toi-même,
> tu te nommes la course à l'exemple de ma faim.
>
> (22; my italics)

The tattooing and the whipping are a kind of inscription. In the passage above, it is the 'indifférence' of 'toi' that 'tattoos itself' in the 'dons'. In another passage, the surmounting of this indifference is the moment of 'parole', which refers back to 'la premier dialogue':

> Dénombrée l'exigence,
> dénommée la fallace,
> les grands se sont trompés
> en fondant une famille.
> L'enfance est née de l'enfance
> dans l'indifférence surmontée

et longuement vécue
sortira sa parole.

(14)

The tattoo is the inscription, that is to say the differentiation, of indifference in the form of the gift. In this passage, 'enfance' emerges out of 'enfance' itself, the indifferent folds into itself, in a structure of 'unfolding folds' that Stein will place at the beginning of her poem. It is the *parole* of naming that overcomes the original indifference: in the first passage something 'dénommée' (named) and 'dénombrée' (listed, or numbered) appears. However, it doesn't quite appear: something is named that in the grammar of the sentence only appears in the 'names', 'l'exigence' and 'la fallace'. This named thing is Exigency, a strict taskmaster, a distributor of 'tâches', presiding watchfully over the workplace with its gaze ('regard particulier'); it is 'la fallace' itself: the paternal *phallus*, named by near-homonym. But, as Lacan insisted was the case with the paternal metaphor, whatever is named has vanished. It is merely 'dénommée', 'dénombrée'. Stein's translation of this line is significant: she reads the prefix 'dé' as a negation, and 'dénommée la fallace' is rendered in her text 'named not alas' (277). The naming in this case folds back into itself, and is at the same time an un-naming. This naming is itself a case of indifference surmounted, of the identity of an object conferred by means of the name, but a name that un-names as well. In this fold of the named object is felt the pressure of the indeterminate and indifferent thing, beyond the economy of names ('dé-nommé') and numbers ('dé-nombré').

'Exigence', this taskmaster, 'la fallace' or paternal phallus, seems to be auto-nomous, or self-legislating; its circular founding of itself consists in this double naming: 'it' is simply 'Dénombrée l'exigence, / dénommée la fallace'. Yet it indicates a position at which Hugnet's 'je' places himself, a name with which he identifies, however ambivalently. It provides the 'je' with the means of saying, '*Je suis* dans mon droit', or that he is

sûr alors d'avoir le droit de parler et de vivre,
le droit d'être dans mon tort par plaisir,
comme la peste et la famine.

(20)

Certain of having the right to live and to speak, the 'je' has claimed his right to pleasure. The 'je' feels itself to be alone, and cruel, in its self-certainty, beyond doubt and doubling, because of this 'oubli'.[109] After the doubleness of sadism and masochism, after the ambivalent identification, the 'je' has stabilized itself.

But this radical attempt to conceal the 'open wound' of division and to deny loss only brings about a mania, a word I borrow not only from Freud but also from Hugnet. The 'girl in mourning' who was discussed above was taken over by 'un manie de la danse'. Another appearance of the 'manie' of the female figure appears in connection with her singular thinking ('pensée'), which is described as 'un[e] manie étrangère à la séduction' (18). Her 'manie' is foreign to the adult sexual relation, characterized by 'seduction' and 'l'adultère'; the abyss between childhood's 'présence sans mémoire' and 'les plaisirs adultes' cannot be crossed, even by 'masturbation'. Hers is a 'manie' (which I also read as a 'maniement' performed by the hand) that occupies itself with something other than the genitals, the 'sexe' of 'nos plaisirs adultes': it is pre-Oedipal, and pre-genital. But it is precisely the gap that both radically separates and radically mingles the two orders of 'enfance' and 'plaisirs adultes' that causes such anxiety to Hugnet's 'je'. The attempt to cross this gap will be the basis of the 'manie' of the 'je', understanding 'manie' in Freud's sense, as the other side of melancholia, but also in the sense of the 'maniement', the handling or manipulation, of objects. Stein's text will stage the forgetting, or 'oubli', that is the condition of the 'manie' of Hugnet's 'je', a mania of oblivion that tries to forget in order to become 'sans mémoire', to abolish the traces of something that cannot be forgotten: a 'pact' incurred by a gift. The most apparent maniacal attempt to destroy all mediating veils of mourning occurs in a passage in which the speaker says that he takes, or holds, 'enfance' by the hand. But that joining of hands is not enough for the return of the 'presence without memory', and continues the hide and seek of memory, 'the work of passion':

> Je te tiens par la main et tu te caches sous ta tête
> cet éclat de mon diadème, ce que fût ma conscience,
> mais ce n'est pas de cela qu'il s'agit ni d'oubli
> ni de souvenirs, il s'agit de ce mot retrouvé
> de ce geste si futile qui font que les souvenirs
> sont morts, morts et sans lendemain

et qui font que la vie vous tient par la main
et ne cache rien à ceux qu'elle oublie.

(30)

Taking 'enfance' by the hand, forgetting and remembering, have nothing to do with 'it' ('il ne s'agit pas d'oubli, ni de souvenirs'). 'Il', 'it', has to do with 'a word found again, and this futile gesture', the murderous gesture, both of which make it so that memories are dead, 'sans lendemain'; they make it so that life takes one 'by the hand', lends a 'main', as it were, and 'hides nothing from those she forgets'. As I said above, the thing has no name; thus its return requires a word 'retrouvé' (refound, remembered, recognized). Along with the murderous 'geste' that kills memory, enabling life itself to put forth its hand and immediately take one's own, this 'mot retrouvé' can recall the missing 'presence without memory'. That immediacy is the pure action of the hand of 'la vie', an action that reserves nothing, hides nothing from the sight, and goes beyond the means and ends structure of the work of passion to realize another order of being.

But this pure act merely mirrors the murderous 'geste futile' that fails to lead beyond such action. Despite its death, the memory, which the word that is 'retrouvé' cannot conjure away, remains like a corpse. The claim of the right to live, to take life by the hand, or have life's hand take one's own, assumes a duality of essence and appearance, and forgets the split or division reflected in the crossing of sadism and masochism in the gift. The duality is represented in the poem largely in terms of sexual difference, but the division is of another order. The forgotten double haunts the economy of pleasure as a missing surplus. Stein assumes the position of this forgotten leftover.

GERTRUDE'S STAIN

Stein's translation begins with the problem of identity and existence summed up in Hugnet's 'je suis' (I am) by engaging Hugnet's poem as it begins, already in pursuit of 'enfances': 'je vous poursuis avant de dormir, sans hâte. / Sans hâte, mais plié sous des tâches ingrâtes...' (10). The 'je' is subjected to 'thankless tasks', and thus to some kind of imperative. Stein doesn't pick up on the verb 'poursuivre' (to follow) until section four of Hugnet's poem, which begins: 'Je suis dans mon droit....' (12). Stein hears these lines perversely, hearing the verb 'suivre' instead of 'être', in the case of 'je suis'; she folds 'je vous poursuis' and 'je suis' together in order to subvert the legal claim of the 'je' and his self-certainty by arriving at 'I follow you'. Moreover, this schoolgirl, 'following' the dictates of the text she is 'copying' or translating, occupies the prior 'I' by taking it over this way: 'I follow you' has two voices, that of the prior 'je' *and* that of the student who 'follows' the 'je'.

In the process, Hugnet's 'thankless tasks' become 'an abusive stain', emphasizing the duplicity of the word 'tâches'. In the same sentence, Stein also picks up on the verb 'plié' (bent, or folded): 'Without the pressure of a place with which to come unfolded folds are a pressure and an abusive stain'. The initial 'without' of Stein's poem does not necessarily serve to indicate a lack, the 'without' of privation, or the loss of objects, since it is also a without, an outside, the 'place' of the pressure of a quantity, that 'to come unfolded folds'. The fold, in order to unfold, to reveal itself, folds itself. Is this fold a doubling of one into two or a folding of two into one? This question will be sustained throughout the poem, reappearing with each of its many doublings and divisions, effects of the ambivalent force of the fold. We have already seen this 'fold' at work in Hugnet's poem as the surmounting of the 'indifference' of 'enfance'. Stein's economy of the fold returns to that moment of indifference, appearing most clearly in her translation of Hugnet's line, 'J'ai payé le prix des mots' (12): 'I have been left to bargain with myself' (276). In the next paragraph this voice can again be heard, in a version of the 'premier dialogue': 'Everything is best of all for you which is for me / I like a half of which it is as much'. There are several ways to stage this; for example, one might hear the bargaining self trying to persuade itself that it is not at odds with itself, that 'what is good for you is good for me, we two are one, we are "myself"'. Yet despite the persuasive tone, there is something odd: 'what is best of all for you ... is for me'. Even in this formulation the folding is several, but the rivalry is evident: even as 'what is best' is given over to the other, it is claimed as 'for me'. In section 5, Hugnet's list of 'tout ce que j'ai tu' begins with 'le partage de la conscience', the dividing or sharing, or rather the folding, of 'conscience'. The list also includes 'notre premier dialogue', which is either shared or divided. This is bargaining, after all, and interests are at stake, interests one might hope could be worked out through this proto-legal form of negotiation, which works at determining the borders of sharing and dividing. The renunciation implied in giving over 'what is best' to the other appears ambivalent at best. But it is not solely a renunciation, since a claim is made on it in the same statement.

What is 'best', and how does this value emerge? Hugnet's poem indicates what it might be, but does not provide an answer. At the time of the sharing or dividing ('partage') of 'conscience', which Stein stages as solitary bargaining, the 'tu' in the dialogue had at her feet 'quelque chose de très rare / que je ne connaissais pas' (14). What is this very rare thing? If we note the interchangeability of 'me' and 'you' in Stein's sentence concerning the bargain, it might appear that 'what is best' is simply agreed upon, or self-evident. But the primacy of the 'for me' in the negotiation claims for the speaker the power of definition and evaluation, of measurement. The claim is, however, already an effort at restitution, at limiting an inevitable loss by coming to an agreement: the 'solitary' bargainer is doubled, and is already forced to share or divide whatever the valuable thing is. Clearly a claim has been made on the thing by the 'you', a claim resembling Hugnet's speaker's appeal to 'droit'. But these claims could regress endlessly, if one were to see in them only claims on what the other has claimed. The form of this statement, this negotiation, is earlier than the content of what is 'best of all', the very rare thing. The 'you' and the 'me' are folded in this case: each person thrown into the bargain can speak these words, 'you' and 'me', shifting positions as in a mirror. The bargaining is solitary, as Stein says, but that solitude is folded: the valuable thing is the effect of a mimetic fold. The first dialogue takes place in a doubled solitude.

The next sentence resorts to a partition, a 'partage', as Hugnet says: 'I like a half of which it is as much' (276). The object divides in half as one generously shares by taking only half. 'A half of which it is as much' would seem to indicate that the division maintains an equivalence of the two parts, a division of the one into the two mirrored quantities, or values. Yet this half is augmented by the 'it': there is a strange force to the genitive in the phrase, 'a half of which it is as much'. The 'it', together with the 'as much', returns back beyond that half, beyond the equalizing 'as much', to the 'it', the whole thing. That is, the 'half' that 'I like' magically returns to the value of the whole thing, becoming 'as much as it'. This resembles the folding of the 'it' that is 'dénommée' and 'dénombrée' in Hugnet's poem, in the surmounting of indifference by means of a circular naming. But that other circularity could not include the unnamed and indeterminate leftover at its limit.

The distribution of a quantity is being bargained over, but its exact measure is unclear. Stein's poem measures this quantity repeatedly in various ways, most often by autonomous comparatives and superlatives such as 'more' and 'most'. Yet, as the preceding few sentences reveal, the conditions of measurement have yet to be determined. The 'best' and the 'most', which imply different kinds of measure, of quality and quantity, are confounded in an almost monetary sense of 'value'. The thing is both the 'rare thing' and mere quantity. It becomes clear as the poem unfolds that stabilized quantities and standards of measure require an effacement of the ambivalent unfolding of the fold, by instituting an economy through which distribution can be regulated. Hugnet's measure will be haunted by an unmeasurable quantity, what is left 'd'oubli', of oblivion, of what is forgotten or excluded in this identification. This returns in Stein's poem as the 'double', which echoes with Hugnet's 'd'oubli'.

The solitary bargaining is Stein's version of Hugnet's 'pact' and 'dialogue'. Its solitude is inseparable from a doubling, or fold. The speaker of the poem says that she 'has been left alone to bargain with [her]self', since 'they went away' (276). In a language that sounds strangely contractual, a legal fiction is apparent: 'Let it be that it is said let me alone'. What kind of solitude is this? Hugnet's opening lines are echoed, 'je vous laisse libres', but the speakers cannot be lined up on either side of the dialogue, with one person leaving the other behind. Stein's 'I' is not only that of 'enfance', abandoned by the 'je' of the other poem; it is also the 'je' in its own solitude, deprived of 'enfance'. What is 'left alone' is doubled, is at once the 'je' and 'elle' of Hugnet's poem, at once mourning and mourned, like the 'fille en deuil' who herself becomes a corpse-shadow. This doubleness indicates a solitude in Stein's poem that makes the economic system of Hugnet's poem much less stable. This appears in the fluctuating measure of the bargaining:

Everything is best of all for you which is for me,
I like a half of which it is as much
Which never in alone is more than most
Because I easily can be repaid in difficulty of the hurry left
Between now not at all and after which began.

(276)

'They' leave something she can bargain with, a little capital to start her off: a patrimony. The word 'repaid' turns the adverb 'alone' into 'a loan'. Hugnet twice refers to a 'loan', thereby authorizing Stein's translation: 'enfance' 'se prête au jeu des phrases' (22); that is, 'enfance' 'lends herself' to the game or play of sentences. The 'game' depends on this loan, or credit, on this original debt or obligation. But the 'game' of 'what is the name' (to echo Stein's concluding lines) will be slightly different from Hugnet's game, which, as we have seen, 'je joue' (12). The other game operates from a place on the other side of the identification of the 'je', on the other side of 'la fallace' – on the side of the remainder.

As this economy becomes more determinate, so does the 'quantity' being bargained over. In the case of the loan, it is not divided in two in the paradoxical manner it was at first. The loan leaves the speaker feeling that 'I easily can be repaid in difficulty' of the hurry left / Between now not at all and after which began' (276). 'I have been left alone', or a loan, yet 'I can be repaid': the loan demands an expense – something was paid out as collateral. This question points to the difference between this staging and the economically less rationalized one presented previously in terms of the standard of measure, in which the negotiation concerned an indeterminate, indeterminable, value or quantity. The initial capital, the loan, in this credit economy, implies an initial debt. Thus, the relation with the other figured in the pronouns no longer seems as symmetrical as it was in the mimetic bargaining. A quantity is 'given', in both senses of that word: it is already there, yet it implies a prior exchange. 'They' have left her a loan. This time, the speaker is 'alone' in a way that was not possible with the scene of rivalry: the division, or the mimetic fold, of the 'myself' is downplayed, and 'myself' as debtor to another takes centre stage.

The identity or name of this other will make a significant difference. The mirroring of the 'I' continues to leave its mark, but the scene introduces a 'they' who have left the loan. The pronoun 'they' signals the new scene that brings the 'I' into one, one who is 'left alone'. The loan and the 'alone' fold into each other: 'I' have been left alone, 'I' am a loan. I am left, I remain. This solitary 'I' is still not, however, the 'I' of Hugnet's 'je suis'. A line in Hugnet's poem indicates the place of the remainder, or 'reste', that Stein calls 'I': '*Restait* à prouver l'irrémédiable'. This irremediable or irreparable involves the little girls who '*restaient* à genoux / devant les garçons déculottés' (my italics). Stein's 'I', when not a schoolgirl, appears in all of Hugnet's other female figures, including the corpses and shadows of the dead or sacrificed. The irremediable, or the irreparable, 'remains to be proven', or undergone: it is not yet available to experience, which is regulated by the pleasure principle. It is the 'reste' or remainder of the symbolization or mediation by which the pleasure principle functions to distance the pain of the thing. The irremediable is an inexchangeable *suffering* that cannot be compensated. Something is lost or sacrificed that can't be 'repaid', or returned, because it is beyond the valuation the economy of pleasure allows, not to be measured in terms of pleasure and unpleasure. It remains to be proven, or undergone, as a pain on the horizon of that economy, excluded from it; but, though it has never been present, this thing returns to haunt the economy of pleasure.[110]

Both poems are haunted by a painful trauma, by irremediable loss. In Hugnet's poem, 'enfance' 'se prête' (lends itself) to the symbolic 'game of sentences'. The 'prêt', or loan, recurs also in a folded form, as 'pure *perte*', a pure loss that cannot be compensated:

> J'ai faim et soif à vie,
> à vie purge ta peine,
> en pure perte.

(24)

'Your pain' is purged into 'la vie'. This clarifies the nature of 'the pressure of a place' to which Stein refers. Pain may be the outer limit of the economy of the pleasure principle, but it has a place in relation to that economy nonetheless, a place 'without', in both senses. It is the place of the thing, which is 'pure loss'.

But it is a pure 'perte' into which is folded a return: it recalls the collateral, the loss involved in the loan, the 'perte' in the 'prêt'. Is pure loss possible, or does something always return? This question invokes the economy of melancholia, which maintains the 'partage', the division or sharing between pure loss and compensation, in a kind of 'presence without memory': 'Restait à prouver l'irrémédiable', the irreparable, what is lost, remains, to be suffered. Or, in another translation, a pain beyond remedy remains to be suffered. Melancholia is 'irrémédiable'. The loan and the loss, the 'prêt' and the 'perte', work the limits of the economy of mourning.

The loan is not money, nor is it an object; it is a mere quantity prior to such determinations. Because of the incalculable measure of that quantity, the debt created by the loan seems to exceed the quantity lent. The loan is offered, but the collateral is taken from the side of the one receiving the quantity. Something is taken at the same time as something is given, and the two are not of the same value; they are not even of the same order of value. Something has been signed over to another name, but it is not a pure loss, since 'I can be repaid'. The loan is a fold, between receiving and losing, paying and acquiring. It is a pact, a guarantee, but one which demands (or 'exige', in French) obligation on the part of the 'I', despite her confidence in the fair deal and the promised returns. 'Now not at all' indicates the negation of the present in this exchange, and the positing of an 'after which began', in the past tense. The after-effects of the loan have already begun, even before the loan is given. The repayment is already underway; the 'I' is losing its quantity. Even in the determinate quantities or objects of experience, in the signs of the economy of pleasure, there is a lack that refers them to what is missing: the incalculable quantity that was exchanged or sacrificed for the regulated economy.

The thing 'they' lend is an unnamed quantity: 'Named not alas but they must lend it for' (277). This line is Stein's homophonic translation of 'dénommée la fallace' (14). This imperative loan does not yet rely upon the institution of the measure, for example in the form of money, but on bargaining, the principle of which is revealed in the adjectives 'best', 'more' and 'most', 'less' and 'least', and so on. Let me focus first on the more determinate aspect of this quantity, the side of the object, rather than the thing: it appears in the patrimony that Hugnet calls 'la fallace'.

This paternal instance is evident in another series working in Stein's poem, as in Hugnet's: the family. The emergence of the self-naming 'fallace' is apparent in Stein's poem, but the moment of identification does not take place in the same manner as in Hugnet's. For the latter, as we saw, the family is the mistake of 'les grands' (14). Stein's family emerges in a particularly complex scene. A 'little one' appears at several points.[111] The birth of this little one takes place, or has taken place in section 12, and the scene of its conception leaves its marks in the poem: 'they need to sew, the difference is that sewing makes it bleed and such with them in all the way of seed and seeding and repine and they will which is mine and not all mine...' (280). The reference to 'seeding' makes 'sew' a pun on 'sow'. The sowing of the (paternal) seed 'makes it bleed'. The bleeding makes a stain, or spot, the 'tâche' of Hugnet's poem.

At the beginning of Stein's poem, the elements of this primal scene are put in place, in a staging of 'the use of passion':

I follow you without it having slept and went.
Without the pressure of a place with which to come unfolded
    folds are a pressure and an abusive stain
A head if uncovered can be as hot, as heated,
to please to take a distance to make life,
And if resisting, little, they have no thought,
a little one which was a little which was all as still
Or with or without fear or with it all,
And if in feeling all it will be placed alone beside
And it is with with which and not beside not beside may,
Outside with much which is without with me, and not an
    Indian shawl, which could it be but with my blood.

(274)

The hot head is 'to please', to regulate pleasure, as well as 'to make life'. This 'pleasure' recalls that of Hugnet's 'je'. Stein's 'I' refuses this 'pleasure' and its economy, refusing to conceal the limit of pain beyond the opposition of pleasure and unpleasure. The sowing of the seed 'to make life', to make the 'little one', leaves an 'abusive stain' which the 'I' links with 'my blood'. 'My blood' is Stein's translation of the 'plaisirs sanguins' that Hugnet's poem ascribes to the 'vous', the 'enfances', of his poem's opening lines. The 'plaisirs sanguins' is pleasure at its limit, the pain of the inscription of a tattoo, in Hugnet's sadistic or masochistic rendition, or the name-stain of the other law that emerges in translation. Hugnet's 'je' refers to 'mon sang' once in his poem as what 'covers' or 'recovers' the schoolgirl's book. This thread of blood leads finally to the game of 'naming' in the concluding lines of Stein's poem, which we will look at later.

For the moment, the patrimony, the line of the father, must be traced: the pun of 'sewing' as stitching and 'sowing' as seeding looks towards another 'stitching' of a sort later in the poem: 'for her to come with him with when he went he went and came and any little name is shame as such tattoo. Any little ball is made a net and any little net is made for mine and any little mine that any have will always violate the hope of this which they wore as they lose' (284). Sewing makes it bleed, the blood leaves an abusive stain. The pricking also tattoos the shameful name. The 'little one' of the family appears in this passage also, as the 'little mine', but also as 'any little name'. The name is a stitching or writing on the body, but also a shameful stain, or 'tâche', of blood or ink. The final lines of Stein's poem echo the 'abusive stain' of the name-tattoo of the first section of the poem:

> And a hope be relieved
> By all of it in case
> Of my name.
> What is my name.
> That is the game
> Georges Hugnet
> By Gertrude Stein.[112]

Gertrude's stain, her shameful name, is Stein. But, as the poem has been reminding us repeatedly, it is not all 'hers': it is the patronym. The paternal 'gift' of the name is a shameful tattoo. It is bestowed by 'sewing', but also by the father's 'sowing', the founding of the family, as Hugnet's poem has it. Recalling Hugnet's 'tâche', this stain is also a task, something demanded, or 'exigé'. If we recall also Hugnet's 'écolière sans devoir', the female student at her desk, without homework or duty, we see where Stein's place is folded into the poem, a place 'without': 'Without the pressure of a place with which to come unfolded folds are a pressure and an abusive stain' (274). Stein's 'copying' of Hugnet's poem rhymes with that student's task, the 'tâches de l'écriture' (16), the stain and task of writing.

The 'tâche' is double: on the one hand, the pain and the stain of blood; on the other the name of the father, 'Stein', and the imperative. The difference between them is marked not only by 'la fallace', but also by 'exigence'. What is 'dénombrée' is not identical with itself: it is 'listed' or 'counted', but is at the same time beyond number. It is 'any little name', naming itself, the innumerable substitutions or translations of the place of 'la fallace'. The economy opens to the pressure of a place where there is a quantity, or a thing, both added and subtracted, that is not 'equivalent' to, because not of the same order as, the patronym. In Stein's poem, there is an explicit refusal of the narcissistic moment of the economy of pleasure, as well as of the 'hot head', the phallus, that would reproduce that economy: 'Believe me it is not for pleasure that I do it' (278). The place of identification in her poem is elsewhere, or on another face of the 'fallace'.

Hugnet's 'fallace' appears in the context of the family, and indicates the founding point of the identity of the 'je'. Such a founding reappears in Stein's translation: 'It was with him that he was little tall and old and just as young as when begun' (282). 'He' is old and young, little and tall; 'he' is father and son at once. Pregnancy is suggested in section 19, where the young and old, little and tall figure appears: 'they have it here it is with much that left by him he is within within within' (283). 'He' is 'within' in a double sense, as child and as the sowing father. If 'he' as sower has left, 'he' also remains, having engendered himself as the paradoxical father-son who is little-tall and young-old. Paternity asserts its founding rights, and the desire of the son-father bestows its name-stain in this self-reproducing economy. But something remains forgotten. In the midst of the economic 'ripeness' of the primal scene of sewing in section 12, the birth and ripening of the little one, there is a reference to 'the way of seed and seeding and repine' (280). The word 'ripen' folds into 'repine'. 'Repining' directs us to an affective focus of both poems: one of hunger, deprivation, suffering, the melancholic side of the large appetite of Hugnet's manic 'je' and his right to the pleasure of eating and speaking. The word 'mourn' appears for the first time in this section, and will recur later (section 16), picking up on Hugnet's 'deuil'. Recall that his mourning girl promptly 'died in the shadow'. Stein's 'I' occupies the place of the corpse, or the remainder that haunts the place of the father's name, 'Stein'. Repining and mourning are an affective diversion from the pleasure of the text. A passage in Stein returns to the sexual relation and the death that was marked by Hugnet's 'fille en deuil':

> Rest it in little pieces
> They like it to be held to have and hold
> Believe me it is not for pleasure that I do it.
>
> (278)

'Rest it in little pieces' echoes 'rest in peace', and reveals the strange quality of some of Stein's 'epithets': 'When this you see remember me'; 'when this you see see me' (279); but especially, 'when this you see think of me. / It is very sad that it is very bad that badly and sadly and mourn...' (281). These are not only epithets, but epitaphs. The poem alludes to a gravesite: 'In all a lent for all when grass is dried and grass can dry when all have gone away and come back then to stay' (280). The parallel in Hugnet's poem is the 'fille en deuil / drapée en deuil' who sleeps with her 'jeune solitaire... / où d'autres verraient que de l'herbe', the grass which has presumably grown over the unmarked grave (24). She had gradually paled into a shadowy corpse, which returns here 'to stay'; the invisible gravestone marks the identification of Stein's 'I' with the haunting, shadowy, corpse.[113]

There had been happier times, it would seem. Following this epitaph is an echo of the wedding ceremony: to have and to hold. Stein's poem emphasizes the ambiguity of Hugnet's 'partage': the loss or division is also a joining; to halve is to hold: 'they have been having that they join as well' (275). The 'having' of the loan also recalls the bargaining scene in Stein's poem. Its structure is that of the original 'having' of the loan. Before learning that the father-son is 'within within within', we are told 'that they like this they have it here it is with much that left by him'. The loan returns in the paradox of having 'here' what one does not 'have' to present, what 'they have': 'they have it, here it is... left by him'. 'It' divides here, or is shared between 'they' and 'here'. 'I' have given it up to 'them', but 'here it is'. It both is and is not identical with itself: the indeterminate quantity, the thing, and the determinate quantity, the patrimony, occupy the same place, named by Hugnet 'la fallace'. Elsewhere, a letter divides the word 'have' right in the middle: 'to have is to halve a beak' (281). If 'having' is also 'halving', it is dividing and losing, or sharing, half. Loss and return coincide, though they do not necessarily share the same value. 'All have gone away and come back then to stay'. This poem is haunted: all that has gone away nonetheless remains, exerting 'pressure' on language; from 'without' comes a 'pressure', not a 'pleasure', a quantity to be discharged, a pain that remains to be suffered. No pleasure is to come from this translation: 'Any pleasure leads to me and I lead them away away from pleasure and from me' (280). The 'pressure' of that place is to be distinguished from the 'pleasure' of the place of Hugnet's 'je'.[114]

What has happened to Hugnet's 'pure perte', the loss which purged childhood of 'peine', diffusing that 'peine' into 'la vie'? This first quantity is found between the gift and the loan, which do not belong to different economic systems as much as indicate a fold within the economy of pleasure. The 'gift' names the economy that would be proper to the regulation of the quantity–thing, but that economy is not to be presented in the work of pleasure. Loans are usually made to the profit of the lender, who invests that quantity in the creditor, expecting a return. Freud argued that the investments we make can normally be recalled in case of death or loss of the object, by means of the work of mourning. But rewrite this in terms of what Stein presents as the original debt, and the 'returns', the quantity that is recalled through mourning, refer elsewhere, to that first incommensurable quantity. On the one hand, this quantity is the patronym, and the economy of pleasure is based on the paternal debt. But on the other, it indicates the thing, an incalculable quantity given and lost, or excluded, at once. The 'fallace', like the sexual relation, is a place of 'leavings', of departures and leftovers, exclusions or remains. The economy alludes to something 'more' or 'extra' that such a regulated economy of restitution or return excludes, or that is always subtracted from it, a point of no return, or 'pure perte'.

In the passage from Hugnet's poem that Stein translates into the bargaining scene, we can see a more determinate economy at work than in Stein's poem, based on an appeal by the 'je' to justice and to rights:

> Je suis dans mon droit,
> on m'a trahi si fidèlement.

J'ai payé le prix des mots
et ce n'est pas un amusement.

(12)

He has been betrayed, even though he has paid the 'prix des mots'; his appeal is based on the sacrifice of something whose return is being demanded, in the name of justice and the right of property. But this thing follows its own law, which is not the law of equivalence. Stein's translation leaves room for the thing that remains, indifferent to the differentiations of the fold. It is not subject to the family, nor is it outside the family and the father's name. The remainder should be renamed, or rather, 'dénommée':

> And a hope be relieved
> By all of it in case
> Of my name.
> What is my name.
> That is the game.

(287)

The word 'relief' returns us to the remainder. Earlier in Stein's poem that hope appears as a 'hope of eating all alike', whose relief is indicated in these final lines. 'Relief' from want is what was most in demand during the Depression, and this is perhaps echoed in Stein's use of the word. The reference to eating came from Hugnet's poem: as we have just seen, Hugnet's 'je' claims the right to 'parler et de manger'. But for the speaker of Stein's translation, the hunger remains, it is not relieved despite the eating, or incorporating, that follows the regulating law of the pleasure principle. Something is missing, left 'without'. In fact, far from leaving us exclusively with a sense of unsatisfied hunger, the reference to 'relief' might actually suggest satiety: 'relief' also refers to the leftovers of a meal, what remains after one can eat no more. Thus 'relief' indicates both too much, and not enough – in other words, the missing surplus, appearing in these lines in the fantasmatic form of the 'all'.

There is also, however, an economic register to Stein's language in the above passage: the word 'hope' in Latin is *sperare*, which, according to Jacques le Goff, 'in the Middle Ages referred to the self-interested hope of all economic actors engaged in a transaction that involved *time*, in other words, that stipulated a remunerated *wait* in return for profit (or loss) or for interest'.[115] Similarly, the word 'hope' implies such an 'interested' perspective, based on what I have referred to as the temporization of temporality, the deferral of the demanded thing. This temporization, as I have argued, is constituted by the economy established by the name of the father, 'Stein'. But the lining of the name is the 'stain', the remainder in which the thing persists: this is the 'case / Of my name' – the 'case', or *casus: la chose* inhabiting the name of the father. The question of the name ('What is my name') indicates the place of the subject as the 'stain' and as the thing, in the position fantasized as the position of 'enfances' as Woman by Hugnet's 'je'. The question, 'what is my name', is posed by what is outside the economy of the name of the father, which is all based on a 'fallace', an imaginary phallus – a mistake. Hugnet answers this question posed by what is beyond representation by insisting that the gap is that of sexual difference. Hugnet writes, 'tu devins femme ... / toutes les fleurs sont à mon nom / dans tes bras ...' (36). As the place of the thing becomes the place of Woman, the flowers in her arms are simultaneously in the name of the imaginary father.

The co-implication of the stain and the name of the father means that the 'relief' that is demanded is intimately connected with the imaginary domination of the father; the demand for 'relief', for the thing itself, for an end to economic mediation, implies the repetition of the sacrifice of the thing. We have seen this repetition at work in Hugnet's poem, by way of Stein's anamorphosis, as the scenes of sadistic violence. The end of Stein's poem doesn't 'relieve' the debt, complete the payments, or satisfy itself with any returns, in the form of a pleasure from the object, the profit that might come from the investment of borrowed funds. It instead recalls the remainder outside the economy of restitution. That remainder can only be figured as another object, perhaps, something else to be incorporated into (or rather, employed by, adapted to) the economy of pleasure, yet it is far from being identical with that object. But that object is also far from being identical with itself. The 'hope' comes up against a limit, the remainder or relief of the object itself. 'Without' the patronym and the patrimony is something not accounted for.

Hugnet opens his address to 'Enfances' by placing them in the 'cent coins de ma mémoire', where they are to be found, 'si ma mémoire est l'oeuvre de la passion'. Stein refers in her translation of this line to 'the use of passion', to which is opposed, in the same passage, 'a pressure and an abusive stain' (10/274). The stain reflects a certain 'abuse' of the 'work of passion', or an abusive use of such an economy of memory, and its work of mourning, founded on the patronym and the debt, the returns of which, in the form of pleasure, Hugnet's 'je' claimed. Stein's translation is an 'abusive stain' of Hugnet's poem, located in one of the 'coins' of his poem, the corner where the schoolgirl sits, as if punished, writing her 'tâches'. It engages another memory to approach what Hugnet calls 'la présence sans mémoire'. This memory is not a 'work', an 'oeuvre', of passion. The presence without memory is a melancholic memory of the thing, which is the ultimate guarantor of the coinage of memory, to which Hugnet's 'je' appeals as his due, but which can never keep its promise, or pact. Such presence cannot be bought with the signs of memory, as the products of the work or labour of passion, but demands another memory, demands a paradoxical economy of loss. This economy is imitated in translation, which registers the 'pressure of a place' of another thing, but Stein's translation also reveals the necessary repetition of the subjection to the name, the subjection that produces the stain, or surplus of the thing, as the lining of the name. Though Stein emphasizes the gendering of Hugnet's economy, she does not value the leftover or missing surplus as a redemptive power for the economy of exchange, because the return of the stain is also the return of the imperative ego-ideal in its imaginary form.

4
'New Deal or Steal'

INTRODUCTION: 'TO ADMINISTER THE PUBLIC TRUST'

According to Spengler's account in *Decline of the West*, as we have seen, the new concentrated forms of capital that began to take shape at the end of the nineteenth century make inevitable 'the coming war between Economics and Politics'. To translate Spengler into more familiar and less bombastic language: the reorganization of the economy makes possible the concentration of the formerly scattered economic energies of the marketplace into the material structures of power known as trusts, monopolies and corporations. The corporation makes the economic force of capital available for embodiment in the universal ruler-will of the leader. But this could not happen in America, since according to Spengler America is incapable of politics as such. This was not simply a cliché of reactionary Europeans: as Robert MacIver argued, for historical reasons America could not transform its 'private', economic energies into a properly 'public', political force. If a political leader is to take over the economic sphere, he must have the institutions with which to do so; the liberal tradition of American politics had virtually guaranteed that no public institutions could regulate the private sphere according to a determined public good. Despite the anti-fascism of political groups of conservative, liberal or leftist tendencies, therefore, fascism was not a major threat in America, as it was in Europe, which had a tradition of corporatist institutions available for reactionary purposes. To be fulfilled in America, Spengler's prediction that monopoly capitalism sets the stage for the authoritarian state would have required a different political and legal tradition, one that placed less emphasis on the individualistic concept of contract.

Stein's fear of 'organization' caused her to conflate the corporate state of fascism and the corporation as such, which she thought would make 'employees' of 'hired men'. Zukofsky, whose political perspective was predominantly Marxist, is more careful to distinguish between kinds of 'organization'. A-8 – written in large part during the period of the Popular Front – appears in its politics to be primarily anti-fascist, even to some extent sharing Stein's anxiety that monopoly capitalism lays the groundwork for the fascist state. But Zukofsky looks beyond Spengler's and Stein's notion of domination as exercised by a paternal figure wielding his powerful ruler-will. In line with Spengler's judgement that America could have no properly public good, no universal term embodying and representing individual wills, Zukofsky recognized what Stein only perceived dimly, that another form of domination was in the making. This was to be a domination exercised not by a universal Man or fascist leader, but a 'No Man' who, in his anonymity and absence, conceals his will in an immanent domination – a false universality with no proper, paternal name. Citing Charles F. Adams, Zukofsky sees the new corporate structure of the economy and of society as dominated by 'a power for which our language contains no name'. By calling this power 'No Man', Zukofsky names the power even while leaving it nameless, to suggest that traditional concepts of power such as Pound's anthropomorphic model no longer apply. If there is a 'person' or a ruler-will in power, it is not the fascist leader but instead a 'No Man' in a precise legal sense. While in Germanic law, the corporation was a *real* person, for the Roman tradition as it was developed in nominalist Anglo-American legislation, the corporation is a *persona ficta*, a 'fictive person'. The corporation had the legal status of a person even as it was legally 'nobody', a mere collection of individual stockholders, that is to say, 'owners' of a new kind of property that provided limited liability and little power. On the one hand, the American corporation demanded recognition as a person, in order to avail itself of the rights of contract legislated in favour of the individual. Yet at the same time, it did not want to be so much a person that it could be considered to have a real will of its own.

Zukofsky chooses the corporation as a synecdoche for the emerging form of domination because the contemporary discourse concerning the corporation raises to the surface and apparently resolves the basic contradictions of American ideology. The paradoxical legal identity of the corporation reconciles the radical individualism of American ideology with the perceived need for and increasing evidence of collective modes of social organization and identity.[116] Zukofsky recognized that this redefinition of the boundaries between the private and an attenuated 'public' sphere in effect took as its model the development of the corporation and the trusts at the end of the nineteenth century. Zukofsky's corporate 'No Man', as we shall see, is a private bank that issues public money. Therefore, it also engages with Pound's analysis of the history of American banking as a record of the progressive transfer of the public good to the forces of usury. For Pound, the conflict of the public and private is most telling in the history of banking. Private banks like the Bank of England and later the Federal Reserve are usurious institutions feeding off the public good, as opposed to public banks like the Monte de Paschi.[117] Pound's opposition of public and private centres on a distinction between a good debt that serves the universal or the public good, and a bad debt that serves exclusionary private interests and is ultimately destructive of the public good. Zukofsky does not accept Pound's unequivocal distinction between good and bad debt because he does not accept the distinction of private and public to which Pound is committed. Zukofsky recognized that such concepts as the 'public' would have to be redefined for the social and political conditions to which economic concentration has given rise. Instead, he focuses on the political contestation over the proper border between public and private of which Pound's concern with debt is an example.

I will begin by examining the ideological conditions of the various group theories and practices that emerged from the obsolescence of the classical liberal market and its individualist ideology. Zukofsky, as we shall see throughout this chapter, contests the dual strategy of American ideology, which exploits the fundamental contradictions, first clearly argued by Tocqueville, that result from the legacy of individualism and the related ideologemes of contract and the marketplace. On the one hand, the new group or 'corporatist' thought found it necessary to critique America's traditional individualist ideology, a critique which would lead to new models of the social that relied not so much on the liberal contractual model as on more psychological or sociological-functionalist categories. On the other hand, the socialist, communist or generally left critique of individualism, the marketplace and the contract demanded a concept of group identities which simultaneously resisted the reactionary possibilities implicit in any corporatist model of the social. For Zukofsky, Pound's fascism was a symptom of the dangers to which the ideological crossroads of American capitalism led. For Pound, as we shall see in the next section of this chapter, the universal required as its guarantee the ruler-will of the fascist leader. In relation to Pound, Zukofsky is a Marxian anti-fascist, looking not to a powerful leader to unify struggling social interests, but instead to forms of collectivity historically articulated by the labour movement and its theorists.

However, Zukofsky is more wary than Pound of any attempt to articulate the public good in a universalizing representative, including the proletariat. This should be kept in mind for any attempt to evaluate the 'Marxism' of the first nine sections of *A*. Zukofsky does not speak as a Marxist in his text. An important distinction must be made between Pound's and Zukofsky's poetics of citation. This difference becomes apparent in Pound's misunderstanding of the final version of *A*-8, when he wrote to Zukofsky: 'it don't show that Marx knew anything about money/ AND I xxpekk the only way to make didactic poesy is to KNOW fer sure' (PZ 187). Where Pound relies at certain points on the authority of a cited speaker to support his economic and political statements or slogans, Zukofsky's authoritative voices (Charles, Henry, and Brooks Adams, Marx and Engels, Thorstein Veblen, among others) are frequently ironized in a manner that does not simply undermine their authority but makes tangible their potential ideological dimension. Instead, the debate he initiates with Pound (among others) extends into the metaphors and ideologemes of the debate not in order to redeploy them, but to make the struggle over their meaning apparent. *A*-8's formal method of citation registers the conflicting impulses and directions of the 'historic and contemporary particulars' of the Depression (P 12). For this reason, it is important to grasp the various contexts in which Zukofsky's borrowed utterances might function. Zukofsky's text functions critically in a way that Pound's does not by exposing the dominant ideological configuration of the particularly American discourse into which these citations can be grafted. The various quotations that constitute the bulk of *A*-8 form a tapestry of different utterances, with no ideologically stable point of view, all of which are capable of being cited in contradictory enunciative contexts.

Despite the predominance of Marxist language, it would therefore be wrong to say that the early sections of *A* are primarily

Marxist: Marxism is one very important discourse, but it competes with different visions of history and of the social whole, not all of which have progressive implications; the selection of Marx's or Marxist texts frequently reflects concerns familiar from the American experience. The most significant effect of Zukofsky's citations of revolutionary discourse is neither to employ it nor to discredit it, but to measure its claims or its implicit desires against the drift of American history. The source of Zukofsky's frequent ironization of Marxist discourse, for example, is his sense of the uses to which history may put the rhetoric. For example, what is for Zukofsky's poem an important quotation from Marx is not at all central to Marx's system as economic science, but is rather essential to a precise historical moment of political organization. Marx, writing to Engels of the American Workingmen's Party, refers with annoyance to 'A good fellow, an old Owenist, Weston (carpenter)', who was

> Continually defending two propositions in *The Beehive*:
> – That a general rise in the rate of wages
> would be of no use to workers
> – That therefore, etc., the trade unions
> are *harmful*. –
> If these two propositions, in which *he*
> Alone in our society believes, were accepted,
> We would become a joke to the trade unions (in England)

(*A* 58)

As I will argue in the third part of this chapter, Zukofsky, more of a Marxist than the Marx of this particular minor passage, recognized the danger that too exclusive an emphasis on 'a general rise in the rate of wages' posed for American labour. American labour unions had helped to simplify the claims of labour into an appeal for purely quantitative goals. As R. Jeffrey Lustig writes, '[w]orking people were said to be fighting for higher wages'; this argument made the labour movement susceptible to corporatist arguments for cooperation between the classes, and the argument that what industry required in order to further social harmony was more efficient management. Power, therefore, should accrue to the corporate directors.[118] Good Marxist political strategy is not necessarily good Marxist science. Zukofsky's Marxism is qualified, as this citation from Marx attests, by the scarcity of language, which is simply to say that no use of language is free of the ideological conditions in which it is produced. Zukofsky's quotations come from individual voices, but these individuals must be seen as in some sense representative of groups. The complexities of enunciation in his quotations emerge from the conflicted identities of the groups that might redeploy them. The voices are dialogical, but the forum is not one conducive to consensus. Instead, speech takes place under conditions of scarcity even in the midst of 'Plenty of eloquence, / Words enough' (*A* 98).

The surplus value of language means that there is a struggle for the appropriation of the surplus. This takes place at the expense of other speakers, by whom the language that was or might have been theirs is perceived to be an alien imposition, or in a more technological, functionalist perspective, an objectivity to which they have to adapt. Such a technological and corporate vision even appears in Zukofsky's borrowed revolutionary call to 'Untiring action... free / From the lie that it can take the place of mass action': though this exhortation may seem entirely unproblematic, it is actually composed of and linked to utterances available for citation in a number of revolutionary contexts, not all of which Zukofsky would be sympathetic with. Though the content of the lines makes them difficult to cite in too many contexts, they share the social vision that would support the developing corporate ideology. This becomes apparent only at the end of the passage, which concludes on a profoundly though subtly ironic note:

> Learn, learn, learn!
> Act, act, act!
> Be prepared, well and completely prepared
> To make use, with all our forces,
> Of the next revolutionary wave.
> That is our job.

(*A* 91)

Despite the explicitness of the revolutionary appeal, one possible context for this appeal to learning and acting is the same vision of a latent social whole that is implicit in the functionalist perspective that was becoming prominent in American social thought and practice. This irony emerges with the notion of 'job', which could imply at the time something closer to a specialized function in a system, performed by what Stein would call an 'employee'. The explicit content of this line seems to distinguish it of course from an apology for the status quo, since this functionalism is in the service of what its agents conceive to be a more just vision of the whole, which would subvert the social order as defined by the implied capitalist class. Nonetheless, to assume that a revolutionary agent speaks does not entirely account for the subject of the enunciation of these particular lines. Who is the 'us' that this voice represents? The sentence 'That is our job', rather than referring to the task of a revolutionary group, might be distinguishing the task of a revolutionary managerial elite from those who have other jobs to attend to; the 'revolutionary wave' may in fact be a revolution in industrial technology. One could multiply the historical enunciative contexts, but the point is that the lines appeal to group and corporate structures without making evident the exact make-up of this latent society.

The conflict of social groups that Zukofsky's citations make tangible also inheres in what might seem to be his own affirmative use of the discourse of science. Though it would be very tempting to read Zukofsky's frequent allusions to science in the light of aesthetic method, it is more important to examine them in light of the political and historical visions to which they are too susceptible of being grafted. Zukofsky refers to such contemporary concepts or values as 'Process: notion about which the researches cluster' (A 56), and seems thereby to be drawing upon the fund of process-oriented aesthetics that began with the Romantics and remain with us to this day. But he is also bringing into the poem the possible historical contexts, or enunciative conditions, for the utterances. As another example, the statement that 'Everything has its time' (A 92) betrays a faith in historical process that is hardly to be reconciled to a Marxist perspective of history. The tension of the Marxist language with the positivist, 'scientific' language of functionalism is evident in the lines immediately preceding the passage cited above: 'But to determine the facts does not / mean to give up the struggle'. While in Marxism, the determination of the facts cannot theoretically contradict the dictates of praxis, since theory and praxis have permeable borders, these lines admit that there is a conflict between what must be a non-Marxist scientific 'determination of the facts' and revolutionary praxis. The revolutionary call to struggle concedes that the determination of the facts may lead one to give up the struggle. 'Fact' in this case is inflected with a positivist meaning: facts, once determined, require adaptation, not revolutionary struggle. Embedded within the revolutionary slogan is a concession to a positivist conception of the social whole as a set of facts produced by evolution.

The social sciences were developing functionalist models of social behaviour and identity that would be employed in conceiving the nature of the social whole along the lines of corporate interests. This line of thought begins with the temporal evolutionary perspective introduced to sociological thought through Comte, which was given a particularly American flavour by William Graham Sumner. Emphasizing social solidarity above models of society based on notions of the liberal individual and the social contract, emerging functionalist thought considered society to be a whole composed of group identities and interests. The theory presupposed a latent harmony of interests that required adaptation or adjustment. 'Everything has its time', everything has a place and a function at any point in history; when its function has been exhausted, it vanishes from the historical stage. A quotation from Henri Poincaré, concerning the presuppositions of the new science, suggests the method to which an emphasis on 'process' gives rise:

> The simple will be discovered beneath the complex
> Then the complex under the simple
> Then again the simple under the complex
> And, and, the chain without sight of the last term, etc.,
> Etc., . . .
>
> (A 47)

As Henry Adams, the source of Zukofsky's quotation above, points out, Poincaré's notion of science as process relies on an implicit vision of history that may be suspect.[119] Poincaré speaks with the authority of a scientific 'determination of the facts', and makes his metaphor available for a naturalization of what is. Zukofsky does not subscribe to any of the ideological possibilities his citations make evident. Instead, by citing science on the verge of being translated into social theory, he holds the vocabulary back before the conceptual shift, making the ideological use of scarce language visible. It will be necessary to keep this in mind in order to understand how it is that Zukofsky's poem makes the 'poetico-political economy' tangible without writing 'didactic poesy'.

'IF THE COMMON MAN GET TOGETHER'

Zukofsky's *A*-8 opens with what seems to be a revolutionary perspective on the 'new announcements of economies' (*A* 51) occasioned by the collapse of the capitalist economy in the Depression. Despite appearances, however, the claim is not unambiguously revolutionary. Zukofsky does not hear 'announcements of *new economies*', but 'new announcements' calling for economization, or sacrifice. As Zukofsky certainly knew, the history of capitalism provides few examples of responses to economic and political crisis that result in the equal distribution of 'economies', understood as economization. The 'economies' thus announced would most likely be new forms of repression enabling a dominant class to economize on the social wealth. The economization required by the Depression, he would have been correct to suspect, would not hit all social classes equally; and if economic reorganization will require economization, then a new political order – new structures of agency representing the old or new interests in the process of consolidating their power – will have to come into being. Would Spengler's prophecy of 'the coming ruler-will' hold true for America, despite his claims that politics was impossible in a nation founded on classical liberal values and principles? Though it is easy to lose sight of the fact after the Cold War, anti-fascism as much as anti-communism determined political and rhetorical strategy during the Depression. Though they hardly constituted an American Popular Front, both classical liberals and left-wing radicals (communists, socialists, etc.) feared, for different reasons, that the spectre of European fascism might also be lurking behind the American political stage; for both the right, with its traditional fear of state power, and the left, with its fear of anti-democratic forms of state power, Franklin Roosevelt frequently bore the burden of this spectral identity.

The fear of fascism in America was therefore composed of various ideological strands, which are reflected in the traditional American anxiety concerning power – an anxiety we have seen in the case of Stein's disavowal of the paternal instance. Tocqueville, it will be recalled, claimed that American individualism atomized potentially collective social subjects; the political agency of such subjects was therefore inevitably sacrificed to the centralized power of the state. For this reason, he, like Stein after him, predicted that during a political and economic crisis America would paradoxically turn to a powerful leader.'[120] Once new 'economies' are announced, when new and more democratic political structures become tangible to Zukofsky's radical desire, the long shadow of the father soon reappears. As in the Spenglerian transmutation of economics into the politics of the ruler-will, these 'new announcements of economies' may be inseparable from a new form of paternal, political domination. Zukofsky quotes Charles Francis Adams, Jr, the older brother of Henry and Brooks, who predicted in 1871 that the political agency of a new kind of leader, 'the coming man', was emerging to resolve the antagonism of capital and labour:

> It, perhaps, only remains for the coming man
> To carry the combination of elements
> One step in advance, and put Caesarism
> At once in control of the corporation and the proletariat.

(*A* 77–8)

This resolution would not be democratic, in Adams' eyes; the emerging political agency would be a representation of concentrated corporate economic power. In the essay Zukofsky is citing, Adams claims that the development of monopoly capitalism in post-civil war America is giving rise to a 'power for which our language contains no name'. In Zukofsky's citation:

> Corporate life and corporate power,
> As applied to industrial development,
> . . yet in its infancy.
> It always tends to development, –
> Always to consolidation . . .
> Even threatens the central government.
> It is a new power, for which our language
> Contains no name.

(*A* 76–7)

The namelessness of the new power reflects the inadequacy of existing American legal and political conceptions to account for the new forms of combination that emerged from the market. Not only traditional political, but above all traditional *liberal* categories could no longer account for or compete with the 'new power'. Adams continues, in lines not cited by Zukofsky:

> We know what aristocracy, autocracy, democracy are; but we have no word to express government by moneyed corporations. Yet the people already instinctively seek protection against it, and look for such protection, significantly enough, not to their own legislatures, but to the single autocratic feature retained in our system of government – the veto by the Executive. In this there is something more imperial than republican. The people have lost faith in themselves when they cease to have any faith in those whom they uniformly elect to represent them. . . . Thus the influence of corporations and of class interests is steadily destroying that belief in singleness of purpose which alone enables a representative government to exist, and the community is slowly accustoming itself to look for protection, not to public opinion, but to some man in high place and armed with great executive powers.[121]

The late nineteenth century witnessed a number of challenges to the ideology as well as the practice of the liberal marketplace and its concomitant form of exchange, the contract. Clearly, the economic as well as the philosophical or ideological foundations of traditional American liberalism, as Veblen pointed out at the end of the century, had for the most part vanished. In retrospect, the liberal marketplace began to seem to advocates of the emerging corporate order to be wasteful and inefficient. As if in concession, classical liberals added their voices to the critique of the marketplace articulated by labour groups as well as more conservative interests. What came to the fore ideologically at the turn of the century were attempts to rethink what had formerly been assumed to be the implicit natural unity or harmony of interests served by the liberal marketplace. The result was an often profoundly ambiguous 'corporate liberalism', in the words of R. Jeffrey Lustig, which attempted to articulate new social and economic theories and practices in order to realize the social promise that seemed to be contained in the emerging economic realities.

The often-noted contradiction between Pound's individualism and his corporatism should be seen in this context, which makes his admiration of Mussolini seem much less surprising than is usually acknowledged.[122] When he wrote that 'the problem of our time is to find out the border between public and private affairs', Pound meant that it was the function of *politics* to protect each sphere from its contamination by the other, while providing for a positive content to itself, the public, political sphere (SP 240). Pound, like a classical liberal committed to entrepreunerial capitalism, respected the private rights of property, but – unlike a classical liberal – not without a limitation in view of the public good.[123] Mussolini, according to Pound, was willing to revive in Italy a concept of the public good that had long since disappeared in America, which in the nineteenth century had seen an unprecedented extension of private status to formerly semi-public institutions. Therefore, for Pound, like Spengler, the condition of the proper private life was a healthy public life, which required that 'Economics', the network of private interests bound together by contracts and money, be subsumed in the immanence of the 'ruler-will' of Mussolini. Only a paternal guarantee could make way for a proper collective as well as private identity, of a public and private life, both of which were in the eyes of such radical conservatives as Pound threatened with destruction, first by the market and then by the development of monopoly capitalism. These twin demons suggest the conflict that would follow: on the one hand, the market represents the danger of social fragmentation or atomization, as well as the unequal distribution not only of wealth but of power; this would give rise in the nineteenth century to labour associations and unions, that is to say, groups that define themselves not as a collection of individuals serving their private interests, but as groups claiming status as public bodies. On the other hand, the monopoly, which emerges on the foundation of the inequality produced by the market, represents a threat not only to these organized groups of labour, but to the individualist ideology of the market, the norm to which even labour would appeal at certain moments of its organization.

This threat against both the private and the public life laid the groundwork for the aesthetic strategies as well as the social and political thought of modernists such as Pound. In its more utopian manifestations, aesthetic and social modernism attempts to represent and recuperate the general or universal condition of the liberal individual, while aspiring or merely claiming to allow for the free development of that individual. The solutions to the dilemma across all political categories were varieties of corporatism.[124] Yet the inevitable result of attempts to resolve the contradiction between the public and private goods was the false or imposed universality of certain institutions (for example, the universality of the state in fascist nationalist ideologies; the universality of the executive in Adams' prediction of the American trend) or persons (Pound's Mussolini), which claimed to represent a public good, but actually served to conceal conflict and contradiction. Such a good required for its legitimacy an ideological justification like that we have already seen at work in Spengler, for whom the creative, political ruler-will was not conceived as a merely legal entity, as it would have been in the Anglo-American context, but as a metaphysical substance akin to the popular, quasi-biological version of Nietzsche's will to power. For its justification, America appealed to what may or may not be a less metaphysical entity, which Adams refers to above as the nation's 'singleness of purpose', also known as the public interest. The task for American thought would be to assuage the public's anxiety over the massive consolidation of private interests or wills. It could only do so by arguing that consolidation would serve the public interest, which would be guaranteed representation and agency. The new theorists would have to demonstrate that the new concentration of economic power would not be detrimental to the values heretofore maintained and assured by the deployment of private interests in the market, which interests included, it was argued, labour. Moreover, if the new forms of power failed to serve the public good, they could be made to do so by reform from within.

Though free of Spengler's Germanic myth, the American analogues for the new political order foreseen by Spengler also required a universalizing conception of the will. The fragmented economic energies or wills of the liberal marketplace, having given rise in the late nineteenth century to the rapidly modernizing corporation, could no longer be considered unproblematically as belonging to individual entities, that is to say, owners of private property (again, including those considered to own their labour power), as evidence mounted that the economy was controlled by corporate structures of agency that were not identical with the owners of the property, who became shareholders. Traditional

American liberals, facing a crisis, responded to the new forms of consolidation by developing a new ontology of the individual as rooted in larger collective identities. However, like its concept of the individual, American liberalism's concept of the group was entirely inadequate to account for the new social and economic structures emerging alongside the corporation. America had little in the way of a tradition of group or corporate theory, and the practical development of organized forms of economic and political life outstripped the ability of liberal theorists to reflect upon them. Historically, the corporations and the labour unions had an advance on the liberals, and provided them with the models which would inflect their reinterpretation of predominantly European forms of group theory (for example, the solidarist corporatisms of Comte and Durkheim). The critical question for group theorists was how to go beyond the contractual model of social life, and therefore how to rethink society according to the priority of group life rather than the abstract individual. No longer could the public good be served by the latent harmony of the marketplace of private interests.

Political, legal and economic debate in America before and during the Depression centred on the problem Pound identified as the most urgent – the determination of the border between public and private life. But group theory of the European variety, which pointed ambiguously in the direction of socialist and fascist varieties of corporatism, held little sway for minds firmly rooted in the American liberal tradition. This became especially apparent in the discourse and legislation concerning the most powerful and identifiable group will of the period, the corporation. Spengler's account of economic development translates directly into the contemporary American discourse surrounding the legal status and social identity of the corporation, a discourse central to the new liberal concern with collective and public social identities. This is not, however, to say that the new ideological and theoretical emphasis on collectivity was simply an effort to justify the corporation, nor that the new theories of groups simply reflected corporate ideology. Simultaneous with the rise of the corporation, labour associations and unions, as well as other groups, were demanding that they be recognized as public, and not merely private, interests. The most important political debates of the period contested the definition of what was and what was not the public good, raising the corresponding issues of representation and the general will. This watershed provided the occasion for a new political thought in America, which had so far lacked the corporate traditions of Europe and tended to conceive all group forms in market and contractual, or in short, individualist terms. Given the ferment of political discussion that once again became pronounced with the Depression, it is important to acknowledge that Zukofsky's citation of C. F. Adams does not simply prophesy a new fascism; the lines point indirectly to the urgent need, felt acutely by Pound among many others, for a new concept of the public good, as well as new institutions designed to serve it. The ferment of anti-liberal thought in Europe and corporate liberalism in America did not point in the single direction of fascism, but opened up a wide area of possible political action and organization. American thinkers recognized the limits of classical liberalism and began to think in a variety of corporatist or socialist categories. However, despite this acknowledgment, Anglo-American legal theory would have difficulty conceiving groups as anything other than collections of private individuals bound by contract. As we will see shortly, this was not to the advantage of radical political desires.

The question of the corporation motivated a vigorous legal and political discussion that was, contrary to intellectual currents in other areas, centred almost exclusively on individual rights. Historically, the corporation did not want to be recognized as a *collection* of individuals, preferring instead to take advantage of the traditional rights of the individual to make contracts. This is in keeping with the history of liberal enlightenment legislation, which did not care to think of social or economic relationships in noncontractual, voluntarist terms. Legislation protecting individual rights against claims to the public good reached a climax in 1886 when the corporation became a legal person within the meaning of the Fourteenth Amendment. Yet even as it became a person, it was acknowledged to be a collection of individuals bound by contract: as Lustig writes, '[a] Holmesean "policy decision" would turn the corporation from a chartered organization and a concession from the sovereign into a private association arising from the compact of its members'.[125] The result was a nominalist conception of the corporation as *'persona ficta'*, a person that was finally decomposable into a collection of individual wills conceived according to the classical liberal concept of the individual.[126] Even as the group theorists were questioning the validity of the classical liberal concept of the individual, that concept, enshrined in the Fourteenth Amendment, was being exploited in the courts in favour of the corporations. Despite the increasing concentration of economic and social life, the individualist model of the contract as the ur-unit of society had won – at the expense, it was argued by traditional liberals, of the economic individuals it was intended to protect. However, the power this legal decision awarded to the corporation would soon make the very concept of contract almost unnecessary. Even as it acquired the convenient status of a fictive person, with individual rights and few duties, the corporation moved beyond the form of the contract in its own organization, providing a model for a new form of feudal hierarchy.[127] While early efforts on the part of business to defeat labour unions appealed to the individual worker's contractual rights and duties, a critical turn took place in the early twentieth century during the Progressive Era, when it became evident that the organization of labour could be beneficial to the goals of business.[128] If concentration in business had proved so productive, the same would be true of the concentration of labour. Developing liberal group theory, which from one perspective threatened the conceptual bases of the corporation's status as a legal individual, proved useful for this reorganization. Rather than being seen as a fictive person composed actually of legal individuals, the corporation demanded, and was increasingly awarded, recognition as a social agent. If during the Progressive era the corporation could be seen as capable of delict, the concomitant is that it would also be seen as an agent of the public good, as a good corporate citizen.[129] The corporation would no longer be a private interest, but would in fact be the representative and steward of the public interest.

One of the most disturbing facts of the history of the period is the extent to which the corporation took over traditionally public domains. It became clear to corporate leaders that there was no need to prevent being absorbed by public interests; all that was required to make it safe was that the 'public good' once again, as in the old days of the market, be the responsibility of what would then be misnamed the private interests. This new public function fulfils Spengler's prophecy in an American fashion: the corporation becomes the guardian of the public welfare. As we will see, Zukofsky's poem attends to the return of the paternalism of the nineteenth-century workplace into the twentieth-century economy; it returns not only in the material but also the subjective relation to the corporation, which is one of dependency. As if to realize exactly what Stein feared of a depressing father, paternalism returns with an economy of the gift. As Richard Sennett writes, the father of nineteenth-century paternalistic authority 'makes a gift of his resources to others. The terms of his gift are wholly in his control'.[130] It was a fundamental truth for John Adams and Jefferson that such dependency was incompatible with liberty. Citing Ambrose Spencer, Pound says that a 'Man who feeds, clothes, lodges another / has absolute control over his will' (C 181). Zukofsky alludes to the similarly captivating power of the new paternalism of the corporation in the following letter to the editor: 'New York, N.Y. / Editor, Times Union:/ I would die for dear old Standard Oil / Ex-Soldier, 12:47 P.M'. (A 93). Of course there is a measure of irony in this quotation, but this irony should not be separated from the truth that it makes tangible. As the corporation becomes a classical liberal individual, the individual becomes corporate. It is not a great step from Zukofsky's 'Ex-Soldier' to the corporatism of Mussolini's Italy.[131] However, in spite of the history of labour associations and other forms of group organization in America, the corporation provided the predominant, or at least most powerful model for group life at the beginning of the century.

For the new social theory that emerged alongside the corporation and the unions, the Lockean individual of liberal economics was an abstraction with no philosophical validity whatsoever. The emerging group theories in America were without doubt philosophically an improvement over traditional liberalism's abstract emphasis on property and contract; there was much to hope for on the part not only of fascist-oriented revolutionaries but also of leftist radicals at the turn of the century. Certainly the Robinson Crusoe that liberal ideologues were so fond of is at best a misleading fiction; whether Robinson be considered an entrepreneur or a labourer, not only his economic activity but his very identity requires 'company', perhaps even *a* company, as Zukofsky puts it, punning on 'company' in an ironic quotation from Marx: 'Company .. can't well live altogether without it, / And that when you get it .. / You try hard to rid yourself of ..' (A 93). The individual, in this case Marx, the prophet of new forms of social and political collectives, requires 'company' in order 'to live'.

However, it was by Zukofsky's time increasingly evident that the political organization of economic and social groups in America worked from the top down, to the detriment of the pluralist liberal democracy to which the rhetoric frequently made reference. After the prosperity of the twenties, the Depression served to disrupt radically the consensus that a corporate social structure, even if it had not achieved the goals of the democratic nation, promised to do so in short order. It once again threatened to become apparent that the contradiction between labour and capital meant that no universality would be possible within capitalist conditions. The option, it seemed, was between revolution or a consolidation of capital.

Though Zukofsky's group language frequently reflects the Marxist insistence on the conceptual priority of the polarization of classes, and therefore the revolutionary claim that labour is the universal social subject, it also appears to test the radical potential of the pluralist liberalism so dear to the pre-Mussolini Pound:

> It is not by the consolidation
> Or concentration of powers (corporate bodies)
> But by their distribution,
> That good government is effected.
>
> (*A* 90)

These lines seem to advocate what Tocqueville advised decades before, namely that power should be distributed across intermediate social bodies so as to avoid a dangerous concentration of power amounting to tyranny.[132] But this begs the very question that American liberal theory has posed since the Revolution, which is the question how such intermediate groups could be conceived in America, with its strong liberal traditions – traditions so powerful that even labour would ultimately appeal to liberal individualist categories rather than lay claim to an identity as a public interest. In America, the state poses the primary threat, not only for classical liberals (who fear that a presumably 'public' interest will destroy the good served by private interests) but also for radicals (who fear that the state serves class interests), because American thought has historically resisted any attempt to conceive group identity in non-contractual, non-individualist terms. The contradictions resulting from this failure are the result of these very strongholds of American ideology, contractualism and individualism. For this reason, the recurrent fear of 'combination' or 'concentration' can be found across the spectrum of social and political interests in America. As Tocqueville argued long ago, individualism and various forms of paternalism or 'tyranny' go hand in hand. Paternalism is rooted in the extension of the contract, conceived in what John Dewey would call an 'individualistic era', to a public space in which it does not properly belong. According to liberal English legal theorist F. W. Maitland, by denying the real personhood of the group, the prevalence of the contract culminates in the fiction theory of the corporation. But contrary to its classically liberal intentions, and therefore contrary to the needs of the corporation, this fiction theory is complicitous with a concession theory, which posits the state as sole author of the group identity of otherwise atomized individuals. As Maitland says, in a claim that voices the concerns of a number of different political and economic interests, this concession model of group identity 'might play into the hands of a Prince or princeling inclined to paternal despotism'. For this reason, the corporation required further protection against the implications of the theory it wanted simultaneously to exploit. The convergence of the fiction and concession theories means that a paternalism is built into the very structure of the liberal marketplace, or into the contract to which the corporations would appeal.[133]

Zukofsky, if he were a Marxist, would most likely desire to transcend the contradictions of a group theory implicitly founded on 'individualistic' contractual relations, and what according to Tocqueville and others was the concomitant paternalist model of the relation of groups to the state. He would argue instead for the autonomy of the group or class identity of labour:

> Workers and farmers are no Roman mob.
> They are not maintained by the State,
> They maintain the State by their work.
>
> (*A* 90)

However, it would be wrong to read these lines, as well as the Tocquevillean lines cited above, as programmatic. Though there can be little doubt of the radical desires motivating Zukofsky's poem, ambiguity infiltrates his citations, proving that the central question to address to his poem is the one he provides himself: 'Who says it, what said, to whom?' (A 73). This vocabulary can be used by a number of different social groups; its potential is not simply radical or necessarily democratic. This language could in fact be used by a corporation concerned to protect its autonomy from intervention by the state; in this case, the phrase 'the workers' would be spoken by a paternal authority engaged in protecting its workers from the paternalism of the state; and of course it is ironic that the workers 'maintain the State by their work', if the state does not serve or represent their interests. Similarly, the Tocquevillean passage also leaves unanswered a number of crucial issues: To whom or what is power to be distributed? How are the intermediate social groups to be constructed or conceived? As I mentioned above, Zukofsky's poem is remarkable not for its contributions to or views of the debate concerning the corporation and the public good, but for the extent to which it performs the task of an objectivist poetics, which, in Zukofsky's words, is to register 'the direction of historic and contemporary particulars' (P 12). A-8 in particular is profoundly American in that it inhabits the historical discourse without using it; it cites without repeating, and so makes tangible the limitations of American discourse. The language of American ideology is in effect spoken by 'No Man', an effaced and anonymous universal that, even though it cannot be identified with a particular class, provides the conditions for the new form of domination Zukofsky sees at work in the emerging economy of consumption.

'THE PEOPLE'S ISSUE OF NOTHING'

Though Pound became a corporatist fascist throughout the thirties, what brought him to such an extreme was not a psychological propensity to hero-worship, nor was it simply a nostalgia for pre-capitalist forms of corporate life. Unlike the regressive mass-psychological impulse of certain forms of fascism, Pound's political desires were articulated almost entirely within the scope of modern, Enlightenment values. As Zukofsky recognized, Pound's political ideas are perfectly consistent with the main trends of corporate liberalism, which was a far cry from the political fantasies of the most regressive European forms of fascism. This commitment would however have provided sufficient cause for Pound's particular brand of fascism. The chief goal of Pound's utopian impulse was the restoration of the public good as a determining instance of political, economic and social life, and he would be willing to require certain sacrifices in order to realize that goal. He considered his programme of 'volitionist economics' to be a rational economic policy, and thought Mussolini's corporate state to be the most likely and efficient means of realizing it. Prior to his commitment to Mussolini, however, Pound thought that technical and administrative means would be enough for social reform. In particular, reforming the technology of money could bring about the efficient production and distribution of wealth that industrial rationalization promised, and so lay the groundwork for new possibilities of cultural value. Though in terms of cultural value Pound was obsessed with the Middle Ages and the Renaissance, his politics was not motivated at all by a desire for the traditional, perhaps feudal relations of authority that were superseded by the mercantile and later capitalist marketplace. In fact, Pound's emphasis on money as the primary institution by which the public good would be restored precludes the possibility of returning to pre-modern, feudal forms of social bonds. There is even a rational dimension to Pound's adulation of Mussolini: authority was not in Pound's eyes legitimated by tradition, nor, despite this adulation, was authority even primarily charismatic. Instead, it required legitimation by 'right reason'. The leader functions like a private bank does in theory, and has his authority on the basis of the goods or things he could call upon or promise as guarantees of the issue of currency.[134] This rational contractual relationship differs from earlier interpersonal forms of exchange in that, when it comes to the distribution of rights and obligations, the contract presumes the prior equality of the exchanging parties. The contract means one has voluntarily given up a certain power which is to be held conditionally by another – as in a bank deposit, for example. This notion of contract is the condition of the rational dimension of Pound's requirement of a leader: the leader holds something in reserve, just as in the social contract the citizen gives up a certain quantity of natural individual will in exchange for political status and rights.

Nonetheless, it would be too generous to Pound to claim that his political decisions were entirely rational. His economic ideas do tend to conceal other, unstated investments; the vicissitudes of the melancholic utopian impulse, which we have been examining throughout these chapters, do not allow him to be entirely aware of the contradictions in which the ambivalence at the root of his utopian desire culminates. Pound's major contradiction is his simultaneous commitment both to a radical individualism and to a corporatism, which is exactly the contradiction that American corporate liberalism attempted to resolve. Pound never became entirely conscious of this contradiction, though it would have been possible for him to do so. Instead, it appeared in his work symptomatically, and in so doing this contradiction revealed much more of its fundamental conditions than a more conscious attempt to resolve it would have. In other words, Pound never entirely accepted the dominant ideological articulation of the fundamental contradiction, which was the opposition of the individual to the collective. Such an articulation of the contradiction in terms of an opposition delimits the 'poetico-political economic' field in such a way as to reduce the ambivalence that motivates its more apparent contradictions and oppositions. The virtue of Pound's ideological stubbornness, like Stein's, is that it gives away its complex conditions whenever it attempts to resolve the crisis that motivates it. This means that their work must be read in the details of its articulation: it must be read not in the direction of its ideological intention, but in the direction of the particulars of its composition.

For example, in spite of the technical and administrative emphasis of Pound's pre-fascist political economy, his programme for monetary reform is also implicitly a new political form: Pound wanted to make money into a new kind of social contract. What Pound has in fact recognized is that money, like a social contract, binds one to a system of social relations, a collectivity not to be found in the more liberal individualist version of the contract as a compact between two equal parties.[135] This new social contract allows Pound to imagine a social bond that is not based on the classical liberal assumption of the private individual, without appealing to the state as the embodiment of the collective subject. At the same time, since he has preserved the basic form of the contract, Pound can turn himself back at any moment into a classical liberal, resisting at certain points the intervention of the state into the private life of the citizen. However, this new social contract would not be conceived along the same lines as the individualist contract of the nineteenth-century market; the person subscribing to this contract would not be the liberal individual, but a corporate individual. This relationship would not be contractual at all in the traditional sense, since the new social contract, embodied in money, would require a founding inequality. Money allows for a system of rights but also, and perhaps above all, obligations. The crucial difference between Pound and a classical liberal is Pound's implicit recognition that an economy founded on such an individualist, contractual basis requires some form of guarantee that transcends the individual acts of exchange; the relationship of the citizens or subjects of the state to their leader cannot be merely one among the many exchanges that take place between equal subjects. The other side of Pound's adulation of the leader is the demand for a strong paternal will in a founding exchange, an utterly unequal and non-contractual exchange which provides the final universal term guaranteeing the economy. This founding exchange is not predicated on the exchange of anything on the part of the subject, which is perceived to have and to be nothing in relation to the all-powerful Spenglerian ruler-will. If money at one level of exchange allows the individual subject to enter into contracts freely, at a more fundamental level that makes exchange possible in the first place, it presumes inequality and radical indebtedness. More than a contract with the state, money is a contract with the father.

The most important institution embodying this contract with the paternal leader was for Pound the public bank, the function of which in Pound's economics is not primarily to hold, guarantee and invest deposits in order to create private capital. Instead, a bank is an institution of credit, and the credit it issues is to be used for purposes that would further the public good. The bank therefore is largely to serve entrepreneurs, and to do so it would use state-issued funds, not capital developed from the investments of its deposits.[136] In relation to the individual citizen or consumer, therefore, the bank would provide no services. A major part of Pound's reform of money was intended to prevent savings, or the hoarding of money, on any scale. Money must circulate, and not be deposited or saved in order to beget more money for its individual possessor. The fact that money can be hoarded is, according to Pound, its most dangerous characteristic, because hoarding diminishes the supply and inflates the value of money. One could only have egotistical reasons for hoarding money; moreover, if one hoards money, one is treating it as if it is private property, and one must also be assuming that the social contract it represents has conferred rights but not obligations. As we shall see, Pound's volitionist economics is designed to discipline the excessive liberal individualism that could give rise to such an attitude. But rather than moralizing about the loss of social values implied by such individualism, Pound proposed concrete monetary solutions for this problem: his solution requires that money serve a disciplinary function even as it makes individual consumption possible. On the level of individual consumption, Pound's economics institutionalized the imperative to keep money circulating: this was the purpose of the 'stamp scrip' he advocated after becoming familiar with the economic ideas of Silvio Gesell early in 1934.[137] Gesell called his money *Schwundgeld* or 'shrinking money' because it was to be in a permanent state of devaluation. This means simply that one's money loses value if it is not put into circulation before a specified amount of time elapses: if one's money were not spent after this amount of time, that money would be worth less unless one were to supplement it with a purchased stamp. It is as if one had to pay a certain amount of interest at allotted times on money that one wanted to save or place on deposit. This disciplinary procedure would therefore prevent the economic advantages of hoarding, which can no longer serve egotistical motives, since it would be tantamount to destroying the value of one's money. After a certain amount of time, if one's money is not put into circulation, it becomes worthless. Most importantly for our concerns, the steady devaluation and the dependency on the supplementary value issued by the state means that the money is essentially borrowed; one cannot treat it, even if it be a wage, as private property. Money belongs to the state, and if one holds on to it, interest accrues, because one is indebted to the state; if one were to hold on to the money long enough for it to be worth nothing, it is simply as if the debt were called in and one were left destitute.

Money is debt because it is issued by the leader, who can back up his issue of money with the substance of his will. Pound's obsession with money therefore also betrays his demand for a powerful paternal leader who is, to borrow a phrase from Canto 36, 'worthy of trust'. Simultaneously, however, Pound's investment in the leader requires a more rational, contractual basis: the leader does not legitimate his power on the basis of charisma or tradition, but on his judgement. He must issue money or credit only if it will be put to a productive use. Money is merely, in this rational aspect, 'a lien on "The Abundance"' (C 211), and the leader will remain in the position of the father only so long as he can measure out capital according to the most likely paths of realization that the promised abundance will take. If he fails to do so, and begins to fail in his public function, perhaps by serving his or other private interests, then the leader, like his subjects, may be judged guilty of a failure in relation to the paternal instance. Having lost his backing in the paternal will, the leader issuing credit is no better than a private bank, creating money on no legitimate basis at all. One of Pound's most insistent refrains is Paterson's claim that the Bank of England, which is private, '*Hath benefit of interest on all the moneys which it, the bank, creates out of nothing.*' In the lines following this passage from Canto 46 Pound links the bank with usurious private capital by referring to the Rothschild money. Both are in turn linked to the question of guilt as Pound puns on the name of 'Rothschild' as 'RothSchild', and Roth-schild' (C 233): *schild* is the past tense of *schulden*, 'to owe', related also to *schuldig*, meaning 'guilty'. Money produced *ex nihilo* violates the paternal will. In Zukofsky's terms, private banks are founded on the authority of 'No Man', a negation of the universal paternal will represented by 'Man'. Zukofsky's 'No Man' appears in a passage of *A-8* in which Zukofsky directly addresses Pound's concerns with banking, money and debt:

> If these banks' moneys come out of nothing
> And take out of all
> Will No Thing – No Man –
> Resign to the people's issue of nothing,
> Or must he devolve upon all?

(*A* 89)

For Pound, private institutions of credit like the Bank of England and the Federal Reserve usuriously 'take out of all', in Zukofsky's phrase, creating bad forms of debt. But notice how Zukofsky makes it impossible to determine whether this institution is a public or a private one: since he does not accept Pound's ideological determination of the border between the public and the private, he leaves the 'issue' of money suspended between the private 'banks' and the public, or the 'people'. 'The people's issue of nothing' could be seen as *opposed* to the bank's issue of money out of nothing, in that it is the 'people' who issue this 'nothing' called money. But the notes are still the bank's issue, which would suggest that this is a good public bank that represents the 'people'. Whereas for Pound the good debt has to be both owed to and underwritten by a universal paternal name, rather than to the proper names tied to private corporations, for Zukofsky, the name and place of the guarantee is fundamentally in question, impossible to place. It has no proper name, and can 're-sign' its name at will, so that one's money never returns; one is always being deprived of value. The pun on 're-signing' is reinforced by Zukofsky later in the poem, in reference to an unnamed 'company' 'Writing its signature different each time, so / you cannot get your money back' (*A* 93). Zukofsky in this case (as in another, which we will consider later) uses the metaphor of the deposit to indicate the surplus that is (usuriously) extracted from exchange as such. Money has been deposited with this company or corporation; however, because it is a 'No Man' without a proper name, it can steal it from its depositors – *resigning* its name at will. The second line of this quotation reveals what Pound knew very well, that such an extraction has extensive public consequences: not only when the bank steals deposits, but even when it *issues* money, it is 'taking out of all', which suggests the usurious extraction of a surplus from what would otherwise be 'all' – a universal, public interest. This bank deprives the social of its wholeness; it vampirizes the 'people'.

The steady loss of value by theft or appropriation is suggested also by the word 'devolve', which means pass on to another, either by the traditional economic form of inheritance or the later, capitalist and contractual version of passing on, which is forfeiture. But when we ask *what* is 'devolved' and *to whom*, the answer is hardly clear. What is devolved or passed on is *either* an inheritance of capital, the people coming into their own, *or* it is the burden of debt. Zukosky's passage does not assume the moral distinction that Pound would insist upon between public and private debt. The proper name of the paternal line of this devolution, or ambiguous inheritance, has been effaced in an anonymity – none of the Poundian names can comprise what is to be passed on. Zukofsky is articulating the ambiguous place of the 'new power for which our language contains no name', a power which seems not to be identifiable with either public or private interests, neither the banks nor the people – and so exceeds Pound's neat distinctions. Money is both capital and credit: what devolves upon 'all' is both a surplus and a lack, and the 'No Man' both gives and takes at once. To a certain extent, this steady devaluation of value is reflected also in Pound's 'shrinking money'. As I argued above, in Pound's mind, any money that can be hoarded is in effect a usurious kind of anti-money, and the desire to hoard money or to capitalize is ultimately a crime against the public good. The possession of money after a certain amount of time makes one indebted in the sense of guilty. Paying a sum on the money one has not spent negates the debt or guilt incurred by hoarding – the debt that, paradoxically, is the result of an accumulation of capital. We have seen in Stein's economic text the conjunction of the miser and the consumer; as I argued in that case, the liberally spending consumer is predicated on a certain miserliness. For Pound, money must circulate; if one is a 'miser', or hoards money for any purpose whatsoever, one also accumulates guilt – a logic which culminates in his anti-semitism. If one has spent one's money, on the other hand, then there is no need to face the guilt of miserliness.

Yet, as Stein's miserly spender suggests, the very act of consumption necessary to propel the economy is itself already a negation, or rather a disavowal, of an accumulating debt to the father upon whose land the brothers live. A borrowed quantity keeps accumulating in the hands of the consumer, one that must be expelled in the act of consumption – which act only contributes to the necessity for expenditure. The very possession of money demands that one pay off the debt for that money every month – unless one has executed the will of the father by *consuming* as one should: by spending the money for real use values. To put Pound's fantasy of shrinking money into the terms of Steinian fetishism: as long as money cannot be hoarded, as long as it is not a corpse-like thing, the father will remain alive, or rather undead, in the place where he has been encrypted by fetishistic disavowal; and as long as the father is undead, there will be order in the community. A tellingly ambivalent moment appears in Canto 33, where Pound quotes a letter from Jefferson to Adams discussing the possibility of America's borrowing money from the Grand Duke of Tuscany, who has 'crowns lying dead in his coffers' (C 161). 'Dead crowns', in Pound's economic imaginary, would be money that is hoarded, withdrawn from circulation. If Stein were to read this, she might comment that 'dead crowns' are also dead *kings*; money is the rational social link that replaces the dead king or paternal leader: the 'dead crown' or dead father is the obverse side of money, which, as Spengler says, destroys the political and paternal will. With the crowned leader of the collective dead in the coffers of the private banks, usury, the parasitical consumption of the public good by private interests, is rampant.

The dynamic process of consumption required by Pound's economics, driven by the need to avoid guilt, demonstrates that money is structured about a 'something' which cannot be so efficiently eradicated. Money itself for Pound implies guilt, which in terms of his economic fantasy is related to the material status of money. Zukofsky has touched upon this in his negation of the 'thing' upon which rational contractual relations are predicated, the 'No Thing'. At the scene of the contract, where the subject makes its deposit and the bank signs and resigns its name, persists the 'No Thing' out of which the money is issued. No Thing is not a *nihil*, but is a foreclosed materiality that issues in 'nothing', in a permanent devolution or inheritance of both capital and debt – or, in short, the positive nothingness of exchange value as credit. The No Thing, like the No Man, serves as a fetish to disavow the 'thing' missing from and yet haunting the heart of the economy. As we shall see, the void that Zukofsky places at the origin of economy is the site of a loss or sacrifice. The sacrificial foundation of value appears in several symptomatic forms in Pound's work. As I mentioned in Chapter 1, chief among them is the narration of loss in terms of the usurious appropriation of value, which leads Pound to develop a political-economic programme that could recuperate upon such losses. However, the recuperation of the thing that is lost must also repeat the sacrifice of the thing that must be excluded from the economy. As we saw in the case of Stein, the thing that is to be recuperated and the thing to be sacrificed correspond to the two sides of the ambivalence that constitutes the economy of the fetish.

Pound's new social contract founded on unequal exchange attempts to construct a fragile political economy that can negotiate the persistence of this thing, which disturbs the economy even as it motivates it. We can see the symbolization of this thing at work in Canto 35, where Pound is discussing a proposal to create a dye works (in Mantua in 1401) in order to create cloth not only to sell, but to serve as money. The passage takes us right to 'the place of contract', which is not only an economic exchange, but an exchange that (since it will also lead to the printing of money) serves as a model for proper social and economic relations. A few lines into the passage, a female figure appears:

> Came this day Madame *hylé*, Madame la Porte Parure,
> Adorned with the Romancero,
> Foot like a flowery branch. That
> Venice be *luogo di contratto* may we say
> the place where the deal is made
>
> (C 175)

'Madame la Porte Parure', 'the wearer of adornment', or 'Madame *hylé*', dressed in the cloth of money, appears at the 'place of contract'. If money occupies 'the place of contract' with Madame *hylé*, it is evident why Pound wanted to speed up the circulation of money, why he thought it shouldn't be held on to for long. The materiality of money means that it is always tied to Madame *hylé*; in economic exchange this means that it keeps becoming thing-like, getting clogged up and lingering around, hoarded. In wanting to accelerate the circulation of money, Pound wants in effect to dematerialize it, to expel the materiality that money, as an 'abstract thing', simultaneously embodies and defers, in order to make it into a pure means of exchange. Dematerializing money would keep the thing away, the thing that is destructive of justice and of social relations. At the same time, nothing will have been given up. A just economy would sacrifice nothing, but such an economy requires the guarantee of a name and a paternal will. Pound wants the assurance that everything will be preserved, even if something essential has been given up. If the father replaces money, if the paternal crown remains undead in its crypt, then everything will remain accounted for.

Pound thought Marx erred in conceiving of money as a commodity in one of its moments, as a kind of substance of value, when money should be only a pure medium of circulation, disappearing with every acquisition (SP 307). But money as such always retains its ties to Madame *hylé*, to materiality. Even the symbolic economy of the father cannot expel it for good; just as there is a 'stain' embedded within the 'Stein', there is a materiality of the paternal name. The acceleration of money is intended to keep something away, but this 'something', figured by Madame *hylé*, returns in the form of the paradoxical abstract thing of money. As Richard Sieburth notes, Canto 30, the conclusion of Pound's first published collection of Cantos, 'closes with a dissonant chord: the vision of the fetishized corpse of Queen Ignez, the ambivalent apparition of Madame hulé . . . and the establishment of Soncino's printing press – an ideogram that rhymes dead (or murderous) female matter with the material mechanization of the letter'.[138] Throughout Pound's text, as throughout Zukofsky's, the issue of printing appears, usually in reference to the printing of money, like the dye-works in Pound's text that would produce a printed cloth to be 'pledged' as money. A parallel text concerning such printing occurs in Canto 32, where Jefferson refers to 'type-founding to which antimony is essential' (C 158). 'Antimony' is the element used in the creation of metal for type, but it is also that which counters money, an 'anti-money', like the Spenglerian Will. This 'antimony' is thus self-divided: as the printing metaphor suggests, it is the material condition of the printing of money, but as anti-money it is also opposed to or destructive of money. Though antimony is the materiality at the foundation of money, it must first be negated and given form in the 'type'. Type-founding is the symbolization of the materiality glimpsed in Madame *hylé*, and the 'type' will be the paternal name. The antimony or anti-money is dangerously paradoxical: it occupies on the one hand the place of the paternal will, as the non-monetary guarantee of the currency printed; and on the other hand it is in the position of anti-money as the usurious, female, element that destroys money and its type.

The place of contract is the place where a bad, usurious debt is incurred; the debt binds one to Madame *hylé*, even though it is the materiality she figures that is to be excluded by the exchange. The condition of a healthy economy is the deferral of the contamination that continues to spread from its core. For Pound as for Stein's Edgar, 'money is not money unless you owe it to any one'. The crucial question for Pound is to whom one owes the money. Where Pound would recommend the healthy possibilities of this debt by giving the power to issue money to the state, Stein would recommend the disavowal of the debt; both, however, meet in their profound ambivalence to a fundamental debt that cannot be regulated by distinctions between private and public, or private goods and the Good. Pound's obsession with money is really an effort to abolish money altogether, and his emphasis on accelerating the circulation of money indicates a horizon of speed at which the circulating object disappears from view. The reform of money, intended to keep it circulating, has as its fundamental goal the disappearance of money into a pure means of exchange. Similarly, therefore, he wanted an economy that would allow for the possession of private property without the dangerous abstract mediation of money and the price system. This requires a paternal will beyond the market that can underwrite and guarantee the value of things, and finally guarantee the private life of the self against devaluation and from appropriation by another. This paternal will, as I argued above, is only to be identified with the leader of the state as long as the leader measures up to the charge placed upon him by the paternal will. Pound's ambivalence towards money extends also to an ambivalence for the state and the will of the leader. In a paradox that points once again to his investment in entrepreneurial market economics, which coexisted with his demand for a strong state power, Pound was ultimately interested only in a state that would be so thoroughly immanent that it would not be an abstract power exterior to the private life, but would bind private life into the collective. Just as the desire to reform money is also a desire to abolish it altogether, the function of the state in Pound's politics is only to disappear. In an important sense, the place of the leader is only a transition to the withering away of such an embodiment: volitionist economics is only a means of diminishing the gap between means and ends, and of realizing the immanence of the universal as the public good.

That this desire should appear in the demand for a powerful leader should not be surprising, since it resembles Stein's turning towards Marshal Pétain in order to avoid another depressing father. The need for a father to maintain the liquidity of money is as important as the need for money to protect what Stein called 'private life'. For Pound, therefore, money should be guaranteed finally by the paternal will, the source of all credit. However, the father's value must be supplemented by a further guarantee: he must be able to fall back on a thing held in reserve – a thing which in the final instance is an object of social fantasy and belief, though it may go by the name of 'the Abundance'. The father and money oscillate in a mutual supplementarity that is designed to maintain the 'something' at a distance while preserving and guaranteeing its presence. However, since the leader embodies a thing of value with which he is not identical, and because of the nonidentity of any embodiment of value with the thing it is required to embody, Pound's political economy is an economy of the fetish. Put in political-philosophical terms, the particular thing can never measure up to the universality it is to embody. Just as no particular thing can embody the thing of most value, so no particular leader can embody the paternal will. As with Stein, melancholic crisis is built into the economy of the fetish, and no economic guarantee can forestall the crisis that constitutes the economy. As Zukofsky puts it, the void at the foundation of the economy comes '[t]o be felt' at times of economic crisis. This fetishistic conflict is played out symptomatically in Canto 33, in which the word 'specie' functions ideogrammatically in order to reconcile the particular and the universal in a false dynamic synthesis. In this ideogram of 'specie' the paternal will as the universal man, or species, is paralleled to 'specie' in an economic sense: he is or has a thing or commodity, like gold in a bank. 'Specie' refers, as the *OED* says, to something in its 'real, proper, precise or actual form; without any kind of substitution'. This definition has two aspects that I want to develop: as an economic term, payment 'in specie' means a payment in something (including 'cash', unless money has lost its value, in which case commodities vie to occupy the position of money-as-specie) that acts as the embodiment of value.[139] But the word also refers to the universality of man as 'species', as opposed to the particular incarnations of man. It has this sense of universality in the quotation from Marx that Pound includes in this Canto. According to the passage from Marx that Pound cites, capital 'cancels individuality' (C 162), that is, concrete labour and particular use values, turning both individualities (labour as such and the labourer) into abstract 'specie' or types. In Marx's text, this abstract universality dialectically prepares the way for the concrete universality of the revolutionary subject of labour. But Pound did not accept Marx's identification of the force of emancipation with the working class. Like other anti-Communist fascists, he thought Marx's utopia required a levelling of individual differences into the universality of *animal laborans* (in Arendt's term). Pound's notion of universality would have to place primary emphasis on the unique, the particular and the local. By insisting on the priority of the individual or particular, Pound – like much modern political theory and practice – could not theorize adequately a universality that was not abstract and sacrificial in relation to that which is singular. This impossibility is in fact the root of his most serious political and ideological contradictions. It is this that led him to turn to a paternal leader as the paradoxical particular incarnation of the universal: the universal is indicated not by a conceptual category such as labour, but by a proper name. The 'specie' is therefore a false synthesis of the contingent particular and the false universal.

The new social contract represented by money, as I mentioned above, must be founded on an unequal relationship between the subject and the leader. This founding exchange guarantees the more egalitarian contractual relationships of the market. Yet this founding exchange, though unequal, must nonetheless be a contract if the values that Pound associates with individualism and entrepreneurialism are to be preserved. That is, the father with whom the founding exchange is made must from another perspective be only a contingent representative of the paternal will. This contractual moment of the founding exchange means that the subject or citizen has rights in relation to the paternal leader, which can be invoked if the leader falls short of what the subject feels the paternal will, or the ego-ideal, demands. The leader in this respect is one subject among others.[140] The ambiguity of this contract is evident in Pound's 'specie', which is at once the universal father, to whom one is tied by obligation and duty, and the particular thing that he merely holds in reserve by virtue of the contract, which provides the subject with rights.

Nonetheless, melancholic crisis looms within the contractual economy of the fetish. This is because what is central to the proper functioning of the economy is credit in the sense of belief. The destruction of money is simply an expression of the fundamental belief or credit that supports the economy; it is one moment of the fetishistic economy of disavowal, which allows for belief to survive all the vicissitudes of the economy. When the universal mediation of money is no longer supported by a belief in money, a demand for the 'specie' sets in, demanding total reform or even destruction of the articulations of the economy. The self-divided, fetishistic 'specie' is the third term that makes possible the turn from money to the father. The Poundian leader is what Stein would call a 'depressing father', who is in control of credit and thus of the issue of currency. But most importantly, as I have suggested, he is also the object of 'credit' in the sense of 'belief'. Thus, as with Stein, 'credit' as belief is the condition of capital. In Canto 36, a translation of Guido Cavalcanti's 'Donna mi pregha' that Pound had been reworking since 1920 or so, Pound locates the authority of such 'lordship' in the perception of pure 'white light that is allness', which is 'divided from all falsity / Worthy of trust' (C 179). This trust or credit is the condition of domination that reveals itself also in Pound's fascism. Pound's Cavalcanti says that Love 'hath ... established lordship', and 'hold[s] his power even though / Memory hath him no more'. This lord or master remains not as a memory but as 'a name sensate' (C 177). This 'name sensate' is not the memory of the figure or of the event, but functions instead like money, which in effect is the memory of a certain quantity of value one has given up in exchange. It has no memory of specific use values or actual things, but is a pure abstraction, pure exchange value. In Pound's Cavalcanti, the 'sensate name' capitalizes or hoards the 'overplus' of the will, which exceeds its natural measure before the object of love. The 'sensate name' serves, like the 'dead crown', as hoarded or capitalized money in that it retains a trace of the thingness that ties it to Madame *hylé*. But, as I have suggested, the thing sacrificed or expelled in this primal symbolization, this subjection to a 'sensate name', will haunt the economy – and will do so as the abstract quantity of exchange value.

Reading Pound's translation through Zukofsky's Marxian revision of it in *A-9*, it becomes apparent that this 'overplus' is none other than Marx's surplus value. The will is 'subjected', Zukofsky will say, to a dominating instance that expropriates its surplus. Zukofsky's version of Cavalcanti's canzone is spoken in part by commodities, a rhetorical device he borrows from Marx. Zukofsky's speaking things, abstracted from their original form of use values, and separated from their cause, are in a permanent state of mourning for what created them, or for the quantity of labour sacrificed in order that that they should come into being. They measure this suffering. But to be more accurate, their relation to this thing is not one of mourning but of melancholia, for which Zukofsky offers little solace. A permanent loss consumes things, but this very loss gives them their positivity, their identity as exchange values. In the next chapter we shall see that the commodities represent their missing cause as alternately labour, love and light.

But this cause is fundamentally lost or missing from its place, just as Marx argued that in a capitalist economy, not only has concrete labour been subsumed as abstract labour by the commodity form, but the sphere of production, the source of real value, has been occluded in a fetishism of commodities. Something has been given up by the commodities in exchange for their identity; but, despite what they have given up, they have *something* in return – namely, their exchange value.

Zukofsky's commodities, therefore, have a fetishized perspective of themselves. A passage in *A*-8 suggests that Zukofsky's commodities speak not only from the abstraction that the market economy imposes upon them, but also from the depreciation of their value brought about by the Depression. With the crash and the Depression, a 'void' opens: 'Should the struck bars of oblong glass be stopped – a *void* / To be *felt*' (*A* 49; my italics).[141] The abstract 'quantity' of value the commodities receive in exchange for giving up their cause, their thing, is being drained from them. The sudden devaluation of commodities means there can be no assurance that the thing of value can continue to guarantee the presence of what has been given up or sacrificed in order for the commodities to come into being. Recall that the steady deflation of Pound's 'shrinking money' is countered by the place of the leader, who has the power to issue a supplementary quantity of value. But Zukofsky recognizes the latent fascism of this economy; instead of following Pound's route, and replacing the guarantee or 'credit' with the paternal name and will to reassure the mourning things that *nothing is lost*, that all is accounted for, he counters this dialectic with a perpetual challenge to the paternal name and will.

According to Zukofsky, what makes commodities fascinating within the sphere of consumption is the fetishistic trace of the very surplus they lack. Commodities themselves are the 'felt void', the embodiment of the missing quantity. To return to Canto 36, the luminous essence that Pound places at the centre of the ethical is exchange value, one form of the universalizing 'specie'. However, Zukofsky does not propose a Marxist or even a 'volitionist economics' to restore concrete labour and use value, as Pound did by imagining a permanent deferral of the abstract thing presented by exchange value, or the 'felt void' of dead female matter. Zukofsky does not provide a model, Marxist, fascist or otherwise, for overcoming the historical fetishism he presents in *A*-8 and 9. In refusing to employ a form of the 'specie', for example the universal man, the paternal name, or even (as we shall see) a universalizing name such as 'labor', Zukofsky appears to be left only with this last option of a fetishism of commodities, which is thus the historical limit inscribed in his text. In the concluding lines of *A*-9 Love consoles the melancholic commodities with a condensed translation of Marx's description of commodity fetishism: 'Weep, love's heir ... related is equated, / How else is love's distance approximated' (*A* 111). The consolation can only provide the commodities a new, tragic perspective on the condition of abstraction from which they suffer. Love explains that it is by the reductive equations, or levelling effects, of exchange value that 'love's distance is approximated', that is, both closed and maintained: things come near to the origin to which they are bound, but not too near.

The universality of the 'relating and equating' exchange value does not liberate things, but continues to feed the 'open wound' of the social. The things are left to mourn what constituted them, that to which they owe their existence – the labour that is sacrificed in their production. They embody the 'felt', or suffered, 'void'. But the consolation of Love's fetishistic perspective does not protect them against the new forms of domination threatened by the economic crisis of devaluation. As in the case of Pound's 'specie', the outcome turns on the 'thing' that will replace gold as the guarantee of the economy. Poundian 'credit' is founded on the belief that the leader is in possession of the sacrificed thing, as a guarantee of the economy, but also that he has abolished it for good even as he holds it in reserve. The leader has never himself incurred the symbolic debt, or given up the thing, so it is both there and not there. Pound's symbolic system demands that the father fill the gap or 'felt void', control its dangerous instability with his name and will. Though Zukofsky's commodities attempt to identify or name their missing cause alternately as love, labour and light, the guarantee is an indeterminate thing, a ghostly quantity, an *unnamed surplus* that can, like surplus value, be appropriated for the purposes of domination.

The unnamed surplus is not in the final instance labour. Zukofsky refuses to name the common substance that could resolve social contradictions. This may seem to conflict with much of the evidence that the early sections of *A* constitute a hymn or song for labour: 'For labor who will sing ... ?' (*A* 46). *A*-8 in fact seems to begin by establishing its terms as those of an anthropomorphic metaphysics of labour: 'Labor as creator / Labor as creature' (*A* 43). Yet labour is rivalled by another concept in *A*-8, which is 'energy': 'Know whatever news the future brings to the world / Should have one constant: Name? – perhaps Energy' (*A* 47). Since one of his sources is Engels, one could argue that Zukofsky follows Engels in considering 'labor' as a form of 'energy'. In this case, referring 'Labor' to 'Energy' as a final instance reifies it even further, as Engels did. The relationship between labour and energy is not, however, one of metaphoric conflation, but rather one of conflict. With this conflict Zukofsky foregrounds the problem of the name of the 'constant' behind historical process. This is already apparent in the name 'Labor' in the lines cited above, in which labour appears on both sides of the equation, at once creator and creature. This would appear to be self-evidently theological or metaphysical, yet it is faithful to Marx's text, which distinguishes between 'labor power' as an abstract capacity and the particular historical forms that capacity assumes. Whether Marx's text is finally 'metaphysical' or not is not my concern at present, but in any case it is not so simply metaphysical as Zukofsky's phrasing would make it seem. The attempt to universalize 'Labor' as a self-originating 'creator', as an ahistorical capacity for production, while particularizing it as 'creature', sets the term off balance in a way that is not regulated even in Marx's text. The doubleness of 'labor' in this splitting resembles the doubleness of capital, as the Father into whom the Son must return. As Anson Rabinbach has argued, Marx's labour power is divided: it is

> both social *and* physiological, historically specific *and* at the same time a form of universal energy, or *Kraft*. . . . First, as an abstract, universal measure and a 'magnitude of value', it is clearly a social phenomenon as 'the labor time socially necessary for its production'. But it is equally a physiological concept, 'devoid of all social and historical elements'. Both a social and a physiological magnitude, it is a measure of value and a measure of energy.[142]

But, more precisely, divided between an abstract 'energy' and its historical, commodified form, 'labor power' is at once measured and measuring. As what is measured, labour power is that which has been transformed into exchange value, which is its measure. On the other hand, 'labor power' measures the surplus that is appropriated for capital and transformed into exchange value. It would seem to be a closed system of relations, in which each term is an adequate measure of the other. Yet it is clearly tautological to say that labour power measures labour power, which is what the second formulation states. That is to say, the name and concept 'labor power' translates a quantity of exchange value into a quantity of labour power, claiming that it was only labour power in disguise.

The important moment in this accounting process is the moment of naming. The point is that 'labor' as a term measures something else that is not entirely accountable as 'labor'. 'Labor' in the final analysis – as Marx knew – is a concept that became dominant with the historical abstraction of labour in industrial production. To refer to all value-making activities as historical forms of a 'universal energy, or *Kraft*', is to impose a historically specific and real abstraction on to discrete forms of activity. On the one hand, therefore, 'labor' names a historical object with revolutionary potential; on the other hand, it abstracts into a single name further, historically submerged, forms of activity, energy and desire. This is the truth that lies in Zukofsky's looking also to the name 'energy' to displace or supplement 'labor' as the name of the missing quantity. Zukofsky's naming is fetishistic: the name 'labor' at once names a determinate historical object, and at the same time points to something that persists as a 'constant' beneath historical transformation – like 'labor' for Marxists – and yet cannot be identified in or with any of its historical appearances or names.

This constant is what I referred to above as the unnamed missing surplus. Zukofsky does not name this quantity, but indicates it with the material mark of the psi – ψ – which is Schrödinger's figure for the wave function. Zukofsky's psi links a number of registers in *A*-8, but one of the most important is economic: the psi or trident designates 'that "something", changes / In which trident stay responsible for the waves' (*A* 50). Zukofsky's nameless figure is a graphic inscription marking a 'something', an indeterminate quantum that is unpresentable in the economy. For Zukofsky this 'something', this quantum, appears as the 'felt void' of the fetish, the 'material clef' of the economy. This 'constant' or 'something' traverses *A*-8 in the form of quanta, appearing in the quotations from Marx, among others. Borrowing from *The Education of Henry Adams*, Zukofsky liquefies the missing quantity of *A*-8 into waves which seem to have the potential for revolution:

> Be prepared, well and completely prepared
> To make use, with all our forces,
> Of the next revolutionary wave ...

(*A* 91)

The primary reference of this quotation is the Marxist identification of the revolutionary quantum with labour. But the waves assume a number of other forms, including the Russian 'herders deserted by their leaders and herds'. Henry Adams refers to these abandoned Russian herders as 'wandering waves stopped in their wanderings', and as 'tribes that had camped, like Khirgis, for the season . . / had lost the means of motion without acquiring the habit of permanence' (*A* 81). But fixed like these tribes, suspended between immobility and motion, these waves (like the unemployed of the Depression) constitute an 'unavailable energy', an energy which has 'lost the means of motion', or of circulation. This indeterminate status repeats what Pound could not reconcile himself to in the case of money, which oscillates dangerously between residual thingness and fluid circulation. For Pound, the issue of money on the basis of state credit was intended to perfect the conversion of energy to use, to make it accessible and liquid. As I argued above, this required a 'specie' as a guarantee: that is to say, it required on the one hand the universal paternal will, and on the other hand a material thing backing the exchanges.

Zukofsky resists Pound's contradictions concerning things and fluids and attempts to imagine an immanence that does not collapse into Poundian fascism. Borrowing from Schrödinger's quantum physics, he isolates the Poundian contradiction between things (or particles) and fluids (or waves) in the 'something' or 'constant' underlying change. Zukofsky immobilizes the wave, or draws attention to its unavailability, its thingly fixity, with the psi. Psi is the mark of thingness that Pound wanted finally to abolish or liquidate in order to overcome the contradiction of thingness and immanence. The contradiction always would require that credit be given to a proper name, which would then serve the function of the universal, the 'specie'. Though Zukofsky's fetishistic psi resists the universalizing proper name and the leader, it does not succeed in realizing the economy of perfect circulation that Pound desired. Nor does it attempt to. Zukofsky's inscription of the fetish stops the wandering wave in its path, but it indicates that what is represented in this figure is not available for use or any other form of economization. In contrast to Pound's model of efficiency, Zukofsky will insist on the importance of a certain 'unavailable energy', which he associates also with what Adams sees as the entropic 'negative luminosity' of Russia and its immobile wandering waves. This energy cannot be recuperated in any political economy: it is fundamentally lost.

'NOTHING OF VALUE'

As we have seen, the speaking commodities of *A*-9 claim that a surplus is extracted from them and employed in their domination. While Marx's speaking commodities only have a fetishistic perspective, Zukofsky's attempt to awaken those who consume them to the fact that '[h]ands, heart, not value made us' (*A* 107). They call for a return to a 'natural use' that is proper to them as 'animate instruments' (*A* 108, 107). However, this perspective rivals another, which is itself as fetishistic as the perspective assumed by Marx's commodities. In the first half of *A*-9, Zukofsky's fetishized commodities, like Marx's, see 'gold' as their cause: 'We affect ready gold a steady token / Flows in unbroken circuit and induces our being...' (*A* 106). The commodities are confused and in a panic, suffering in the midst of economic crisis: 'should the struck bars of the oblong glass be stopped – A void / To be felt' (*A* 49). In the Depression, the guarantee of their value has collapsed, devaluing their very substance. For Zukofsky, economic crisis makes tangible the 'felt void' at the heart of the economy – the originary loss which is not subsumed in the guarantee of the name, and is not to be countered by 'the coming man'. Yet the rival perspectives can be reconciled: the speaking commodities merely 'affect' gold as their 'ready token' only because they have little faith in labour, which has itself been induced by gold, and become abstract: 'labor takes on our imprecision – / Bought, induced by gold at no gain...' (*A* 106). Zukofsky's alteration of the commodities' perspective measures the distance capitalism has covered since Marx: though the commodities first look to labour as a potential 'constant' or 'something' that will survive the crash and emerge as the real basis of value, they are anxious that labour is already lost as a potentially emancipatory substance, that its revolutionary moment has passed.

The crisis allows the commodities to look upon labour with critical, demystified eyes: they reveal that labour is 'induced by gold' into the industrial mode of production 'at no gain' to itself. The form of exchange such an inducement calls upon is not compatible with the capitalist market: the inducement of labour 'at no gain' to itself would require that labour make a 'gift' of itself for the Good of the corporate body, the larger whole of which it is a part. We have seen this form of self-sacrifice at the authoritarian extreme of Stein's politics. However, in Zukofsky's version of such an inducement, it is not the father or the ego-ideal, but *gold* that occupies the place of the Good. Where such an authoritarian inducement of labour would require a collective Good operating without reference to 'material abundance', Zukofsky's labour sacrifices itself for the production of a material value from which it does not benefit. Workers are induced by gold even though this thing of value emerging from their labour does not return to them in the form of economic gain, but is instead appropriated by another class. If their sacrifice of labour is 'at no gain', whether in gold or in other terms, workers must have been induced into production by an ethic of sacrifice. Labour is induced not by appeals to self-interest, but to a public Good, defined in terms of the 'gold' that can be produced by its self-sacrifice: the production of gold is a Good in itself, worthy of sacrifice, even when another class will profit from it. This identification of gold and the Good is characteristic of the emerging capitalist culture of consumption. Zukofsky's poem, as I will argue in this section, attends to the production of the consumer through the social promise figured in the offer of 'gold' as increased wages. In contrast to Marx's conclusion that wages inevitably drop to the level of bare subsistence with the rising demand for surplus labour, workers are historically induced into the American economy as *consumers* by means of increased wages for the purpose of increased consumption.

However, as I argued in Chapter 1, despite the increase in wages and material abundance, the extraction of surplus value and the structure of sacrifice persist in the economy organized about the Good of *bien être*. In the culture of consumption, 'gain' and 'no gain' operate simultaneously, though in such a regime of *bien être* the moment of sacrifice is not as tangible or apparent as it is in the authoritarian inducement. Zukofsky encodes the suffering inflicted by the capitalist requirement of sacrifice in the figure of the worker subjected to the 'machine's terror' (*A* 108). The condition that makes possible this 'terror' is the abolition of the pre-industrial (for example, artisanal) forms of property that made possible the autonomy of the worker. This autonomy is destroyed when industrial capital subsumes these pre-capitalist means of production into itself. In Marx's analysis, 'labor' is the only 'property' to which the labourer can lay claim, the only commodity he or she owns and can exchange on the market for the means of subsistence or of the reproduction of labour power. Zukofsky's revision of Marx, as we shall see, changes the emphasis in this exchange of labour for wage, and sees the wage as the only form of 'property' available to labour. Rather than merely a means to reproduce labour power, the increased wage promises access to more than reproduction: it promises access to private property beyond one's own labour. The reason for changing the emphasis from one side of the equation to the other is to indicate the way in which not only higher wages, but also the development of institutions of consumer credit, seem to compensate more than adequately for the sacrifice of a quantity of labour in the production of surplus value.

Historically, in Marx's analysis, the industrial machine expropriates the property – the tools – of the artisanal worker, in effect making him or her dependent on the machinery owned by the capitalist. Autonomy then only comes in the form of the wage. Zukofsky treats wages as a historically new form of the tool as a *means of consumption* rather than the production proper to tools as such. As I argued above, Zukofsky is concerned at this point not with the diminishing quantity that Marx understood the wage to be, but the increased wage that would prepare the culture of consumption by interpellating labour into the class of private ownership. Though the wage might seem to provide a semblance of the autonomy lost to the worker, it nonetheless reflects the structure of domination that it is intended to conceal. This question is raised in Zukofsky's text by means of a series of juxtaposed quotations from Marx, which confuse several different kinds of property. The elusive and diminishing 'quantum' we examined in the last section returns in its economic sense, as Zukofsky turns to Marx's text:

> As defeats gaged economies...
> That quantum of the means of subsistence which leaves
> No surplus to command the labor of others,
> The communists see no need to abolish that,
> Growth of industry is destroying it daily...
>
> (*A* 50)

Zukofsky here collapses two sentences of Marx's, the first of which describes the goods that wages can buy:

> that quantum of the means of subsistence which is absolutely requisite to keep the laborer in bare existence as a laborer.... We by no means intend to abolish this personal appropriation of the products of labor, an appropriation that is made for the maintenance and reproduction of human life, and that leaves no surplus wherewith to command the labor of others. All that we want to do away with is the miserable character of this appropriation under which the laborer lives merely to increase capital....

Instead, Marx says, 'that quantum' should be 'a means to widen, to enrich, to promote the existence of the laborer,' whereas capital enforces the reduction of the quantum, in order to keep 'living labor [as] but a means to increase accumulated labor'.[143]

But in the passage cited by Zukofsky ('no need to abolish *that*'), Marx is referring not to this minimal property, though Zukofsky's quotation makes it seem that he is; Marx's 'that' refers to the property 'of the petty artisan and of the small peasant, a form of property that preceded the bourgeois form.... There is no need to abolish *that*', Marx writes, since 'the development of industry has to a great extent already destroyed it, and is still destroying it daily.' This quantum is being abolished for good, rather than being subsumed into the process of the reproduction of capital: this form of individual property is being consigned to an era now past. Both of Marx's quanta refer to diminishing quantities of very different kinds (the means of subsistence acquired by the wage awarded to the worker at the end of the working day, on the one hand, and a form of private property that 'preceded the bourgeois form', on the other); but by juxtaposing them as he does, Zukofsky makes them refer to an emerging kind of property, the structure of which is indicated by *wages* at the time

Zukofsky is writing. During the Depression, wages, the very means of subsistence of the worker, are being diminished or destroyed. According to the Marxian perspective Zukofsky borrows, wages (suggested to him by Marx's 'means of subsistence') must diminish historically and not only in the particular crisis of the Depression. The diminishing quantity of wages is to be referred to the logic of surplus value. Marx's analysis of the contradictions of the capitalist mode of production led him to the conclusion that the declining rate of surplus value would force wages downwards. The value haemorrhaging from the worker's wages continues to function as the 'surplus wherewith to command the labor of others'; it continues to accumulate as that other quantum called capital. Zukofsky's quotations would therefore seem to fit in with Marx's analysis of capitalist crisis, in which the growth of industry leads to a decrease in wages and abolishes the means of consumption; as Zukofsky says, 'there are no consumers' (*A* 65). The growth of industry, based on the expropriation of surplus value, is thus a Depression in the making, according to the Marxist analysis Zukofsky performs in miniature.

Zukofsky's collapsing of the two quanta seems to lead to a shorthand Marxist analysis of the Depression as capitalist crisis, with a Poundian emphasis on underconsumption. But the effect of Zukofsky's collapsing of the quotations is to make his 'quantum' something very different from the various quanta Marx is discussing. With the implied comparison of wages as means of subsistence with 'the property of the petty artisan and of the small peasant', Zukofsky participates in a mystification of the relationship of labour and capital. The effect of the quotations is to say that wages, 'that quantum of the means of subsistence', *should* enrich the life of the worker. Zukofsky makes Marx sound like Proudhon, for example, or other reformers who recommended the redistribution of wealth without taking into account the total mode of the production of capital. How is it possible to turn wages, which are based on the commodification of labour, into a form of property that can enrich the life of the labourer? The economy that produces wages for labour, as Marx emphasized, cannot be reformed from within. Yet Zukofsky, in implicitly comparing wages to an older and quickly disappearing form of property, seems to hold open the possibility of a kind of property which does not produce a surplus that can command the labour of others.

Zukofsky's citations from Marx attempt to locate a quantum that is not particular to a class, that belongs neither to the worker nor to the petty bourgeois nor to the artisan. In his citations, the quantum that is being abolished every day and the quantum of the means of subsistence are one quantum, which is particular to the *consumer* in so far as the consumer was becoming the ideological figure of a *classless* person. Labour must have the means of its subsistence, but must also be able to partake of the pleasures offered by the new economy of mass production, which makes available an 'enrichment' beyond mere subsistence. In Zukofsky's citation, Marx says that 'quantum should be a means to widen, to enrich, to promote the existence of the laborer', and this is precisely what was undertaken in the early twentieth century. The increased capacity for consumption serves to conceal production. Labour itself is mystified to the extent that it acts as if labour is a commodity, or private property, to be sold on the market in return for the means not only to replenish itself but also to enrich itself beyond the reproduction of labour power. That is to say, the labourer is not a labourer as much as he or she is a consumer, in Simmel's terms, sacrificing one thing for another. However, the transformation of the labourer into the consumer is more than merely ideological obfuscation, in that it reflects a new organization of the economy. The resolution of the economic crisis caused by underconsumption demands that the labourer find his or her place in the economy at a level beyond that of subsistence or need; therefore, the concept of labour itself undergoes transformation.

Zukofsky is not simply reproducing ideology uncritically. His increasing isolation of the quantum maintains a Marxian edge: Zukofsky's quantum is seen steadily in the light of Marx's insistence on the diminishing of wages that intensified industrialism makes inevitable. In the face of capital's recognition that wages must increase, Zukofsky sees the 'quantum' as something that is essentially, in its very definition, being 'abolished'. It is a diminishing quantum that has loss or depletion embedded within it as an irreducible structural feature. Because of this, it resembles the wages of the labourer in Marx's analysis, in which the capitalist crisis was already implicit. The most important aspect of Zukofsky's quantum appears in the contradiction of a quantum that diminishes even as it increases; this means that another aspect of Marx's analysis of wage labour persists into the new consumer economy:

even the quantum of the means of consumption, the private property of the consumer, must be understood in terms of surplus value. Not only production, but also consumption, produces value; consumption yields a surplus. The loss embedded within the diminishing quantum of the wage means that the wage, as money, is not a positivity, but is a kind of credit; as Gertrude Stein says, 'profit and loss is always loss'. As we shall see in the next chapter, the analysis of surplus value that Marx discovered in labour under the conditions of capitalism must be transferred to the analysis of desire in the culture of consumption.

Though America resolved the economic crisis without resorting to an authoritarian politics, the question of domination within the developing consumer economy must still be posed; the analysis of the culture of consumption must keep in view the genealogical connection of this economy with the authoritarian politics of the thirties in Europe. To understand the significance of the diminishing quantum particular to the consumer economy, it is necessary to understand the material and cultural conditions that made the interpellation of the producer as consumer possible. Zukofsky had little of Stein's fear that America would go fascist, but was more attentive to the political implications of the domination of the American economy by private interests. Where Stein chose to focus on the army and the state as the paternal structures which would absorb the 'private life', Zukofsky was more prescient: the state and its institutions, for Zukofsky, were secondary to the private corporation. Where Stein feared the 'gift' of the depressing father who answered the needs of his subjects, Zukofsky attends to the economy of the gift that persists even in the wage that Stein thought would return the employee to the status of 'hired man'. Zukofsky recognized that the benevolent corporation was an ambiguous confusion of private and public interests with the power to define the public Good. Like other attempts to construct a nonconflictual public or society, the corporation functions by transforming the remnants of nineteenth-century paternalism and its patterns of identification. This can be seen in the transformation in the status of property in the early part of the century; even as the prospect of private ownership is extended to the working class, the concept of property is being transformed so as to preclude the traditional 'right of action' that provided the basis for the traditional liberal defence of property. As Jeffrey Lustig writes, we have not really 'socialized' property because Americans can buy an array of consumer goods and (sometimes) draw a pension in their old age. The status of ownership traditionally never indicated anything about rights to a median income or to new household gadgets.... What ownership did entail [in its earlier concept, in the writings of Adam Smith, Thomas Jefferson, and John Taylor] was a stake in productive wealth, a chance to exercise initiative, do valuable work, and earn a standing in the community. Similar promises were at the heart of socialism. But modern producer wealth confers none of these things on the producers. And consumer commodities – rootless, weightless things whose values change according to distant developments – hardly even support the concept of possession. They are essentially conditional holdings; if one's income falls they can easily be 'repossessed.' The modern promise is really of commodity-holding, not property-holding. That means that the new world of 'position,' rather than signifying the emergence of a new kind of freedom ... actually reveals the evolution of a new kind of hierarchy.[144]

As Daniel Boorstin argues, the corporation was becoming 'the democratizer of property' in that it was owned by private citizens who were the stockholders. By 1932, Boorstin writes,

it was a commonplace that in modern America the very experience of owning property had become something new – in one sense plainly more democratic, but at the same time more occult. In this 'people's capitalism,' more and more millions of citizens 'owned' the means of production. But what did they own?[145]

The corporate redefinition of ownership recalls the corporate dimension of Pound's private property. It will be recalled that Pound intends private property to maintain its ties to the social whole that makes it possible; therefore, private property in the final instance belongs to the leader who represents that whole. Whereas private property used to imply right of action, and therefore power, ownership in corporate culture is separate from power, which is distributed among salaried managers.

Therefore, what Zukofsky (after C.F. Adams) calls 'corporate life' (*A* 76) mimics Pound's corporate state down to the structure of property – and also to the system of credit that contributes to the redefinition of property and ownership. The increased wage of the worker seems to promise the unification of all classes by democratizing private ownership, yet in order to fulfil that promise it must exploit the structure of credit that Pound insisted must remain public. Pound, of course, would never have approved of the private appropriation of the general structure of debt. But both popular and academic economists agreed that not only increased wages but also a new system of consumer credit was required to increase consumption adequately to avoid future economic crises. 'Installment buying' originated with Ford's scheme to sell cars to his employees by allowing them to exercise their thrift by saving five dollars a week until they had saved enough for the price of the car. But, as Daniel Boorstin argues, '[w]hat was really needed was some scheme allowing people to "own" cars before they really owned them.... If a costly new product like the automobile was to become a common possession, Ford's old-fashioned morality, with its calculus of abstention, thrift, and foresight, would not do.' The instalment plan allowed consumers to own what they had not yet paid for; and this form of consumer credit would eventually be issued by credit corporations, beginning with the Guaranty Securities Company, whose remarkable success led the major car manufacturers 'to set up their own financing firms'. As Boorstin points out, 'Ford finally changed its policy in 1928 with its Universal Credit Corporation....'[146] The paternalism of Ford's factories can be extended to the paternalism of a new system of consumer credit, which, by way of this new form of property, ties the subject to the agencies that issue value.

For both Zukofsky and Stein, the corporate state advocated by Pound and the corporate culture of consumption that developed in its place share a common foundation and structure despite their different forms of domination. That foundation is the general system of credit and debt. For Pound, the Depression and all such economic crises result directly from conspiratorial combinations of individuals, who manipulate the general structure of credit and debt for their own private interests. But Zukofsky, motivated by an insight into the development of the consumer economy that Pound did not have, goes further, and sees that the Depression, even as it raises the possibility of revolutionary resistance to capitalism, also makes possible a rearrangement of the general system of credit and debt. Nonetheless, A-8 can seem at times profoundly Poundian in its concerns. For example, Zukofsky's cited account of the programme of 'business-like management' might have been taken directly from *Eleven New Cantos*:

- limitation of supply with a view to profitable sales;
- obstruction of traffic with a view to profitable sales;
- meretricious publicity with a view to profitable sales.

(*A* 79)

However, Zukofsky concerns himself with the conditions that make Pound's structural distinctions possible. Even as he draws very near to Pound's economic perspectives, his perspective always allows a space for critique. As another example, one of Zukofsky's versions of the Great Depression is provided by Brooks Adams' introduction to Henry Adams' *The Degradation of the Democratic Dogma*. In his introduction, Brooks focuses on the problem of debt and inflationary measures. In a passage that is partially cited by Zukofsky (*A* 81), Brooks provides a synopsis of his philosophy of history around 1893, and it is one with which Pound would have agreed wholeheartedly (I have italicized the lines quoted by Zukofsky):

Mostly *men work unconsciously*, and *perform an act, before they can explain why; often centuries before.* Throughout the ages, it has been a favorite device of the creditor class first to work a contraction of the currency, which bankrupted the debtors, and then to cause an inflation, which created a rise when they sold the property which they had impounded. The question to me was, how fully was I justified in applying these admitted facts of history to the crisis of 1893. Beginning with the panic at Rome under Tiberius, I had a long list of precedents stretching through the crusades to the present time. And the common way for many centuries, in which an advance after a depression had been secured, was by an adulteration or debasement of the currency, and at a later day by an issue of paper. But the men who had usually conducted such vast movements had to be supremely adapted to the business.[147]

In quoting from this passage, Zukofsky might appear to be suggesting that the Depression could also be understood as such a monetary conspiracy on the part of creditors to bankrupt debtors. Pound's views of such conspiracies are well known, and can be summed up in a phrase repeated in Cantos 52 and 53: 'licit consumption impeded' (C 213, 216). For both Brooks and Pound, consumption has been impeded in the population in order to increase the production of usurious profits for the consumption of the few. This is not only the structure of the Depression for Pound, but the structure of industrial labour in general, which requires the appropriation of surplus value. Quoting Thomas Jefferson's comments on the monarchist party, Pound expresses concern with the exercise of power through unproductive consumption of the surplus extracted from workers:

> to take from them, as from bees, so much of their earnings
> as that unremitting labour shall be necessary to obtain a sufficient surplus barely to
> sustain a scant life. And these earnings
> they apply to maintain their privileged orders in splendour and idleness
> to fascinate the eyes of the people ... as to an order of superior beings. (C 158)

Zukofsky echoes this passage in *A*-8, citing C.F. Adams, who writes in 'Chapters of Erie' that '[m]odern society has created a class of artificial beings who bid fair soon to be the masters of their creator'.[148] As is the case with the class division made possible by the extraction of surplus value, the relation of creditor and debtor is reversed: though 'society' (Pound's 'people') has created these beings (that is to say, the Goulds, the Vanderbilts, but above all the corporations that do not bear such proper names), fetishism inverts the relations of debt between these conspicuous consumers and the other class of 'workers'. More important than the fact of conspicuous consumption is the general structure of debt exploited by the corporate culture, and the fetishistic inversion of debtor–creditor relations.[149] Moreover, Zukofsky's citation also allows us to place the entire structure of domination in the framework of commodity fetishism: though the monarchist party is a figure, for Pound, of the usurious class of finance capitalists, 'an order of superior beings' with the capacity 'to fascinate the eyes of the people', one cannot help but see these beings as commodities, which fascinate the eyes even of their producers, who are unable to perceive the real relations that are their condition. The fascination exercised by the 'superior beings' is the fascination of commodity fetishism, which precludes the possibility of 'licit consumption'.

But Zukofsky's text does not align itself with Poundian polarities. Instead, Zukofsky questions the revolutionary demand to correct the inverted perspective and restore the proper relations of credit and debt, for the fetishization of *labour* as the source of value would conceal the further condition, which is the original debt to the father. Zukofsky makes this further condition apparent in his citations from Henry Adams, which work in counterpoint to the more Poundian lines taken from Brooks Adams. The structure of debt is revealed in the economic crisis of 1893. As would happen in the early years of the Depression, banks were closing as there was a run on the gold supply in anticipation of the repeal of the Sherman Silver Purchase Act and the return to a single gold standard. The spectre of absolute debt was glimpsed by Henry Adams in the crisis of 1893, when the banks too were threatened with destitution:

> Blindly some very powerful energy was at work, doing something that nobody wanted done. When Adams went to his bank to draw a hundred dollars of his own money on deposit, the cashier refused to let him have more than fifty, and Adams accepted the fifty without complaint because he was himself refusing to let the banks have some hundreds or thousands that belonged to them. Each wanted to help the other, yet both refused to pay their debts, and he could find no answer to the question which was responsible for getting the other into the situation, since lenders and borrowers were the same interest and socially the same person. Evidently the force was one, and its operation was mechanical... but no one knew what it meant, and most people dismissed it as an emotion – a panic – that meant nothing.

Henry was touring through Switzerland when he received 'letters from his brothers requesting his immediate return to Boston because the community was bankrupt and he was probably a beggar'. Adams found it difficult to understand 'how any man would be ruined who had, months before, paid off every dollar of debt he knew himself to owe...'.[150]

This absolute or fundamental debt implies that, as Brooks put it, 'men work unconsciously' – that is to say, the subjective structure phenomenalized in industrial labour extends to other domains of experience, and serves as their condition. Stein tried to distinguish between 'hired men' and 'employees'; we have seen how the distinction serves to disavow the general structure of debt. 'Men work unconsciously', whether they are 'hired men' or 'employees'. Zukofsky raises this issue immediately after the passage on 'the people's issue of nothing' and the 'No Man', and immediately before the passage concerning the Tocquevillean distribution of powers:

> By what name you call your people
> Whether by that of freemen or of slaves . .
> That in some countries
> The *laboring* poor were called freemen,
> In others slaves . .
> *Workers producing a surplus* . . .
>
> (*A* 90)

The unconscious work is labour for a master, a 'superior being'. As Pound writes, citing Ambrose Spencer, 'Man who feeds, clothes, lodges another / has absolute control over his will' (C 181). The superior being in the economy of mass consumption is, however, not a 'master', or a ruler-will, but is 'No Man': the corporation has the fantasmatic power of induction with (no) gain. The increased wage of the labourer binds the subject to an economy of immanent domination and sacrifice. The 'new announcements of economies' point to an economization within mass consumption, as investments or deposits are made to corporate structures of agency which only apparently serve the interests of the subject. Therefore, despite its promise of *bien être* and the minimization of sacrifice, the culture of consumption requires an unconscious ethic of sacrifice: 'I would die for dear old Standard Oil' (*A* 93).

The structure of sacrifice does not appear explicitly in Zukofsky's poem, but through a series of exchanges which would seem to represent a diversity of economic or social relationships. Yet even as each of them relies on the rhetoric of exchange, it appeals to the structures of debt, gift and sacrifice – the complex ties of desire, and not the (apparently) rational, self-interested relationships of exchange. For example, an advertisement for the 'Flanagan and Phepoe / Lottery and Insurance Office', to be found in New York '[o]ne hundred sometime years ago', attempts to induce the consumer, presumably at a gain for both parties, with a time-piece of gold:

> A superb Double Cased Gold Watch
> Chances sixpence
> Unequalled Policies by which the Holder
>   has 4 chances of obtaining 50,000 dollars
>   & 100 dollars, if last drawn.
> These unparalleled advantages to be obtained
> For the truly trifling risque of one shilling...
>
> (A 55)

The ad solicits an investment of wages in the 'risque' of obtaining 'advantages'. In the course of an argument over the definition of the 'commodity', Pound points out to Zukofsky that the word comes from the Latin *commoditas*, meaning 'advantage, benefit' (PZ 170). This use of the word by Zukofsky suggests that this passage concerns not an exceptional but rather an exemplary relationship between the consumer and the commodity: the commodity is a reward that far exceeds the investment required. The economic ambiguity of the exchange, however, cannot be understated: since this is a lottery, there is no guaranteed return, but the act is still the *purchase* of a chance. One may get something for almost nothing; the prize is *almost* being given away, but not quite. This implies that, if one wins the lottery and receives the prize, there is no need to feel grateful, obliged or indebted; it is the payoff from an investment of one shilling. Chances are however that one will have paid *something* for *nothing*. The mere chance purchased has no value once the lottery is over. If one does not receive the prize, one cannot claim a right to it; what was purchased is the chance. Besides, the investment is so small that one cannot insist on the right to more than the mere chance of winning. All parties are free in this exchange, and the sacrifices are minimized all around.

But if we pursue the 'risque' as a figure of consumption, as a figure of the act of purchase, it becomes apparent that more archaic forms of domination persist even in the modern capitalist economy of abundance. To see the relation between the consumer and the commodity in terms of this kind of lottery suggests that the 'risque' extends throughout the consumer economy, providing a clue to its subjective structure. The ad continues, in Zukofsky's quotation, to convince the reader that 'Now is your time'; 'now', the time of Stein's 'continuous present', is the time to 'Choose a firm cloud before it falls, and in it / Catch e'er she die, the Cynthia of the minute' (*A* 55). The value of what might be won or given far exceeds the minimal required sacrifice of one shilling. But since the chances of receiving anything in exchange for the sacrifice are slim, something else is being exchanged in this act of consumption, and the relation established is more important than the thing that might be acquired. The prize itself indicates the important relation: the 'Gold Watch' (which is both a piece of value, like the money offered, and a commodity) may not be valued so much for the 'gain' of gold it represents, but for the fact that, like Gold as the commodity of commodities, it embodies the temporization or economization that is crucial to the act of consumption. The continuous present is just out of reach; its presence is the presence of temporization, time as deferral and promise. The mode of the *promise* reveals the sacrifice concealed even within the acquisitive act of consumption: *enjoyment* is impossible, is endlessly deferred, even within the *satisfaction* provided by the purchase and/or consumption of the commodity. The crucial moment is the establishment of the relationship in the 'now' of the purchase, and not the deferred 'now', the future present when the gift is given away. The gift is poised, holding in reserve the enjoyment deferred by satisfaction, or *bien être*.[151]

But it is important not to forget that the offer is made by a 'Lottery and *Insurance* Company,' which offers 'Unequalled Policies', presumably as guarantees against any future loss of property or destruction of value. The purchase of a chance at winning is simultaneously an investment in the guarantee of value; the investment of a shilling can guarantee the value of your property, perhaps even your life, *against* the operations of chance. At least up to the price of the Gold Watch or $50 000. Such are the unequalled policies: one shilling may get you $50 000. But what really is being given up with this investment in the Lottery and Insurance Company? The word 'unequalled' is especially significant, given that Zukofsky places it after a passage in which Marx says that 'The every-day exchange relation need not be directly/

Identical with the magnitudes of value' (*A* 54). The ad claims that only a 'trifling risque' can provide 'unparalleled advantages'. Yet this 'every-day exchange relation' hides the real 'magnitudes of value'; if the price of the risque is merely one shilling, which is *almost nothing*, what is the *real* value of the investment, and how is it to be measured? The fourth characteristic of 'business-like management', according to Zukofsky's citation, is 'the marketable right to get something for nothing' (*A* 79). This lottery and insurance company, which by the 1930s would be a corporation, establishes its guarantee, like the bank discussed above, in No Thing and the signature of No Man. It can create value *ex nihilo*, but the *nihil* is the 'felt void' that structures the economic relationships of desire. The No Thing does in fact serve as a guarantee of value, because it is the trace of the disavowed thing sacrificed or given up in exchange for something, a piece of property which Zukofsky here reduces to a chance of enjoyment.

This changes the question we have been asking, and requires us instead to consider what is the value of this chance, this 'nothing' that the consumer gets in exchange for the 'something', represented by the mere shilling. Zukofsky links back into the series initiated with the 'No Thing' by means of a citation from Brooks Adams, in which Brooks appeals to his brother Henry to measure the value of the manuscript of *The Law of Civilization and Decay*, an analysis of Western history that attributes the decay of civilization to usury. Brooks' letter allows Zukofsky to add to the series that begins with the 'people's issue of nothing' a 'nothing of value':

> 'Please read this manuscript . . tell me
> Whether it is worth printing
> Or whether it is quite mad.
> Probably there is nothing of value in it.'

(*A* 79)

Brooks cannot be certain, after his persistent defetishization of economic value, if his own text has any 'thing of value' in it. Unlike Stein's Roosevelt, he cannot assure himself of an 'other meaning inside of him.' His concern over the value of his words is raised in the context of the nineteenth-century debates over 'sound money'; the gold-bugs claimed that only gold was 'sound money' with some 'thing of value' in it. Brooks challenged such a fetishism, and as a result provided for Zukofsky a glimpse of the 'nothing of value', that is to say, the *real value* underlying the prices of the everyday exchange relation. But the emergence of the real of value from behind the No Thing also raises to the surface the constitutive guilt about which Pound, as we have seen, constructed his political economy. Zukofsky's citation from Henry's response to Brooks' manuscript also indicates the threat of a sacrificial social logic: 'The gold-bugs will never forgive you.' Brooks is 'monkeying with a dynamo', a fetishized creation *ex nihilo*, or as Henry says of the dynamo, a *fiat* of power much like the *fiat* of faith.[152] What threatens to become tangible in the economic crisis of 1893, as in the Depression, is the 'felt void,' or the *'nothing of value'*, the void materialized. Through Henry Adams, Zukofsky raised the spectre of absolute debt, or the No Thing as the positivity of the material void remaining where the thing, which is the real of value, was formerly. We will see in the next section how Zukofsky has inscribed the gap between the real value and the price of the commodity of labour into the act of consumption, whether licit or illicit.

5
Animated Things

'LICIT CONSUMPTION IMPEDED'

As I argued at the beginning of the last chapter, Pound's politics is taken by Zukofsky as one example of a larger crisis in American liberalism. This crisis both makes possible the 'didactic poesy' that Pound wanted to write, and also undermines it from within. The ambiguous contexts of enunciation of his citations allow Pound falsely to resolve the ambivalence that motivated his political economy. For example, in Canto 37, Pound says that a 'Man who feeds, clothes, lodges another / has absolute control over his will' (C 181). From the perspective of Pound's liberal tendencies, it would seem that he is criticizing a neo-feudal economic and political institution, and implicitly insisting on the need for institutions to guarantee the independence of the worker. Read in terms of exchange, therefore, the man who is fed by another only gains access to consumption in an unfair exchange, by giving up or sacrificing his will to the commands of another. However, with the ambiguity characteristic of many of Pound's statements, this statement could easily be reframed in order to describe the fascism he supported. Read according to the Steinian economy of the gift, therefore, we return to the ethic of sacrifice: the worker gives up his will to the control of the Leader *in order to* be fed, clothed and lodged.[153] The gift puts the recipient in debt to the paternal instance, Stein's 'filling' father.

It is at this more complex level of utterance that Zukofsky is able to engage Pound beyond the content of his statements or his beliefs. What Zukofsky learned above all from the work of his mentor was the power of a poetics of citation to explore the potential contexts of utterances and their implications. It also allowed him to perceive the poetico-political-economic conditions that the contradictory ideological investments of corporate liberalism intend to resolve. Like Stein, Zukofsky fears that the political and economic crisis of the Depression will force a melancholic solution upon the nation, a solution which would be both a symptom of and an attempted cure of the fundamental ambivalence that gives form to the economy. In particular, for Zukofsky, the crisis of the loss of value threatens that labour will be commanded by paternalistic gift structures of debt and obligation. As we have seen, one form of this 'absolute control' is revealed in Zukofsky's notion of the inducement of labour by means of 'gold at no gain' to itself; the further condition of this is the ethic of sacrifice. Recall the lines I cited in the last chapter: 'New York, N.Y. / Editor, Times Union:/ I would die for dear old Standard Oil / Ex-Soldier, 12:47 P.M.' (*A* 93). As I argued in that chapter, Zukofsky examines the question of 'control' or domination specifically in the American context. His focus is therefore not the return of Spengler's ruler-will or Pound's corporate state, but the emergence of a corporate culture of consumption, structured about the fetishistic concealment of the paternal function: though it would appear in the consumer economy that the individual will has not been given up to a paternal leader, Zukofsky suggests that the culture of consumption is regulated by the corporation, which like Odysseus assumes the paradoxical identity of 'No Man'. The 'No Man' as a principle of identification allows for an implicit collectivity that does not openly contradict the appearance of liberal individualism.

In this chapter I will follow Zukofsky as he traces the migration of the worker from the sphere of production to that of consumption. We have already seen the basic outlines of this migration: the culture of consumption induces labour into the economy as a consumer by means of 'gold' *at a gain*, that is to say, as the increased wage. But in order to pursue the domination by the 'No Man' implicit in the culture of consumption, it is necessary to return to the question posed in the last chapter: how is it possible that a consumer economy, predicated on material abundance, requires sacrifice? As I argued in the last chapter, the exchange of wage for labour is simultaneously a loss to the worker, no matter how 'just' the compensation might be, no matter how high the wage. The assumed restitution does not add up. In Zukofsky's analysis, the Depression reveals that a certain loss is inherent to the quantum that is exchanged, and that an increase in the quantum does not diminish the loss. Even in the midst of material abundance, there will be scarcity – just as Stein's barbarians, even when well-fed, suffer privation. This means, as I have been arguing, that Marx's analysis of surplus value must be extended into the act of consumption. But in accepting the increased wage, or the gain of gold, and submitting to a certain sacrifice, labour gets much more than mere economic value. Citing C.F. Adams, Zukofsky suggests that recent legal and economic history, as we saw at the beginning of the last chapter, resists '[t]he old maxim of the common law, / That corporations have no souls...'.

> Corporate life and corporate power,
> As applied to industrial development,
> .. yet in its infancy.
> It always tends to development, –
> Always to consolidation..
> Even threatens the central government.
> It is a new power, for which our language
> Contains no name.
>
> (*A* 76–7)

Though it is unclear from Zukofsky's citation, Adams more specifically argues that the modern corporation '*illustrates the truth* of the old maxim of the common law, that corporations have no souls'.[154] By leaving out that judgement, Zukofsky implies that the old maxim has been proven untrue, that the corporation, though it 'has no name', does in fact have a 'soul'. Given the omnipresence of Marx throughout Zukofsky's text, one cannot help at this point but think of this passage in connection with the commodity endowed with the 'soul' of exchange value. To confirm this suggestion, Zukofsky also cites C.F. Adams' claim that '[m]odern society has created a class of artificial beings who bid fair soon to be the masters of their creator'.[155] The 'artificial beings' to which Adams refers are the robber barons and the corporations of the nineteenth century. However, Zukofsky is citing in order to perform a double function: on the one hand, he adopts Adams' point of view on nineteenth-century finance capital; on the other hand, he measures the distance between the 1880s and the 1930s by displacing the reference of this passage. The result is a simultaneous insistence on the continuity of and the gap between one historical moment and an earlier one. In the thirties, therefore, the referent of 'artificial beings' has become commodities, which in Marx's analysis 'bid fair soon to be the masters of their creator', as producers come fetishistically to perceive the products of their labour from within the sphere of consumption.

The two halves of Zukofsky's *A-9* are spoken entirely from within the perspective of fetishism, a perspective dramatized by Marx's rhetorical strategy of allegorizing commodities: 'If commodities could speak, they would say this: our use-value may interest men, but it does not belong to us as objects. What does belong to us as objects, however, is our value. Our own intercourse as commodities proves it. We relate to each other merely as exchange-values.'[156] Zukofsky imitates Marx's rhetorical device of giving voice to commodities. While Marx's fetishized commodities speak in order to confirm their fetishistic status, those in Zukofsky's poem attempt to destroy their appearance in order to reveal the hidden conditions of their production: 'unspoken wealth labor produces' (*A* 106). However, Zukofsky's fetishes once again fetishize themselves in their very effort to demystify: the 'cause' to which they demand the eye be 'joined' (in Zukofsky's phrasing) is not in the end identified with human labour, but with light (as a 'quantum of action') and love – specifically a troubador or courtly love modelled on Pound's translation of Guido Cavalcanti's 'Donna mi pregha'.

Yet this refetishization of productive agency as love and light, I will argue, is not simply fetishistic: its perspective is in the final analysis critical. Zukofsky's ambivalence to Marxism emerges most powerfully in his concentrated critique of the metaphysics of labour, aspects of which we explored in the last chapter. Contemporary Marxist arguments based on the universality of labour as a critical-utopian category for social analysis and transformation implicitly appeal to a phenomenology of labour that refers back to artisanal production.[157] The intervention of the machine, however, has transformed subjectivity such that the artisanal model of labour is an impossible ideal, merely a metaphor to organize a discourse. The assumption of a primal unity of head and hand cannot serve, as it does for Pound, as the normative reference point for a critique of capitalist production. A Marxist critique of the society of industrial production would need to take into account the place of the machine without reference to the organizing metaphor of the unity of the hand and head, a unity that is built into Marx's abstract model of labour. As we shall see in a detailed reading in the next section of this chapter, Zukofsky counters Marx's model of subjective intentionality with Thorstein Veblen's 'machinic' account of causation.

It was on the basis of the artisanal model of production that Pound and Zukofsky were forced to confront their political differences. Pound and Zukofsky could not agree on the fundamental Marxist and capitalist tenet that labour under industrial capitalism necessarily became a commodity. For Pound, '[a] commodity is a material thing or substance/ it has a certain durability'. Labour is not such a thing: '[t]he workman can't store it/ it is not a product, that he can put on shelf for a month. It is not something he can dig up and keep'; nor, presumably, could labour be a thing to be sold on the market (PZ 168). This refusal to acknowledge the material determination of labour as a commodity is characteristic of Pound's persistent confusion between descriptive (or critical) and normative concepts, that is to say, his tendency to see what ought to be, to the detriment of what is. Zukofsky saw that Pound allowed his normative concept of labour to interfere with a critical analysis of its particular historical identity as a commodity, and challenged him to acknowledge his naivety:

> read Charlie [Marx] and find out for yourself why *labor* is the *basic commodity* (if that word is to have any consequential meaning at all) and how the products of labor are just the manifestations, and money yr. capitalistic juggling, of that commodity. (That money *shd.* be just a medium of exchange is another matter, but you write as if it is to-day, when you know perfectly well it isn't.[)] Marx put it: Commodity–Money–Commodity (what exchange *shd.* be): Money–Commodity–Money (what the *exchanges* are).
> What do you think labor *is* aside from what you say it does – 'transmute material' – just automatic exhilaration in the best of all possible – to-day – economic worlds? (PZ 171)

Zukofsky perceived a connection between Pound's nostalgic artisanal or artistic concept of labour as 'automatic exhilaration' and the spiritual and erotic metaphorics of 'energy' that Pound had been elaborating since *The Spirit of Romance*. Pound had very recently elaborated upon this metaphorics again in his essay on

Cavalcanti, the final version of which was completed in 1931 and published in 1934. In this essay Pound looks back to late medieval culture as a 'radiant world where one thought cuts through another with clean edge, a world of moving energies' (LE 154). Labour could not be a thing because it was one of the privileged ties, for Pound, to this 'world of moving energies', providing the possibility not only of economic but also of cultural value. To acknowledge that labour is a commodity would be to lose this energy by objectifying it as a thing, on the one hand, and abstracting it, on the other, as a mere fuel for the machinery of production – as Pound seems to think Marx had done conceptually when he analysed the levelling of labour in industrial production. It will be recalled that Zukofsky resists giving to the 'constant' underlying the economy the name of 'Energy'. One reason is surely that the term 'energy' is readily available for regressive political ideologies like Pound's fascism, and can serve to obfuscate the historical structure of labour (by spiritualizing it as 'automatic exhilaration', as Pound did theoretically) as well as its emancipatory possibilities (by abstracting it into a uniform power, as capitalism did historically). But another reason is that 'Energy' is perfectly fitting as a concept for the economic concentration of power prior to the Depression, leading to 'immaterial wealth' and a dematerialization of things and property. Energy is capital, and capital is energy. Judging from his translation of Pound's 'overplus of the will' into surplus labour, Zukofsky seems to have thought that Pound had bought into this ideology of energy.

Nonetheless, as Zukofsky knows, Pound is aware that there is some meaning to the word 'commodity', and that the concept should remain distinct from what he calls, in the letter to which Zukofsky responded so stridently, 'wares'. In his essay on Cavalcanti, Pound distinguishes between 'the fine thing held in the mind', produced by an artist, 'and the inferior thing ready for instant consumption', which is mass-produced in conditions which require that the specific qualities of the energy of labour be destroyed (LE 151). Just as Pound's political economy thrives on such qualitative distinctions as that between good and bad debt, or licit and illicit consumption, it requires that distinctions be made between good materiality, the 'concrete', 'natural' object, and the bad materiality or abstract materialism that results from the historical division of spirit and flesh at the opening of the modern world. For Pound, as is well known, usury is the cause of the destruction of the 'moving energies' of the late medieval world, and for the commodified expression of that abstracted energy in the 'inferior thing ready for instant consumption'. According to Pound, usury 'impeded' 'licit consumption' (C 213, 216). It did so in a number of ways, but one of the most significant ways was by destroying the conditions under which the objects of licit consumption were produced. From one perspective, then, illicit consumption is bourgeois consumption, which was for Pound, as for Veblen, largely a degraded imitation of historical forms of aristocratic consumption. Yet there is a worse form of consumption than that of the bourgeoisie. The usurer is its cause, but he is also its best example: rather than being a producer, the usurer is a consumer who does not consume things as much as he consumes the immaterial value they bear in order to produce more capital. He therefore defers consumption altogether in an ascetic and unnatural denial of desire that allows him to accumulate capital. Pound, like Bataille and other contemporaries, objected strongly to the ascetic, 'protestant', accumulation of productive capital, of abstract 'immaterial wealth' and 'intangible assets'.[158] The usurer consumes 'illicitly' because he does not consume use values, or things, but consumes only in order to accumulate reserves of the abstract energy called capital. His form of exchange makes the thing consumed into abstract exchange value.

Moreover, when the usurer accumulates enough capital to turn from exchange and primitive accumulation to industrial and mass production, he will produce only 'inferior things', contaminating things at the productive source with the abstract matter he consumes. However, Pound cannot regulate the opposition, implicit in this hierarchy of 'things', between the spiritual materiality of the 'fine thing' and the abstract material of the ready commodity. Pound's opposition of 'the fine thing held in the mind' and 'the inferior thing ready for instant consumption' excludes any mediating term that would allow for the material thingness of the spirit or the energy of the 'radiant world', but at the same time each category of thing is tainted with traces of the other. As we saw in the case of Pound's opposition between moving fluids and hoarded things, the problem is not with kinds of things as much as it is with thingness as such, which is inherently dangerous. This is because both categories of things are too deeply implicated in historical conditions dominated by the structure of the commodity. As was the case with the 'specie', the economic conditions Pound so detests prove to be the ones that also make possible his own categorical distinctions. Pound's distinction between kinds of things as differences between kinds of value cannot be made to bear up against new forms of capital, Zukofsky's 'immaterial wealth' and 'intangible assets'. New forms of capital raise problems for Pound's distinctions since such metaphors as 'immaterial wealth' can without difficulty be translated into the spiritual registers that he employs in his notions of cultural and economic value. From one perspective, 'immaterial wealth' can be valued as a purely spiritual value, like 'the fine thing held in the mind', or like 'moving energies' that resist becoming things. This spiritual capital would provide the basis of a system of values that could serve as the foundation of a proper economy and a proper politics, and therefore a 'licit consumption'. Without such a guarantee, the material objects of consumption are, according to Pound, prone to corruption or decay, as is the economy as such. From the opposite perspective – which is Zukofsky's in his translation of the 'overplus' of the will of Canto 36 into surplus value – the 'immaterial wealth' and 'intangible assets' that Pound affirms as cultural and spiritual values are made possible by the accumulation of capital.

'Licit consumption' cannot be distinguished from 'illicit consumption' in a capitalist economy, which requires that circulation be based on the expropriation of a surplus – that is to say, on commodity fetishism. The commodity requires a new kind of materiality, one that bears the trace of the missing surplus, and is animated by the soul of exchange value. The split that gives the commodity its ghostly quality means that it withholds something, a missing surplus, from the consumer. Consumption in a fetishized economy is predicated on the delay that withholds the 'something' – which is an 'enjoyment' that is deferred by the satisfaction or *bien être* demanded of the economy. The temporal delay we saw operating in Stein's miser is characteristic of *both* of the things that Pound attempts to distinguish: just as the 'fine thing' is '*held* in the mind', the 'inferior thing' is held in reserve, '*ready* for instant consumption'. This temporal delay, as I have argued, constitutes consumption, which only subsequently becomes evaluated in terms of licitness. The structure of the commodity is therefore fetishistic, in Freud's sense: the material fetish bears with it the 'felt void' of the maternal phallus, just as the Marxian commodity bears the surplus 'soul' of exchange value, or 'felt void' of surplus labour. Materiality and the spirit are related chiastically, not oppositionally, in the fetish; the maternal phallus is not immaterial and intangible, but constitutes another kind of matter, 'a void to be felt'. It is at once thing and 'No Thing', guaranteed by the immanent paternal will of No Man.

Pound saw the troubadors as models of a healthy love and sexuality that had not been destroyed by a usurious economy that circulates commodities that are neither material nor spiritual. As my discussion of Canto 36 in terms of surplus value suggests, to speak of courtly love and 'the spirit of romance' is also to speak of economics, politics, culture and spirit. For Pound, the illicit consumption of usurious quantities also implies a kind of usurious sexuality, figured above all, in true medieval fashion, as sodomy, which one could consider a form of 'illicit consumption'. In this case, courtly love resembles Pound's ideal model of 'licit consumption'. Though courtly love is evidence of the translatability of Pound's economic, political, cultural and spiritual values, a discrepancy appears when we translate the economic notion of 'licit consumption' into the spiritual-erotic terms of courtly love. It becomes apparent, as Robert Casillo has convincingly argued, that the love celebrated by the troubadors is in fact 'usurious' in its mode of increasing and transforming the value of the thing to be consumed. Courtly love is actually an artificially impeded consumption (or consummation) opposed to Pound's economic ideal of 'unimpeded consumption', which, as Casillo says, is 'a free circuit of exchange facilitated by abundant money'. Like the usurer, the troubador exploits the temporal delay: '[j]ust as the usurer gives credit to a client and waits for the higher realization of the money's value, so the troubador invests in his lady, credits her with the highest spiritual and aesthetic powers, and hopes for the ultimate realization of his investment of time and emotion: not monetary but sexual possession'. Thus, as Casillo points out, '[w]hatever their supposed differences, usury and interest manifest essentially the same temporal structure as troubador love'.[159] The licit consumption of courtly love is thus exactly analogous to the illicit consumption of usurious quantities of abstract value in monetary form; like money, the Lady occupies the position of the good, or the commodity of commodities, and is therefore both the presentation and the deferral of the 'nothing of value'. The love of the Lady guarantees 'immaterial wealth' and 'intangible assets' as spiritual value. In this system of value, which is entirely analogous to Pound's political and economic systems, the Lady, rather than the leader, serves to hold in reserve the missing thing.

However, like Pound's 'fine thing held in the mind', and Stein's fetishistic 'master-piece', the Lady is split by the form of exchange value, the ghost of an expropriated surplus, and cannot overcome the internal chiastic division of the fetish between the abstract and the material. As was the case with Pound's 'specie', this fetishistic structure serves the useful economic function of maintaining the very systems of value that are designed to overcome it; when these structures collapse, another object can occupy the place of the missing thing. There is always a reserve to which the subject can have recourse because not everything is invested in the 'commodity of commodities', or the object that merely occupies the place of the thing.[160] The fetish only serves to guarantee something else, which in the Freudian version of fetishism is the impossible hallucinated maternal phallus. To serve as a guarantee, the Lady, the Leader and Gold must be possessed of a kind of immortality, or a second body made of another matter. The guarantee must be absolute, and able to withstand any economic collapse of the sort that gave Stein such a fright in the Depression. When Stein saw herself on screen, the fantasy of the incorruptible quantity of the second body emerged in a kind of economic crisis. Stein's 'shock', I suggested, should be understood in relation to the circulation of commodities on the market: it was caused by a sudden awareness of herself as commodity, with the double implication that her value was subject to the market (and therefore subject to deflation), and that her value (her thing or second body) was eternal, without being identical with herself. The second body becomes tangible the moment that her own contingency and death, or devaluation, become possible. Pound provided a stay against economic collapse in the political and economic sphere with the supplementary duplicity of his 'specie', which is at once the material guarantee of economic value and also the universal will of the Leader. In Stein's words, this political-economic structure is predicated on a belief, or credit, in something (Zukofsky's 'constant') beyond the internal division of the specie. Beyond the material embodiments of the Good is what I have been calling (after Marx) the 'real value' at the basis of all economic transactions in a commodity economy; both halves of the specie are haunted by a *second body*, or the 'constant' that Zukofsky in *A*-9, which is based on Pound's translation of Cavalcanti's 'Donna mi pregha' in Canto 36, calls 'the perfect real – / A body ready as love's steady token' (*A* 109).

Zukofsky's primary model for the 'constant' underlying the fetishized appearances of economic forms (including the commodity) is concrete labour and use value. According to 'The First Half of *A*-9', commodities, which, as in Marx's text, are mistakenly identified as exchange values, are to be 'proved' – to be exposed as illusory appearances which conceal their true status as use values and products of human labour.[161] 'The First Half of *A*-9' attempts to demystify the appearance of commodities by appealing to the (simultaneously expressive and instrumental) concept of human labour as the 'will' that, in an original relationship to things, produces 'animate instruments' to answer its needs (cf. *A* 62). The speaking commodities therefore describe themselves as 'animate instruments', as tools with an occluded use value. Only when commodities are invoked as instruments or use values, created by and for labour as *will*, can they 'wake searing / The labor veering from guises which cloak us' (*A* 107). Commodities must be 'invoked' and 'proven' as use values, to overcome the 'scission of surplus and use corroded' (*A* 108).

Zukofsky seems in 'The First Half of *A*-9' to be appealing to an organic, artisanal model of labour as the foundation of an emancipation from capitalist fetishism. Zukofsky's *A*-9 maintains a steady parallel to Canto 36, which concerned the production of the 'formèd trace' from the 'overplus' of the will. The parallel develops an extended, ironic analogy between industrial production and courtly love. According to Marx's abstract model of labour, which is based on artisanal production, the worker 'gives up' his will to his 'image' of the end of the process, or, to return to our terminology, Pound's artisanal 'fine thing held in the mind'. The analogy between industrial production and courtly love suggests that, just as the labourer gives up his will to the 'image', so the courtly lover gives up his will to the beloved, the sublimated feminine 'image' or object. But Zukofsky's point proves more radical than the ironic analogy. The analogy also requires that we consider that the artisanal structure of labour is transformed historically, and what remains of its subjective intentional structure is transferred to the total system of factory production. Industrial production is characterized by an intensive division of labour that does not require anyone to 'hold in the mind' the 'image' of the determining end or product. In the case of industrial labour, therefore, we need to ask what has happened to 'the worker's image', which functioned as the good determining the relationship to the means as tools. If 'the worker's image', the good of the work, is no longer the determining instance of industrial labour, something else comes to occupy the end. This historical break informs Zukofsky's version of labour-as-courtly love in *A-9*, which, I will argue, allows us to see the structure of desire historically emerging from behind its appearance as labour. Zukofsky has presented the new subjective structure of industrial labour not in revolutionary Marxist terms, but as the inducement of desire into the system of production and consumption. Just as the desire of the courtly lover is induced by the Lady as the 'image' of 'the perfect real, love's steady token', so is labour induced by means of the fetishized 'steady token' of gold, as wage (the gain for the worker) and as corporate profit (at no gain for the worker).

But even these objects or images only allude to the 'intangible assets, immaterial wealth' that economic forms are to guarantee. Zukofsky emphasizes the fetishistic, hallucinatory eternity of the commodity, thereby drawing an analogy to the eternalization of the female body in courtly love. The 'perfect real' of the incorruptible body is the 'steady token', or the gold standard, the 'specie', of the investments of love or desire, rather than of labour. For this reason, Zukofsky's commodities underwent a radical transformation during the eight-year span between the composition of 'The First Half of *A-9*' and 'The Second Half'. Whereas in the first half of the poem, commodities are to be disproved or demystified by being 'proved', or consumed as use values, in the second half they are to be *disproved* not by consumption-as-use, but by consumption-as-love: commodities are no longer tools or means, but have become exactly what Marx said they must appear to be within the capitalist economy: eternal objects of love. In 'The Second Half of *A-9*', Zukofsky follows Marx's personification of commodities into the religious sphere, and raises consumable objects to the level of idols or saints. Zukofsky's commodities say they can only be 'disproved',

> ... as things of love appearing
> In a wish gearing to love's infinite locus,
> [...]
> No one really knows us who does not love us,
> Time does not move us, we are and love, searing
> Remembrance – veering from guises which cloak us,
> So defined as eternal, men invoke us.
>
> (*A* 110)

The revolutionary concept of 'use' is no longer, it would seem, valid for Zukofsky. 'Natural use' in fact is a '[d]issembl[ing]' (*A* 108):

> the resemblance
> (Part, self-created, integrated) all hues
> Show to natural use ...
>
> (*A* 108)

This distinction between the pure source of light and its spectral radiation makes direct reference to Pound's 'white light that is allness' and that is '[w]orthy of trust'. The 'hues' of the spectrum indicate their white source, which appeared in the first half of the poem as 'light's infinite locus' towards which 'the will' of labour was geared (*A* 107). This light reappears in the second half as the object of a 'wish' rather than of the will (*A* 110), and a metaphor of the 'use' that hides behind the 'hues' of value. The transformation of 'will' into a 'wish' means that the 'animate instruments' of the first half of the poem formerly available for use in productive consumption are now hallucinated objects which merely '*show* to natural use'. Their essence is exchange value. Poundian 'natural use' is an ideological '[d]issembl[ing]' based on the system of 'trust' or credit in the pure 'white light' behind 'hues'.

If in the first half of this poem, commodities were to be disproved by being *proved*, that is to say, actively used or employed in some kind of project or task, a 'natural use' that would demystify their fetishized appearance as commodities, in the second half they are to be disproved by being *loved*. But the love of things does not reduce the suffering that was to motivate labour to reclaim its missing surplus. Instead, the site of sacrifice pays off in masochistic pleasure. By the end of *A*-9, the suffering of labour has become, via Cavalcanti, the suffering of courtly love, which implies a certain pleasure:

> Broken
> Plea, best unspoken, a lip's change produces
> Suffers to confuse this thought and its loci,
> the foci of things timelessly reflected...
>
> (*A* 109)

Courtly love stages the extraction of the surplus in a manner analogous, according to Zukofsky, to the exploitation at the basis of capitalist production. Zukofsky's 'loci', which also alludes to Pound's 'formèd trace', mark the traces of what Zukofsky interprets as the expropriated surplus. This object, a commodity or an idealized woman, is produced out of the suffering of the lover and of the labourer.

If Zukofsky is indeed advocating the (dis)proving of commodities by means of love as a utopian vision, he is in effect advocating that labour fetishize its products entirely, separate them from the sphere of production and see them as appearing *ex nihilo*. That is to say, he would seem to be advocating that the labourer become the consumer. Nothing, it would seem, could be farther from contemporary Marxism. In revising his earlier model of 'disproving' commodities on the basis of 'proving' them in consumption-as-use, Zukofsky reflects the fact that the tool and the hand that uses it are no longer the basis upon which labour works, and consequently that a historical rupture from an earlier relation to technology means also a rupture in the continuity of 'labor' – that the historical moment can no longer be understood in the terms provided by contemporary Marxism. The notion of use value, and of its corollary, an originary and original relation of means to ends, cannot serve as the normative reference points for a critique of capitalist production. Machinic production, Zukofsky suggests, abolished the grounds of any appeal to 'natural use' as a revolutionary category: 'In machines' terror a use there averted – '. The 'terror' of the machine abuses use by means of the intensive production of exchange value; industrial production undermines the conditions that would make possible an emancipatory appeal to consumption-as-use, or productive consumption.

Zukofsky's figure of the labourer-lover is more than rhetorical. The analysis it performs suggests that there is a missing representational link between the labourer's act of machinic production and the act of consumption. In occupying that gap, the figure of the labourer-lover, the producer-consumer, demonstrates not so much that the producer must also be a consumer, as that even in the act of consumption as such, 'men work unconsciously'. The subjective basis of industrial production provides the foundation for mass consumption. Most importantly, the theorization of mass consumption requires that Marx's analysis of surplus value be retained even as it is displaced. At the most general level, Zukofsky's critique of the discourse of economization is based on the insight that exchange (including substitution and translation) implies sacrifice; economy is based not upon balance, but upon a steady and continuous loss that feeds surplus value. Zukofsky's analysis of economization means that a revolutionary or even reformist discourse based on the notion of a restitution to its proper source of what is sacrificed must provide a name for the remainder. Such names represent the remainder in order to reappropriate it, but in so doing do not overcome the structure of sacrifice implicit in exchange and restitution. Such an act of naming is of course always historically specific, and must be measured against the material conditions of exchange. Zukofsky's analysis of Marxist discourse and of the object that it attempts to represent suggests that the name of Labour will not serve as an adequate representation of the remainder in the era of mass consumption. The reason for this, I am arguing, is that the name of labour pins together a system of representation that does not account for the transformation of the 'energy' that it used to represent in terms of (for example) concrete labour and use value. Zukofsky's deployment of Marxist discourse and the figure of labour serve to designate the remainder, not to name it and reappropriate it in a model of subjective agency that implicitly refers to the intentional structure of artisanal labour.

If courtly love encodes the suffering of the labourer at the industrial machine, it also encodes the 'sacrifice' proper, as Simmel claimed, to the consumer. Zukofsky's analogy between labour and love is fitting in so far as proper love of the Lady requires a temporal delay, and thus the suffering of deprivation. As I mentioned above, the analogy adds another dimension to his interpretation of industrial labour under capitalist conditions: in courtly love, the suffering of deprivation simultaneously occasions a certain pleasure, which cannot be called satisfaction or *bien être*. It is peculiarly masochistic pleasure in suffering that Zukofsky perceives as the link between industrial labour, courtly love, and the domination implicit even in the non-ascetic gratification advertised by the culture of consumption. For, despite this advertisement, what fuels the culture of consumption is not the promise of wealth or of material abundance as an 'other meaning' (Stein), but the pleasure of sacrifice or expenditure. If the worker can work for gold 'at no gain', that is, will work even if the wage and the capacity for consumption do not function effectively as a reward for the sacrifice, then it is necessary to ask what the worker acquires from the sacrifice of labour. For Zukofsky the act of purchase, which as we saw in the last chapter is the model of consumption, is a giving up of something for nothing in a 'trifling risque'. What is important in the 'trifling risque' is not the possibility of reward, but the fact of loss, of expenditure, of giving up.

The figure of the labourer-as-lover in effect provides an analysis of Stein's later political position, which assumes that sacrifice or privation is an end in itself, and can provide a perverse 'pleasure' that is bound to the domination exercised by the father. The relationship established by the sacrifice or expenditure, as I argued in the case of Stein, is to the paternal will as guarantee. The expenditure is in fact an investment in the father as a guarantee that what is lost will be held in reserve; paradoxically, this implicit contractual relation (at the basis of rights) is also a condition of debt and, by extension, guilt. The guilt is the correlate of masochistic suffering. In Zukofsky's analysis, even the consumer, like the courtly lover, has a masochistic relation to a dominating instance; the question of pleasure makes it possible to perceive how the domination embodied in the historical symptom of the 'machine's terror' functions within the sphere of consumption. Marx describes what Zukofsky calls the political 'terror' of the machine:

> The separation of the intellectual faculties of the productive process from manual labor, and the transformation of those faculties into power exercised by capital over labor, is . . . finally completed by large-scale industry erected on the foundation of machinery. The special skill of each individual machine-operator, who has now been deprived of all significance, vanishes

as an infinitesimal quantity in the face of the science, the gigantic natural forces, and the mass of social labor embodied in the system of machinery, which, together with those three forces, constitutes the power of the 'master'.[162]

The worker confronts the results of intellectual labour, the actual working machine, as an alien objectivity. The new model of production or labour requires a supervising and regulatory instance, an ego ideal that displaces 'the worker's image'. The analogy Zukofsky draws between courtly love and machinic labour requires that we move from the labourer as subject to the imperative of the machinic law to the function of the imperative in the case of the consumer: the 'law' of the superego. Zukofsky marks out the place of this imperative in *A*-9, which refers to a 'joy enjoined to least death' (*A* 110). '[E]njoined' echoes 'en*joy*ed', and thereby recalls the object of John Quincy Adams' longing, the 'something of awful enjoyment' (*A* 72). But more importantly, it recalls the role of the imperative: to 'enjoin' is to command. 'Joy enjoined to least death', the superego's imperative, does not liberate the subject from domination. However, the discussion of this imperative must wait until we explore the missing link, which Zukofsky fills in with the labourer-lover, between production and consumption.

'THE WORKER'S IMAGE'

With his figure of the labourer-lover, Zukofsky takes his critical analysis to the outer limit of Marxist discourse, where it addresses an object that has changed dramatically since the years Marx was working on *Capital*. Though Zukofsky's figure insists on the continuity between the old and new economies, the name of labour will not serve as an adequate representation of the source of value in the era of mass consumption. In Marx's case the concept of labour rests on a model of labour derived from artisanal production, a model which assumes a unity of head and hand in production, which buttresses an anthropomorphic model of the creation of value. The initial model therefore sets up a discourse of alienation and reappropriation, which deploys the economic forms of exchange that are the source of the alienation.[163] Marx's discourse is not of course entirely limited by his choice of an initial model of labour, and in fact the central focus of his analysis concerns the point at which that model is irreversibly superseded. Marx himself did not finally appeal for the reinstitution of use value or productive consumption as the means or the ends of revolution, but recognized that the abstraction of labour effected by industrial production transformed it such that there was no going back to the older economic forms and modes of production that utopian socialists valued. The abstraction of Labour was in fact for Marx the condition of the revolutionary self-recognition of the proletariat as the real creators of capital. The figure of Labour provided contemporary Marxism with an image of the worker that promised the universality that Enlightenment values also promised but failed to deliver. At the same time, Marx is aware that the very abstraction that the revolution requires is also the condition of Enlightenment universality.[164] What is uncertain in Marx is what becomes of labour in the post-revolutionary economy; will it be possible to restore what has been lost in the abstraction of concrete labour and not give up on the advantages of industrial production? Is it a matter of 'restoration' at all? What emancipatory form of universality can emerge (dialectically) from the abstraction of 'humanity' which at the same time does not require the material conditions of that ideological form of universality?[165]

In Zukofsky's poem, this universality appears in several guises, chief among which, as we have seen, is the concept of 'energy'. Zukofsky's analysis suggests that there is no going back to Marx once the new technological conditions of capital have taken over: while the development of industrial production leads to a qualitative transformation of the subjectivity named Labour, a further division in that subjectivity gives rise to an 'Energy' that cannot be absorbed or reappropriated entirely into labour, use, or even 'humanity'. This 'Energy' is employed not in production, therefore, nor even in the circulation of exchange value among owners of commodities. In Zukofsky's metaphorics, this 'energy' figures the missing social substance the possession and restitution of which have been contested among social groups since the Enlightenment raised the spectre of universality. Borrowing from nineteenth-century physics, Zukofsky provides a remarkable metaphor for the phantasmatic substance that constitutes the collective:

> (I imagine that this elastic fluid
> Is more and more dense

> As it approaches the surface of bodies
> And for some distances within them,
> As is likewise observed
> in the air surrounding the earth.
> Cadwallader Colden).
>
> (*A* 102)

The representation of this circulating energy requires the invention of a nonanthropomorphic, non-humanistic figure, such as an 'elastic fluid'. But Zukofsky derives his most resonant figure above all from Thorstein Veblen. I have said that the social substance is no longer embodied in the sphere of production; I will not argue that it has entirely migrated to the sphere of consumption. Instead, Zukofsky's 'energy' is the missing link that ties the two spheres together, requiring such a crossed figure as the labourer-lover to represent the subjectivity of consumption. Beyond both use (as productive consumption) and exchange (consumption as such) is what Zukofsky calls the 'idle concomitance of variation' (*A* 56). One can see already from the phrase (cited from Veblen) that the 'idle concomitance' is a 'constant' in the midst of historical 'variation', and is therefore related to the 'one constant' whose name shall (perhaps) be 'Energy' (*A* 47). If we imagine this Energy in terms of courtly love, we see that it is not realized in 'use' (in this case, erotic consummation), but derives its effectivity from a certain uselessness. As we will see in the third section of this chapter, which will begin by exploring Zukofsky's thermodynamic metaphors, the 'Energy' required to open up the sphere of consumption to its full effectivity is an *idle* energy 'unavailable' for 'use'.

As I mentioned, in order to figure the subjectivity of this idle energy, Zukofsky does not appeal to Marx's abstract model of labour, but instead points to its limitations in the era of mass production and consumption. The critical perspective on Marx's model comes from Veblen's critique of the 'pragmatic-barbarian' culture and its correlate, the ethic of workmanship. This may seem an odd choice for a critique of Marx, but it is important to recognize that Veblen was as significant a figure as Marx in the American political context of the thirties. My claim may also seem odd, however, given that Veblen, who is above all known for his critique of the leisure class, is often considered to have placed a high value on 'the instinct of workmanship'. However, the fact that Veblen also inspired a generation of 'technocrats' who affirmed the new industrial order and its possible political forms suggests that there is more than one Veblen. The Veblen called upon by Zukofsky is not the economist and sociologist who critiqued the leisure class and absentee landlords, but a Veblen affiliated with values that would seem anathema to the technocrats of the thirties who rallied together under Veblen's name, as well as to the romantic anti-capitalists who read Veblen (as well as Marx) as an advocate of the ethic of 'workmanship'. Zukofsky implicitly critiques contemporary technocracy and romantic anti-capitalism by foregrounding an anti-utilitarian and anti-pragmatic Veblen who had a very ambivalent relation both to traditional, artisanal 'workmanship' and that which was rendering it obsolete, industrial technology. In this section, I propose to discern what Zukofsky's understanding of Veblen must be that it would permit him to juxtapose and link his ideas and texts to those of Marx.

During the thirties, Veblen was considered by the leaders of the technocracy movement to be a 'pragmatist' whose critique of the 'leisure class' was based on reference to a normative state of utilitarian efficiency. But Zukofsky's Veblen, the author of 'The Point of View of Science' and 'The Evolution of the Scientific Point of View', essays which advance a perspective that is not assimilable to any of the Veblens circulating in the thirties, has a more complex notion of instrumentality and of science than the one the technocrats proposed to press into their service.[166] Contrary to the technocratic Veblen constructed by the thirties, Veblen's attitude toward 'pragmatism' is severely critical. Though it is true that the value of efficiency as opposed to wastefulness is crucial to Veblen's economic and sociological thought, it is not accurate to say that this value leads Veblen to a technocratic advocacy of a 'soviet of engineers' as the leaders of society. This may represent one moment of his thought – but there is also in his thought what appears to be a very traditional defence of the values of what Stein called 'the human mind' against the 'pragmatic-barbarian' values of efficiency and utility:

> Under the barbarian culture, as well as on the lower levels of what is currently called civilised life, the dominant note has been that of competitive expediency for the individual or the group, great or small, in an avowed struggle for the means of

life. Such is still the ideal of the politician and business man, as well as of those other classes whose habits of life lead them to cling to the inherited barbarian traditions. The upper-barbarian and lower-civilised culture ... is pragmatic ... with a thoroughness that nearly bars out any non-pragmatic ideal of life or knowledge.[167]

In order to defend a 'non-pragmatic ideal of life or knowledge', Veblen develops a concept of science intended to resist its reduction to instrumentality and utility. For Veblen, science is rooted in the opposition of two kinds of knowledge to be found in the development of human culture: one is pragmatic, teleological or interested, while the other is what he calls 'idle curiosity', a disinterested attempt to account for 'what happens'. Though they are opposed modes of cognition, pragmatic thought and idle curiosity originate in the same moment, which is based on a Darwinian premise. The organism, in order to survive, must have a capacity for a 'pragmatic attention' which can determine how to react to a given situation. In Veblen's model, the appearance of a 'reasoned line of conduct' is the result of a natural process of selection from among the most effective responses. That is to say, rationality is an effect of natural selection. But this means that the originating moment of intelligence is characterized by a set of responses not all of which are efficient, pragmatic and reasonable:

> If credence is given to the view that intelligence is, in its elements, of the nature of an inhibitive selection, it seems necessary to assume some such chain of idle and irrelevant response to account for the further course of the elements eliminated in giving the motor response the character of a reasoned line of conduct. So that associated with the pragmatic attention there is found more or less of an irrelevant attention, or idle curiosity.[168]

Unlike idle curiosity, teleological thought operates according to traditional models that result from the process of natural selection and habit: certain means have proven efficient in achieving certain ends. Idle curiosity, on the other hand, is 'closely related to the aptitude for play, observed both in man and in the lower animals'. Though the origin of 'idle curiosity' is also to be accounted for by Veblen's apparently Darwinian premise, the notion of struggle in conditions of scarcity cannot account for this idle curiosity, which is not directly motivated by a concern for survival. The constituting moment of knowledge is not a defensive and goal-oriented motor response, but the attention or curiosity that attends (to) the play of a chain of such responses, which are gradually 'eliminated' from what will become the pattern of reasonable responses. The Darwinian metaphor does not imply struggle, but allows for idle 'play' in the same conditions that demand the 'tropismatic reaction' that will become 'the reasoned line of conduct' through selection.[169]

This 'play' at the origin is the basis of Veblen's notion of science. Strangely enough, however, rather than leading to a body of scientific knowledge considered as disinterested and objective, idle curiosity originally leads to folklore and myth, which attribute a 'pragmatic animus' to things:

> This idle curiosity formulates its response to stimulus, not in terms of an expedient line of conduct, nor even necessarily in a chain of motor activity, but in terms of the sequence of activities going on in the observed phenomena. The 'interpretation' of the facts under the guidance of this idle curiosity may take the form of anthropomorphic or animistic explanations of the 'conduct' of the objects observed. The interpretation of the facts takes a dramatic form. The facts are conceived in an animistic way, and a pragmatic animus is imputed to them. Their behavior is construed as a reasoned procedure on their part looking to the advantage of these animistically conceived objects, or looking to the achievement of some end which these objects are conceived to have at heart for reasons of their own.[170]

For Veblen, the idle curiosity emerges from the plurality of non-rational responses of the organism to a situation in which its survival is at stake. Though idle curiosity does not reason about the relative value of each response (since the most 'rational' responses are selected naturally, presumably by the survival of the organisms whose responses were the fittest), it does attend to the drama in which the organism finds itself involuntarily playing a role. Since idle curiosity is the concomitant of the drama of self-preservation, the organism may be seen as interpreting an entirely unpredictable situation, which unfolds without the participation of the subject of the idle attention. Veblen's 'idleness' cannot serve, then, as a traditional humanist defence of the values destroyed or devalued by the hegemony of utility. If we are to characterize it as a state of mind, we could say that, though the attention is 'idle', it may still be motivated by the suspicion, anxiety, and fear of a subject unable to act since it is in control neither of its body's 'idle and irrelevant response' nor of its more efficient responses. Whatever its relation to the 'play' of childhood or of the adult, aesthetic variety, this play in the origin can be seen also as related to a certain *panic* or fear, prior to the institution of the utilitarian structures of agency, means and ends characteristic of the pragmatic-barbarian economy. Idle curiosity watches very carefully the world in which it finds itself, knowing that it is divorced from the capacity to act in response. It must trust the rationality of its learned responses. In Veblen's description, it attends to the behaviour of other agents in a world of 'animated things' (to borrow a term that Zukofsky uses). Things as such require a curiosity that is drawn to ends unknown to the organism, the 'end which these objects are conceived to have at heart for reasons of their own'.

I have emphasized that the idle curiosity is incapable of action; instead, it attends to a process unfolding outside of whatever will the subject might be conceived to have. Idle curiosity is responsible for the illusion of subjectivity as agency: it projects on to things and others the capacity for action that it lacks. Idle curiosity is therefore in a certain sense responsible for the dominance of the pragmatic-barbarian world of which it should properly not be a part: agency and instrumentality would be inconceivable were it not for the projection to which idle curiosity is prone. Veblen's defence of science as idle curiosity is therefore very far from a humanistic defence of disinterestedness. It could be seen rather as an attempt to discipline the tendency of idle curiosity to impute agency where there is none. This possibility becomes apparent in the second essay of the pair I am discussing, in which Veblen is concerned to develop aspects of a worldview more in line with the era of 'machinic process', a worldview which will prove to be incompatible with the world assumed by both the pragmatic-barbarian era and its attendant idle curiosity alike. Veblen argues that

> [t]he machine process has displaced the workman as the archetype in whose image causation is conceived by the scientific

investigators. The dramatic interpretation of natural phenomena has thereby become less anthropomorphic; it no longer constructs the life-history of a cause working to produce a given effect – after the manner of a skilled workman producing a piece of wrought goods – but it constructs the life-history of a process in which the distinction between cause and effect need scarcely be observed in an itemised and specific way, but in which the run of causation unfolds itself in an unbroken sequence of cumulative change.

For Veblen, the concept of causation itself is a remainder of the era of handicrafts and of the animistic dramatic conception of cause based on the model of artisanal production. What, then, is a machinic concept of causation, which 'constructs the life-history of a process in which the distinction between cause and effect need scarcely be observed'? Let us read Veblen's reply in a lengthy footnote as cited (selectively) by Zukofsky:

Process: notion about which the researches cluster.
[. . .]
In so far as the science is of modern complexion,
In so far as it is not of the nature of taxonomy simply,
The inquiry converges upon a matter of process,
And it comes to rest,
Provisionally, when it has disposed of the process.
Whereas it is claimed that scientific inquiry
Neither does nor can legitimately, nor, indeed, currently
make use of a postulate more metaphysical
Than the concept of an idle concomitance of variation, such
As is adequately expressed in terms of mathematical
   function.

Consistently adhered to, the principle of 'function'
Or concomitant variation
Precludes recourse to experiment, hypothesis or inquiry –
   indeed
It precludes 'recourse' to anything whatever. Its notation
   (however)
Does not comprise anything so anthropomorphic.

(*A* 57)

In this note, Veblen criticizes the claims of the most advanced science to be beyond the metaphysical thinking that Veblen sees as its heritage from animism, the dramatic expression of idle curiosity. Though these scientists claim to be 'making use of' a mathematical and statistical model of causation which supersedes outdated concepts of causation with the noncausal, statistical notion of function, or 'idle concomitance of variation', these recent theories 'must be admitted still to show the constraint of the dramatic prepossession that once guided the savage mythmakers'.[171] A phrase like 'idle concomitance of variation' cannot disguise the fact that in their practical work, scientists appeal to the concept of causation, which has been passed on to them not only from the era of animism, but from the early modern institutions of a culture of 'workmanship' and artisanal labour:

> In their polemics with their antagonists, such scientists, defenders of the non-committal postulate of concomitance find that postulate inadequate. They are not content, in this precarious conjuncture, simply to attest a relation of idle quantitative concomitance (mathematical function) between the allegations of their critics, on the one hand, and their own controversial exposition of these matters on the other hand. They argue that they do not 'make use of' such a postulate as 'efficiency', whereas they claim to 'make use of' the concept of function. But 'make use of' is not a notion of functional variation but of causal efficiency in a somewhat gross and highly anthropomorphic form.... Consistently adhered to, the principle of 'function' or concomitant variation precludes recourse to experiment, hypotheses or inquiry – indeed it precludes 'recourse' to anything whatever. Its notation does not comprise anything so anthropomorphic.[172]

It is unclear from his critique whether this is the 'humanist' Veblen speaking or the Veblen of whom the technocrats were fond. Does he demand that science be more rigorous in its attempt to purge itself of anthropomorphism, or is he declaring that science has reached the outer limits of its epistemology, where it still finds the human subject? He appears to prescribe that science not fall prey to the illusory metaphors of a bygone worldview, and that it be rigorous in purging itself of its disavowed anthropomorphism. At the same time, his critique points to the regrettable inevitability of anthropomorphism. Though a machinic culture must think causation beyond the anthropomorphic fantasies of subjectivity as agency, the figure of 'man' will always haunt the concept of cause; idle curiosity will always project the will it lacks on to the things of the world. Veblen's defence of 'idle curiosity' may, from this point of view, even be an attempt to keep idle curiosity in its place, on idle as it were, safely ensconced in a quasi-aesthetic sphere where it will do no harm to the emergence of a machinic worldview.

Before we can understand Veblen's strategy in these essays, and what it is that Zukofsky is attending to in this lesser-known Veblen, we need to pause and consider the fact that, in citing Veblen on the 'idle concomitance of variation', Zukofsky is also implicitly and ironically drawing into his text Veblen the technocrat, the theorist of the 'leisure class'. The formula 'idle concomitance of variation', quoted by Zukofsky, could in fact be adopted to describe the leisure class, which is composed of those who lag behind technological innovation, or 'variation', because they have no pressing need to adapt. As for 'idle curiosity' (which Zukofsky does not refer to explicitly), Veblen was certainly not unaware of the economic conditions that are required for such intellectual or aesthetic play, and devoted the final chapter of *The Theory of the Leisure Class* to it. It is not by accident that 'idle curiosity' resonates also with the activities of the 'leisure class'. As Adorno would perhaps suggest to Veblen, 'idleness' may figure the utopian moment of a nonetheless barbaric culture. That Veblen might have concurred becomes apparent with a fourth appearance of the theme of 'idleness'. As Adorno points out, Veblen, despite his arguments for the normative value of the instinct of workmanship, allows himself to imagine the life of savages as characterized by a certain idleness – as if there was a time of abundance before the regime of scarcity that made the barbaric struggle for life necessary.[173] Though Veblen refuses any utopian speculation or image, the return of the notion of idleness in his version of the savage state is symptomatic of a utopian impulse, which brings 'idle curiosity', 'idle concomitance of variation', the leisure class, and savage 'indolence' together under one semantic horizon. What Veblen is in fact resisting is the Darwinian premises upon which he constructs his entire conceptual apparatus. At the limit of his Darwinism are an original 'idle curiosity' and idle savages who have managed to avoid scarcity. Economically speaking, subjectivity and agency are associated with need and desire; socially speaking, life can only be 'full' if the conditions that require subjectivity (and competition, rivalry, etc.) are abolished. 'Idleness', therefore, suggests a utopian dimension beyond utility, beyond scarcity, that Adorno thought to be lacking in Veblen's reflections.

Yet in his critique Veblen does not provide an alternative way of conceptualizing that which is of most value. This 'other' Veblen only becomes tangible at the limit of his texts. He remains entirely within the assumption of scarcity, which is the condition of the subjectivity that the machinic worldview should abolish. Moreover, we should not lose sight of the fact that the dominant note in the citation and context Zukofsky chooses is fundamentally anti-anthropomorphic and anti-humanist. Veblen's ambivalence towards the 'human' or to 'man' emerges very powerfully in these passages. Clearly, that which is of value cannot go by the name of 'man' or of the 'human'. The radical anti-humanist Veblen who interests Zukofsky forgoes naming this value or substance and so provides a critical perspective on the ideological strategies of Enlightenment humanism. A powerful anti-subjectivism runs through Zukofsky's social critique, as it does through Veblen's. But it is simultaneously important to emphasize that this anti-humanism in the final analysis serves the fundamental values that humanism intended to guarantee. By focusing on the 'idle concomitance of variation' Zukofsky demonstrates the symptomatic return – in the name of 'idle' – of that which Veblen attempted to foreclose. Only the most rigorous interrogation of the ideological forms in which the thing of value presents itself can be adequate to the desire that determines that value. What is of value cannot, however, be guaranteed in the form of the human or of subjectivity conceived as agency. With the concurrence of the various themes of 'idleness', Veblen's contradictions become most apparent: his call to the sacrifice of subjectivity, or its suspension in 'idle curiosity', and therefore also the effacement of 'man' as agent, is paradoxically intended to preserve the very value that has been foreclosed from various Enlightenment economies of restitution or reappropriation that economize upon the loss of the social substance, and therefore cannot escape the condition of scarcity they presume.

At the same time, of course, the rigour of the critique risks sacrificing that in the name of which it acts. Though Zukofsky is clearly sympathetic with the ambivalence of Veblen's critique of anthropomorphism, he also recognizes that much must be given up if one is going to remove subjectivity and agency from the notion of 'process' – particularly if that process is history, and if history is to realize the fundamental goals of the Enlightenment. The formula 'idle concomitance of variation' concentrates all of the ambivalence associated with a critical historical and theoretical juncture, where it seemed that Enlightenment humanism was to sacrifice its notion of reason and of subjectivity to notions of 'process' in, for example, an authoritarian functionalism. Despite what might appear to be an affirmative citation of Veblen's notion of 'process', Zukofsky is of course aware that such a concept is an ideological extension of the 'process' of industrial labour, or machinic process. Such a sacrifice of the subject would institute the authoritarian functionalism that Zukofsky fears of machinic process. Marxist that he is, Zukofsky recognizes that a concept with such roots cannot be emancipatory. But the most important point to draw from this is that Zukofsky does not follow Pound into the past and advocate a return to artisanal models of production and their neo-feudal social and political institutions.

Nonetheless, the 'idle concomitance of variation' brings to a focus the utopian moment of Zukofsky's poem, and allows it to exceed the technocratic vision of an efficient industrial society that his invocation of Veblen might suggest. What this leaves to Zukofsky, as we will see, allows him only to walk a very fine line at the limit of the economy of the fetish. Every concept and figure he deploys is split into its ideological presentation and its utopian promise. This becomes especially apparent, as I have suggested, with his citation of Veblen, which ties together a number of different referents into a knot of ambivalence. In the rest of this section, I will focus on the form of 'idleness' with which the name of Veblen is most often associated. Zukofsky's citation and inflection of 'idleness' situates him neither with the traditional defences of the aesthetic as a disinterested activity or play, nor with the technocratic critiques of waste Veblen inspired. Instead, it provides him with a profoundly ambivalent term to designate the utopian moment (beyond 'use' and 'labor') as well as its most ideological appearance, leisure. Zukofsky was aware that the culture of consumption required the promise of leisure time as the time to consume. We will see shortly one of the forms in which leisure appears explicitly in *A*-8, but first I will examine an example of what has come to be ironically called 'enforced leisure'. Zukofsky never loses sight of the transformation brought about by the Depression; for this reason, one of the most explicit appearances of idleness in *A* is the Depression's 'armies of the unemployed'.

Labour is historically reduced to an undifferentiated 'energy'. Let me say hypothetically and metaphorically that, with the emergence of mass consumption, it was recognized that this transformation into energy left something behind. That is to say, the translation did not exhaust the 'energy' of the productive classes entirely, but left behind a desire which could be productive of further surplus value. Socially and culturally speaking, it left behind the qualitative differences of specific forms of labour and the symbolic social investments, constitutive of personal and collective identity, that went along with them. This remaining 'energy', not usable in industrial production, would be attached to a medium of exchange (the increased wage) and rechannelled into consumption and leisure. With the mass unemployment of the Depression, this energy is put on idle. As we will see shortly, 'idleness', borrowed from the semantic registers in which Veblen places it and reframed in terms of unemployment, must be conceptualized as an unusable 'energy' or 'idle concomitance of variation'; though it is not available for 'use', for productive consumption, it will nonetheless be 'converted to use' by the culture of consumption.

How is it possible for 'labor' to become an 'energy' available for consumption? The answer as far as Zukofsky's text is concerned begins with his citation of Marx's description of 'the labor process apart / From its particular form under particular social conditions'. Zukofsky develops the implications of the model of labour in order to trace the continuity between the subjective intentional structure of the worker and that of the consumer. Marx's abstract description of labour posits a mental conception on the part of the worker, 'Which when the process began / Already lived as the worker's image' (*A* 61). The word 'process' serves as a concept rhyme with Veblen's notion of 'process' as discussed above, but beyond this what ties Marx and Veblen together is the repetition of the artisanal model of labour. In the case of Marx's abstract model of labour, the reference to the artisan is not explicit; nonetheless, the artisan is the historical figure that presupposes a mode of production that does not require a radical separation of mental and manual labour, and so serves as a norm implicit in Marx's model. The abstract worker of Marx's model is responsible to a 'mental conception' which then in turn regulates the production process: Marx says that the concept of the end product of labour defines the 'purpose [that] determines the mode of [the worker's] activity with the rigidity of a law [to which] he must subordinate his will...'.[174] The worker then gives up his will to his 'image', which then becomes the source of an imperative. Zukofsky exploits the ambiguity of the phrase 'worker's image', and the rifts that Marx's own description introduces into the phenomenology of the production process (for example, the exteriority and alterity of the image). The image at once belongs to the worker, as his mental product, and is also an image *of the worker*. If we read the line with both meanings in mind at once, the implicit identity of this worker with the image 'that / Already lived' before the work was undertaken makes the act of giving up one's will to the purpose ambiguous; what 'already lived', as we will see, functions as a wraith or a vampire sucking energy from the worker. In this context, the worker's 'giving up' his will might evoke Stein's anxiety about 'giving up', about sacrifice:

> And he realizes his own purpose
> To which he *gives up* his will.
> Nor does he give it up to the crick of a second...
>
> (*A* 61; my italics)

If we ask where the worker's 'own purpose' comes from, we discover that the identity of the 'worker' depends on an image that is originally outside of him. We have already seen how the structure of surplus labour extends in Zukofsky's citations into the structure of exchange. In his citations of Marx's discussion of labour, Zukofsky is again concerned to reveal the sacrificial structure that gives rise to a remainder that returns to haunt the worker not only in the form of capital but in the psychic-cultural form of the 'image'. The worker's image functions like the image of psychoanalytic theory, in that it provides the necessary condition for the constitution of the identity of 'the worker'. Implicit in the purpose and image that 'already lived' is a transference and identification which takes place across the split between the worker and his image, a transference of will to another agency. This transference serves as the condition of the proper will and purpose of the worker. Read with wilful naïveté in this context,

Marx's language sounds like corporatist ideology attempting to interpellate the subject as worker: Give up your will and you will realize your purpose, you will recognize yourself.

In Marx's text, the recognition of labour as Labour and of the worker in the worker's image is mediated by the productive consumption of use values, which is consumption 'for a purpose' – namely, the purpose of realizing the worker's image, which 'already lived'. Zukofsky continues to quote Marx on the need to redeem the products of labour from their

> 'death-like' sleep.
> Bathed in the fire of labor
> Brought into contact with living labor
> Things animated, consumed, but consumed for a purpose
> In which living labor itself is consumed.
>
> (*A* 62)

The use values to be seized upon by living labour are in a state of '"death-like" sleep', and are to be roused by productive consumption. Already, prior to Zukofsky's citation of it, a curious dialectic of living and dead labour complicates this passage from Marx.[175] But the description of these use values echoes the definition of commodities as fetishes, as 'animated things' in which labour is congealed. From the first perspective, the 'things' are seen within the abstract model of labour as the production and productive consumption of use values; but lurking within these metaphors are the 'things' seen purely from the perspective of the consumer of exchange value – the fetishist of commodities. In the first case, productive consumption animates these dead things; in the second case the consumption of exchange value fetishizes these things, animates them otherwise. As I argued in the last section, Zukofsky's poem does not posit the first as a revolutionary alternative to the second form of fetishism.

The gap that Zukofsky reveals between the worker and his 'image' does have some historical specificity. The inducement of desire into consumption instead of labour into production depends on a complete reorganization of the relationship of ends and means, but the reorganization is nonetheless based on the structure that is characteristic of industrial labour.[176] Industrial labour is based on the radical split between intellectual and manual labour, a division that culminates in the disappearance of the 'mental conception' or 'worker's image' from the productive process. The sphere of consumption is constituted by the final displacement of 'the worker's image' from the artisanal task to a purpose external not only to the worker but to the sphere of production as a whole. Zukofsky's text argues that the abstract model of labour not only persists under the conditions of industrial production, but extends also into the postindustrial sphere of consumption.[177] In order to understand the effect of Zukofsky's citation of Marx, the description of 'the labour process apart from its particular form under particular social conditions' must be qualified by the particular social conditions that concern Zukofsky. He has focused on the particular separation of ends and means in modernity as constitutive of the separation between work (or production) and leisure (or consumption). In industrial production, quantity, whether of goods or profit, is the end in view, at least for the capitalist, not the Good or end of the work, as it is in Marx's abstract model of artisanal labour. For the labourer within the culture of consumption, the Good is the wage, which links the labourer to the sphere of consumption. The fantasy structure of consumption is determined by a displacement of 'the worker's image' as the end or aim of the process into the sphere of consumption. In machinic production, work is pure means, and the end in view is no longer within the work process itself, but is directed to another sphere, namely to that of consumption, which takes place outside of the work-process itself.

The displacement of the worker's image gives rise to a new temporality founded in the opposition of work and leisure, or rather the time of work and the time of consumption. The temporality and subjective structure of consumption is articulated in the voice of an old man singing a Blakean song of innocence, haunted by the perspective of experience:

> He is an old man whose lips whisper an infantile verse:
> I-was-early-taught-to-work-as-well-as-play-
> My-life-has-been-one-long-happy-holiday-
> Full-of-work-full-of-play-
> I-dropped-the-worry-by-the-way-
> And-G-g-g-God-was-good-to-me-every-day.

(*A* 63)

The division between work and play is that between work and consumption. Yet the man's infantile play-time singing is characterized by repetition by rote. The source of his words is a cultural authority, such as a teacher: Zukofsky hyphenates the words in order to indicate his machinic stuttering. Just as the worker is subjected to the machine as to a 'master', so is the consumer of 'idle', unemployed, unoccupied time subjected to a concealed authoritarian instance, the ego-ideal.

That the opposition of work and leisure is rooted in the subjective structure of industrial production may seem an unlikely argument, given that, as Marx says in Zukofsky's citation, 'the less attractive [the worker] finds the work in itself, / The less it frees him body and mind – / The more is his care glued to the grind' (A 61). According to industrial reformers and Taylorist efficiency experts, the workers should be freed of this grind. But their answer was the automatization of the worker: in reducing the need for 'fixed attention', and in fact abolishing the demand for any use of mental operations at all, the automation of the worker's body was to free the worker's mind for a productive leisure *on the job*. As Edward Filene wrote in 1929, '[e]ngineers have found . . . that most workers prefer to perform a simple, specialized, repetitive operation. It leaves their minds free to ruminate on other things. They do not abhor monotony, but desire it'.[178] Once the worker 'gives up his will' to the monotonous repetition of the machinic task, Filene imagines, the resulting *distraction* can become an *attention* to the 'other things' that nourish the mind. The division between head and hand should be introduced not only into the workplace, but should reorganize the relationship of the worker to his or her body, which should function as an automaton.

Though Filene's fantasy of the worker acquiring culture on the worksite was not realized or realizable, his understanding that industrial production establishes the subjective potential of 'idle curiosity' is accurate. In Marx's artisanal model of labour, the worker's attention is absorbed by 'the worker's image' as the end of the process. In industrial production, 'close attention' is paid only to the means that lead up to the end, the 'image' that is no longer the intentional object of the labourer. Zukofsky's poem reveals that the radical division of head and hand in which Filene places so much confidence does in fact alter the structure of attention, though it may not free the worker from the grind. The new mode of attention is structured about the split between the time of work and the time of leisure. Rather than the immanence of ends to means implied by Marx's model of labour, the intentional structure of industrial labour in the era of mass consumption is divided between production and consumption, the former serving as the means of access to the latter. The 'worker's image' is peripheral to the sphere of production: it is now 'image' as commodity in the sphere of consumption. The missing thing of value cannot be reappropriated in the name of Labour, nor, as an 'unusable energy', can it be reappropriated in what Zukofsky calls 'natural use'. It is only available to consumption. Commodity fetishism preserves the missing thing in the 'animated things' of the market. One of Zukofsky's important commodity-'images' indicates the structural fetishism of the consumer economy:

> The Museum (New York) owns little of Bosch, but for
> The Virgin's peacock hair.
> The pearl sexes, the prepuce-leaves,
> Of the old and original establishments of Europe –
> They remain in the galleries of Brussels.
> Not in the importing offices of –.

> (A 64–5)

In a classic example of Freudian fetishism, the New York Museum only 'owns little of Bosch', only a part, a tuft of hair. The word 'prepuce' refers both to the foreskin of the male genitals and to the 'leaves' that conceal the clitoris; the 'prepuce leaves' that cover the sex of the Virgin suspend the question of sexual difference and castration. The tuft of peacock hair conceals a thing of value – or rather a 'nothing of value': the proving of commodities in consumption reveals the 'felt void'. Just before quoting Marx on 'the labor process' and his 'proof' of the necessary appearance of the 'dictatorship of the proletariat' from the contradictions of capitalism, Zukofsky indicates the place of the missing thing:

> If you know all the qualities of a thing
> You know the thing itself;
> Nothing remains but the fact
> The said thing exists without us;
> And when your senses have taught you that fact,
> You have grasped the last remnant of the thing in itself.

> (A 60–1)

The 'last remnant' is the irreducible exteriority of the elusive 'quantity' (*A* 58) of '[t]he said thing'. According to one of Zukofsky's citations, workers are to be 'converted [not] by lecturing', but by 'experienc[ing] it on their bodies' (*A* 72): by suffering the inscription of value. What can be 'taught' by the senses is not identical to what can be learned by lecturing; what is taught by the senses is that 'Nothing remains but . . .' the exteriority of the missing thing, 'the last remnant'.

'LET HIM BE CONSUMED . . !'

In the revolutionary rhetoric cited by Zukofsky, the productive body of Labour returns in the ideological form of the worker's image as emancipatory cultural hero. Soviets portray Lenin as a New Man displacing the Old Man, Adam:

> He (Lenin) came to this earth, to drive out Kuchak, Tajiks! Kuchak (Adam).
>
> He slays the dragon, with golden arms
> Born of the moon and stars,
> When the world was made he helped, too
> Comrades of Uzbekistan.

(A 60)

Though Zukofsky does not place his trust in the universal figure of a 'coming man' (*A* 77), whether as Poundian leader or as the subject of Labour, he recognizes that the ghost of an abstract universal persists after the demise of its viable names and figures. Even as revolutionary rhetoric produced its figures of Man as Labour in an attempt to recall labour to its proper sphere, the consumer culture created its own 'image of the worker' in order to interpellate the labourer as a consumer. This image is provided by fetishized commodities exercising their fascinating power from the sphere of consumption. In the consumer economy, the social substance is dispersed as a promise embedded in what Zukofsky calls 'animated things'. In order for Marxist revolution to be avoided, workers must not think of themselves primarily as workers, but must be provided another 'image'. The fetishism of commodities must be so total as to leave no trace of the causal relation with labour.

As I have argued, Zukofsky's poem ultimately presents the total fetishization of commodities, which divorces them entirely from the labour that produced them. The worker's image is no longer the image or idea found in Marx's model of labour, but is divided entirely from the sphere of production: the end of labour is an ideal that is a matter of fantasy, as Dewey puts it. If the image is entirely divorced from production, it appears *ex nihilo* within the sphere of consumption. But to emerge from the darkness of nothing it requires light to 'animate' it. For Pound, the 'the white light that is allness, worthy of credit' is the one constant, or 'idle concomitance'.[179] For Zukofsky, on the other hand, the constant is the instantaneous luminescence of radium, along with its black waste product; the white light emerges against the darkness of the *nihil*. The breakdown of radium gives off luminosity, which 'animate[s] things', or commodities, and projects 'the worker's image' entirely into the sphere of consumption: 'Let him be consumed . . !' (*A* 101). Zukofsky literalizes this eucharistic consumption in *A*-8: 'What we eat actually is radiation' (*A* 63), recalling that for Henry Adams radium is 'parricidal'. If 'what we eat actually is radiation', then we eat the corpse of the father. The consumption of the father's corpse leaves a remainder in a melancholic reserve, 'a void in which nothing was dead' (*A* 51). The consumption of radiation increases the reserve of otherwise 'unavailable energy', 'an idle concomitance of variation'.

The social substance leaves its traces but not its name. Nonetheless, the abstract universal is the ghost of the father that haunts the political and economic spheres as their utopian promise and their totalizing threat. Zukofsky presents this ghost in metaphors of entropy, conceived as the degeneration of 'substance' into 'heat' and 'wraith': 'Heat, not substance. Simmer, not wraith. / Battle drains off like work; unavailable energy increases' (*A* 52). In terms of entropy, 'heat' is the 'unavailable energy' of an expended 'substance'. Historically, this 'idle concomitance of variation' manifests itself as 'the armies of the [unemployed] poor' of Zukofsky's poem. Zukofsky's thermodynamic metaphorics figures the economy of consumption, which increases the reserve of heat, thereby suspending the 'wraith' of substance as a lingering promise. Zukofsky cites Henry Adams' evaluation of pre-revolutionary Russia as giving off a 'negative luminosity / As though she were a substance whose energies had been sucked out' (*A* 81). The social 'substance', like surplus value, measures something that has been lost or sacrificed. The loss that inheres in the social substance appears in the economic crisis of the Depression as the 'void to be felt'. For Zukofsky, the presentation of the void in economic crisis held revolutionary possibilities:

> The void fills, the music of old glass is playing new
> Announcements of economies. As one object
> Speeding in the light in a calculus of speed,
> Revolution is the pod systems rattle from,
> Yet no frame breaks, being elastic, the column
> Of the wake continues into the wave, Disdain
> To shunt aims, To each his needs, the Manifesto.
>
> (*A* 51–2)

Zukofsky had hopes for the revolutionary 'wave', the 'constant' (ψ) of '[s]ubstance subjected to no human prevision' (*A* 109). It would seem to promise the return of what has been lost: the 'void to be felt' is also 'a void in which nothing was dead'. But the economic crisis leaves only the 'wake', a melancholic attendance upon the loss that constitutes the promise of the social substance. The citation of Adams' account of pre-revolutionary Russia also frames Zukofsky's ambivalence to post-revolutionary Soviet Russia, which may not have escaped 'the negative luminosity' of the melancholic substance, despite having named it Labour. The 'wake' of mourning extends into the 'revolutionary wave' (*A* 91).

It will be recalled from the second section of this chapter that Zukofsky also imagines the social substance as an 'elastic fluid / [which] Is more and more dense / As it approaches the surface of bodies' (*A* 102). Ether, the 'elastic fluid', was also conceived to be the medium of electricity. For one charged moment in Zukofsky's poem, this substance seems to be reappropriated in a potentially revolutionary event. In a sentence that is split by the parenthetical citation of Cadwallader Colden on the 'elastic substance', Zukofsky translates the ether into a figure for a kind of immanence of technology:

> And the effect of the day was like a shock of electricity..
> [. . .]

.. arousing every man .. placing him erect ..
solidly on his center ..

(*A* 102)

The shock of electricity would seem to transmit the substance that is the condition of 'every man'. But this reappropriation seems to be tied more to fascism than to Marxist revolution. 'Energy' as electricity seems to provide the foundation for 'the coming man', who, like a 'super-Nazi' (*A* 100) will stand erect and at attention, 'solidly on his center'.

But Zukofsky is not identifying the economy of consumption with the fascist politics of 'the coming man'. Even as the culture of consumption exploits the wraith of the substance of universality, it requires the fragmentation of subjectivity. 'Man' is consumed as a universal term, but he is in fact easily 'broken down', or digested by the corporate body. From Henry Adams Zukofsky borrows an image for the fragmented or 'broken down' subject of industrial production. Considering the threat posed by the new psychology to the value of unity, Henry Adams argues that nineteenth-century metaphysics, even at its Schopenhauerian darkest, 'had been content to turn the universe of contradictions into the human as one Will, and treat it as representation'. From contradiction it was possible to salvage Man as Will. The new psychology, however, presumes no such unity of Man and offers little solace to those who desire it; instead, it

> seemed convinced that it had actually split personality not only into dualism, but also into complex groups, like telephonic centres and systems, that might be isolated and called up at will, and whose physical action might be occult in the sense of strangeness to any known form of force. Dualism seemed to have become as common as binary stars. Alternating personalities turned up constantly, even among one's friends.[180]

What Adams calls the 'electro-magnetic civilization' produces a psyche fragmented into 'telephonic centres and systems'. But for Zukofsky, this fragmentation does not preclude 'the coming man' of the fascist state from continuing to haunt the culture of consumption. Like the fascist politics of reappropriation, the revolutionary culture of consumption refuses to mourn for the loss that is the condition of the social. Instead, it disavows the disappearance of the social substance by accelerating the object to the speed of light: 'the wake continues into the wave', the light wave, the diminishing surplus. The object missing from the centre of the emerging economy travels at the speed of light 'in a calculus of speed' (*A* 51).

Film, which requires a 'calculus' of small differences, records the 'calculus of speed'. In a line that could just as well be from Benjamin or Eisenstein as from an official of the culture industry, Zukofsky announces that, 'Of all the arts the wind can blow / The most important, in my opinion, is the cinema' (*A* 54). With film, the revolutionary wave of light casts its images; in the 'perpetual revolution' of film, 'no frame breaks, being elastic' (*A* 51). In a collage of various texts, Zukofsky indicates the function of the new medium of film:

> Technology throws light upon mental conceptions.
> 'intervals of gradualness'.
> Quantity into quality.
> Or sweetness: where there is more light than logic.
> A full number of things in a very few words.
>
> (*A* 58)

It is above all film technology that 'throws light upon mental conceptions'.[181] If we recall once again Marx's abstract model of labour, it becomes apparent what has happened to the worker's image. The 'mental conception' of the worker can no longer provide the condition for a revolutionary self-recognition of Labour, because the power of realizing that image lies not with Labour but with Light. The extreme and irreversible moment of commodity fetishism is the total interpellation of the labourer into consumption; this requires that the subject be fragmented so that it cannot recognize itself in its revolutionary and universal name. But the fragmentation of the subject into 'telephonic centres and systems' remains in subjection to the melancholic ghost of the universal: the transformation of the 'energy' of 'labor' into the electricity that will produce the 'light' in which things appear requires the lure of universality. In *A*-12, written in 1950–51 (just after completion of 'The Second Half of *A*-9'), Zukofsky examines the process by which the figure of Man emerges as a 'genre body':[182]

Athlete with anatomical belly
In love with his own genre body –
Paradoxically *transcendental*.
Said the blest, such terms
Arise from the fact
That the limited body
Can form in itself
Only a certain number of images,
If more are formed
The images begin to be confused,
If exceeded, they become entirely confused.
The mind then imagines
Without any distinction,
                        under one attribute –
A universal –
Man, not
The small differences,
And predicates concerning an infinite number of individuals.

(*A* 203)

In Spinoza's account, the calculus of 'small differences' is confused and blurred in order to produce the image of an imaginary Man. This later passage serves to illuminate the references to film in *A*-8: the 'pulse of light ... timed to / The speed of the film' (*A* 92) projects the still images that make up film, and turns small differences into movement. Moreover, film demonstrates the process by which 'A universal – / *Man*' is brought into being despite the fragmentation into small differences.

Zukofsky does not simply take sides in such oppositions as this one between universality and small differences, nor does either term define his aesthetic. For Zukofsky, the opposition assumes only particular historical forms; to advocate an aesthetic of 'small differences' would be to fall prey to a particular historical form of fragmentation rather than to affirm the supposed ontological primacy of multiplicity or singularity. Contrary to this, in fact, Zukofsky's political imperatives demand that the value that has gone by the thoroughly ideological name of the 'universal' (for example) must be retained for any political action or emancipation to be possible. What haunts his poem in the form of exchange value and the 'idle concomitance' is the substance of collective life that has been contested in a struggle that assumed its modern form in the Enlightenment. That Zukofsky affirms such a notion of universality becomes apparent in a discussion of Charlie Chaplin's aesthetic method, written by Zukofsky at the same time (1936) as he was writing *A-8*. Zukofsky is interested in Chaplin as an example of an artist attempting to realize the goals of the Enlightenment, conceived also to be the goals of history. Notice in the following statement how Zukofsky both extends and restricts the claim he would make for Chaplin: 'Chaplin's *technics* . . . now embraces a tradition of the film, as much as any one man can who moves to grasp its whole being at once in the present' (P 63). The antecedent of 'its' is unclear, and seems to include at once 'technics', 'a tradition of film', and most importantly, 'one man'. But this one man is implicitly a particular example of a universal, of the species 'man', the missing antecedent implied by the others: Chaplin, 'one man', 'moves to grasp [the] whole being [of 'man'] at once in the present'. Yet what is to be grasped is not represented in Zukofsky's sentence: 'it' is the hybrid object of Zukofsky's concern, which is embodied in the history neither of *technics*, nor of 'humanity', yet is immanent to the history of each.

In this essay, Zukofsky constructs a perspective on the universality of 'man' in three concluding passages from Dante. In the first passage, Zukofsky defines *technics*: '"Adornment," says Dante, (and he might have used the word *technics*) "is the addition of some suitable thing" . . . "everything which is suited to us is so either in respect of the genus, or of the species, or of the individual, as sensation, laughter, war."' In the second quotation, Zukofsky focuses on the species that *technics* is to serve. According to Dante, 'man has been endowed with a threefold life, namely vegetable, animal and rational'. Each of the three parts of the human has a specific kind of object which will satisfy it: 'in so far as he is vegetable he seeks for what is useful, wherein he is of like nature with plants; in so far as he is animal he seeks for that which is pleasurable, wherein he is of like nature with brutes; in so far as he is rational, he seeks for what is right – and in this he stands alone . . .'. Finally, in the third quotation from Dante, Zukofsky focuses on the 'movement' of this seeking, and in connection with his statement concerning Chaplin's attempt 'to grasp its whole being', 'movement' becomes a figure for the history of the universal 'man': 'Everything that moves, moves for the sake of something which it has not, and which is the goal of its motion; ... Everything that moves, then, has some defect, and does not grasp its whole being at once' (P 63).

These comments invoke Dante's anthropology in order to recall the post-Enlightenment (including Marxist) image of the human as *homo economicus*, as determined above all by the 'defects' that must be answered by objects of use and pleasure. Even as it institutes the forms of political economy that will allow it to produce and distribute such objects, this species at one level of determination invents Chaplin's art 'to suit [its] need'. The species attempts 'to grasp its whole being at once in the present' through this individual's aesthetic method, itself a response to the 'tradition of film'. The *technics* the species creates for itself in its history constitutes a system of needs, providing objects of use and pleasure. But this determination of political economy and aesthetics leaves out the third term of Dante's hierarchy of the needs of man, one that interested Zukofsky as much as the needs of *homo economicus*, which is the need for 'what is right'. The emphasis on the question of justice or rightness undoubtedly motivates Zukofsky's interest in Marx, but at the same time this need could not be answered by the Marxist science and critique of political economy that in its foundations foreclosed the ethical question of 'what is right'. I will argue in the following – concluding – comments that the question of 'what is right' ultimately exceeds the anthropology of *homo economicus*, which institutes an economy of need or lack that is at the very root of the forms of domination I have been examining in this book.

What motivates 'movement' in Chaplin's films is a matter of justice, which cannot be reduced to any of the psychological or political categories that are suggested by use and pleasure. Moreover, this notion of reason is entirely immanent to the formal method of Chaplin's films. That is to say, aesthetic method is related to an immanent rationality of justice. This is why Zukofsky emphasizes that 'Chaplin's *technics* developed with respect to his work as an individual, alongside of other technics invented to suit the need of the species...' (P 63). The technology or technics of film, which are deeply imbricated with historical conditions, are also imbricated with the reason or rationality of the species, which exceeds the rationality of any of its individual artists or thinkers. What this implies in Zukofsky's work is that the 'species', a form of universality that may or may not go by the ideological name of the 'human', is immanent to technics and its history.

In his essay on Chaplin, Zukofsky outlines an aesthetic that puts him on a very different track than that which most modernist aesthetic pronouncements would follow. His essay is particularly interesting for its notion of the relation between historical conditions and the formal methods of art: 'Art does not rise out of thin air. Certain conditions existing, the thought (e.g. the art) which reflects them in the topographic air will make it alive with relations of method embodying them' (P 57). The 'topographic air' is Zukofsky's figure for historical relations that may perhaps not be theorizable or available for reflection, at least in existing discourses, but which are embodied already as the composition of lived experience. A continuity exists between lived historical experience and the aesthetic and theoretical structures of meaning that can only incorrectly be said to reflect the first. What is important in Chaplin's work, for artists concerned with the progressive possibilities of aesthetic method, is therefore not 'an attitude toward history', but a 'material thoughtfulness' (P 59) and 'inventive existence' interacting with other existence in all its ramifications: sight, hearing, muscular movement, coordination of all the senses acting on the surrounding world and rendering it laughably intelligent' (P 60).

But this inhabitation of history is not a precondition for a consciousness or a practice that could lead to a revolutionary transformation of the conditions of production. The question of revolution is suspended, as is, to a certain extent, the notion of critique. Zukofsky provides a list of examples of the 'inventive existence' that Chaplin (both as director and as actor, the traditional distinction not really holding here) demonstrates in his films. I will focus on two examples:

> *Behind the Scenes*, in which Charlie scabs on his fellow stagehounds and wins the girl according to pedestrian expectation, reaches the end with Charlie kissing her. Yet the very last shot is Charlie winking at the audience – *close up*, and *irised out*. In *Shoulder Arms*, Charlie embodying a transformation in Ovid camouflages himself into a tree. The metamorphosis which Charlie poetically senses is not his sole achievement. He becomes the man-tree to destroy the human foe.

In the first example, Zukofsky appears to admire a moment of self-consciousness in Chaplin: just as the plot satisfies 'pedestrian expectation', Chaplin winks at the audience, as if to say, perhaps, 'All the world's a stage.' But more important than this traditional self-consciousness is the technical qualification of such self-consciousness, when the camera too winks, or rather closes its eye, 'irising out' the final scene. The wink of the camera is not a parallel to the self-conscious wink, but rather frames that wink in another, different one, which I will examine in more detail below. In the second example, Zukofsky focuses on a transformation that is really a camouflage, in which the human becomes the natural, in order to 'destroy the human foe'.[183] Common to both is a framing of the human in other terms: the appeal to self-consciousness is framed by an appeal to a technological wink, and the human is transformed into the natural. This transformation is, however, only a 'camouflaging' of the human, not its loss or supersession. Nonetheless, the 'human' as such is left behind, even as technology and nature reserve what it is that historically has been held under the name 'human'. Though the 'substance' of what was named 'human' remains behind (camouflaged as, for example, a tree), Zukofsky will not provide it with a proper name (such as Labour), unless that name be considered a camouflage and the substance be considered in hiding. Zukofsky's inquiry is well-summarized by the epigraph to his essay: 'Mark Twain (over the embalmed Egyptian): "Is he dead?"' (P 57).

A-8 explores this notion of camouflage in its references to film. It will be recalled that this discussion of Chaplin began with Zukofsky's citation of Spinoza ('the blest') in *A-12*, which I read as a reference to the 'universal Man' produced not only by confused thinking but also (in Zukofsky's metaphorics) by the filmic illusion of movement. In the elaborate network of *A-8* and *A-9*, the references to light and to film also evoke Pound's 'white light that is allness', and translate that medieval substance into the pulsing quantum of light that produces the image of Man on the film screen. The question that now must be addressed is: Given that Zukofsky sustains a critique of the universality of Man, while at the same time he paradoxically attempts to preserve the substance of universality, what is his historical imagining of the way in which substance has camouflaged itself in the emerging economy? As we will see, the temporality of the pulse of light will be important to Zukofsky's attempt to envision the possibilities of liberation that remain once the Marxist utopia of emancipated Labour can no longer be supported.

Since Zukofsky has rooted his analysis of the emerging subjectivity of the economy of consumption in the superseded economy of industrial production, it makes sense that his attempt to delineate the camouflage does not evade the form of industrial production. Let me return one last time to the question of 'the worker's image', or the 'cell in [the worker's] head' (*A* 61), which is at this point, as we shall see, celluloid or an animation cel. According to Marx, the worker, in throwing light upon this 'mental conception',

> ... realizes his own purpose
> To which he gives up his will.
> Nor does he give it up to the crick of a second...
>
> (*A* 61)

Once again it is important to insist on the paradox, which Zukofsky makes the most of, that in giving up his will the worker 'realizes his own purpose'. As I have said, Zukofsky plays off two possible interpretations of this paradox: on the one hand, such a sacrifice is an alienation of the productive 'will' that will provide the basis for the radical division of labour upon which industrial production is founded. In this case, 'his own purpose' is identical with that of the 'master', to use Marx's word, or the machine. On the other hand, Zukofsky also emphasizes that the notion of the 'will' is ideologically suspect for its anthropomorphism: the human will, and the productivist economies that privilege its rule, should be sacrificed for the purposes of furthering the inventiveness of the species. It should be clear at this point that Zukofsky can maintain both positions at once, since to affirm either separately is to give in to the most reactionary and dangerous political and economic forms of modernity.

Film embodies these contradictions, as does all aesthetic method, by virtue of its relation to its historical conditions. Zukofsky's interest in Chaplin focused on the question of movement; the significance of this is reflected in the fact that *A*-8 summarized the varieties of fetishism under the rubric of 'animated things [that] move' (*A* 73). Zukofsky and Chaplin were both of course aware that industrial labour regiments and inhibits movement. Both were also aware that the technology of film played a role in the intensification of the regimentation that Taylor's revolution in production pursued. The Gilbreth chronometer was a device which recorded on film the movements of the worker at the factory machine in order to isolate unnecessary gestures that were wasteful of energy and to identify any 'idleness' in the worker.[184] This aspect of film subordinates it entirely to the rationality of the political and economic system, and Zukofsky's metaphors, seen in this light, are metaphors for domination.

It is because of this regimentation that the worker 'gives up his will' to the higher purpose embodied in the machine, and not 'to the crick of a second', not to a spasmodic, unnecessary immobilization of the body. A crick is 'a sudden stiffness which makes it more or less impossible to move the part' (*OED*). It is opposed to the 'pulse of light', the temporality of the production of the worker's image on film, to which the worker gives up his will; it is a spasmodic interruption of smooth operations. Zukofsky's film thus functions doubly: on the one hand, as the Gilbreth chronometer, it figures a totally determining technic, so thoroughly rationalizing of the production of surplus value that it exhausts all remainder. The will is entirely given over to 'the worker's image' and the master's 'purpose'. The Gilbreth chronometer has isolated the moment of resistance, the crick, and realized the potential of this unproductive energy. In this regard, we could recall the old man, whose mechanical repetition of infantile verses indicated not only the radical separation of work and leisure effected by industrial production, but also the generalization of the discipline of repetition into the free time of the unemployed old man, who is related to the signifier as to a repeating machine. He was 'taught-to-work-as-well-as-play', and learned the lesson well. His repetition of the infantile verse is addressed to a disciplinarian, to a master. His infantilization enables the execution of a superegoic imperative. The apparent 'idleness' of the old man conceals the work he performs; as Brooks Adams says, 'men work unconsciously' (*A* 81). He embodies the entropic remainder, the 'unavailable energy' whose only 'work' is not actually production but repetition and redundancy. His 'breakdown' (cf. *A* 52) is the result of the analytic decomposition effected by such a device as the Gilbreth chronometer, which isolated the moment of resistance, the crick, and realized the potential of this unproductive energy. All the gaps in his language are filled by the hyphens that direct his energy to the completion of the task.

There is more to this crick than might first appear. It is not as immediately evident that a 'crick' is the wasteful gesture I have just suggested. Zukofsky's grammar is puzzling, since it affirms that the worker both does and does not give up his will to the crick, even as he gives it up to 'his own purpose'. His grammar allows Zukofsky to straddle two possible readings of the 'crick'. The crick provides the image of another kind of motion that does not fall into the opposition between work and 'idleness' that the Gilbreth chronometer is designed to regulate: it provides a perspective on the resistance offered by the worker. In the second reading of this passage, the worker's will is not entirely 'given up' to the purpose or will of the master as embodied in the machine. '[T]he crick of a second' leaves space for a moment of resistance, a moment that does not fit into the dialectic of fragmentation and totalization or universality that drives consumption. If the worker does *not* give up his will to this 'crick of a second', he presumably puts something of the will in reserve. The crick in time is a momentary rejection of the appropriation of the will, or a concealing of something from the master.[185]

Remaining entirely within the metaphorics he has developed out of Marx's abstract model of labour, Zukofsky has identified a moment of resistance within the subjective structure of industrial production. As I have argued, this subjective structure is the foundation also of the emerging economy of consumption. The displacement of 'the worker's image' into the sphere of consumption should be understood as an extension of industrial labour into the structure of the unconscious. There is, as it were, a Gilbreth chronometer at work also in the sphere of consumption; there are 'animated things that move in the light' that cannot be accounted for entirely by 'the worker's image', the image of the worker at the machine within the sphere of production. We have seen how Zukofsky's labourer-lover provided the link between the two spheres. This is not to say that the interpellation of the labourer into the sphere of consumption is liberating or is the condition of resistance. In fact, Zukofsky's analysis has suggested that the structure of domination persists right into both spheres – but that there is a space of resistance between them.

Zukofsky's film presents the two moments of the split second of the crick. The crick is a constitutive gap or failure in the smooth operations of the machine, but it is a gap upon which the technology of film functions in order to produce its own commodity-images, 'animated things [that] move in the dark. / In the light

(*A* 73). In film, the constitutive crick makes possible the illusion of movement. '[T]he pulse of light' (*A* 92) projects the filmed *immobile* image on the screen as movement; it casts light on a series of still photographs, which themselves record the analytic breakdown of movement. Between each frame is the 'crick of a second', the dark between pulses of light. In *A*-8, Zukofsky presents this space of resistance in the form of a well-known 'animated thing': Mickey Mouse. A voice, recalling that of the infantile old man, responds to an implied question concerning his identity: 'Sure .. I am Mickey Mouse .. why do you have to ask?' (*A* 63). A number of issues are raised by this line. One of the most interesting is, of course, the implied question to which the speaker is responding: is it really Mickey Mouse who is speaking, or is the speaker being ironic? Do we trust that the speaker is really Mickey Mouse? Perhaps the speaker is even deluded into thinking he is indeed Mickey Mouse. Whoever has posed the question may or may not be satisfied with the response, but clearly the question is not satisfactorily answered by the speaker. The reader too is implicated in the scenario implied by this response, unable to disentangle truth from deceit or delusion. But a closer look at the response of 'Mickey Mouse' suggests a complication to the scenario. The speaker in turns asks a question in response to the question posed by the other: 'Why do you have to ask?' The original question seems to challenge 'Mickey Mouse'. That is, rather than asking 'Are you Mickey Mouse?', the questioner would seem to have asked, 'Are you *really* Mickey Mouse?' This second form of the question suggests that the original questioner does not believe that the speaker is who he claims to be. The implied questioner is suspicious, and 'Mickey' clearly senses the challenge. He would seem to have something invested in being or appearing as Mickey Mouse.

At the same time it is necessary to ask who the implied questioner might be. Perhaps it is a child who sees someone costumed in a Mickey Mouse outfit, bringing his or her childish suspicion to bear on it. Perhaps the implied questioner is rather a social agent of surveillance, such as was embodied in the Gilbreth chronometer. If this were the case then we could translate the response: 'Yes, I am Mickey Mouse, I am not the guilty party you are looking for.' All of these scenarios are equally plausible, and all are equally valid. The point is that the subject is camouflaged in the 'animated thing' of the film screen, and that this camouflage is the condition of multiple but indeterminate relations with other subjects, which are indistinguishable from the 'animated things' of the economy of the fetish.[186] Zukofsky locates this subject-thing in the form of a commodity that perhaps would have pleased Mickey Mouse:

> It-began-to-be-desirable
> That the cheese show eyes in the cut
> And after, for that 'little bite' to complete the evening's
>   enjoyment...
>
> (A 64)

When the commodity, in this case cheese, begins to 'show eyes', to look back at the consumer, the ambiguous moment of fetishistic identification has arrived. There are two moments of this identification: first, the eyes emerge 'in the cut' of castration; second, the trauma of the cut gives rise to the gaze, which is the founding condition of the many valences of the trauma. The gaze emerging from the cut is profoundly ambivalent, like the identification upon which it appears, and of which it is the limit-point. The eyes that show in the cut are not the eyes of the subject, but of the Other. It is a point at the limit of subjectivity in that the subject can never occupy that position. For this reason, this position may be occupied by the various agencies of surveillance, such as the ego-ideal. But the ego-ideal or the master does not exhaust the possible functions of this position. This is why I am suggesting that this moment is also the limit-point to the economy of the fetish, and therefore also the political economy based on an ambivalent identification with the father. Let me be clear, however: the idea of a limit-point does not imply that there is a human or subjective or essential quantity that escapes the economy of the fetish. To say that the subject's identifications are restricted to the economy of the fetish means that there is no outside to the economy founded on an ambivalent identification with the agency I have been calling the master. Though this enunciation signals the point at which the subject resists the domination of the 'image', the subject does so by way of camouflage.

In the extreme moment of fetishism, commodities look back, embodying the gaze which can never be reappropriated. What the subject meets in the gaze is the traumatic split that is its condition; what is presented in the 'cut' is a part of it that it can never recover, a primary alienation of something that cannot be named or recognized. Let me return for a moment to Mickey Mouse. The response of the subject to the question betrays anxiety, self-doubt, even as it asserts itself with certainty. The question that the subject poses in the second half of the reply, 'why do you have to ask?', has a very unstable emotional valency. The question posed by the Other reveals a slight distance or split within the subject, which the subject may or may not have been aware of. That is to say, the response of the subject might be interpreted as: 'Sure, I am Mickey Mouse; are you suggesting that I have reason to doubt it? Who else could I be?' Whether the subject is or is not Mickey Mouse, a distance has opened. This is the moment where the structure of camouflage becomes apparent, whether or not Mickey Mouse is the self-conscious disguise the subject assumes or not.

The subject is responding to the 'cut' that is the condition of its relation to the Other at the point where that relation loses its particular historical determination; the other is at this point not the father or the law of value. The implied question is posed in the gaze of the Other prior to its historical determinations; at the same time, however, this undetermined relation only becomes tangible within the historically determinate relations to the law of the father and the law of value. Zukofsky's cheese places this gaze in the sphere of consumption, in the commodity-fetish. Moreover, since the subject is Mickey Mouse, the subject itself is immanent to the sphere of consumption as one of its commodities. Since the subject is identified as an 'animated thing', as Mickey Mouse, there is no spectator positioned outside of the film screen upon which the image is cast. Mickey Mouse is a 'thing' that is 'animated' by the technology of film, and is not a subject that is in control of the technology that projects it. If the subject is identified with Mickey Mouse, and there is no spectator of this commodity-subject, then commodity fetishism has absorbed all that might otherwise be considered to be its outside or its mystified condition. Yet a question has been asked, a challenge posed, to the camouflaged subject. The uncanniness of Zukofsky's line can be attributed to the fact that Mickey Mouse is not observed by a subject in a position we can occupy, but is suddenly exposed to the gaze of the Other, which does not speak its lines. Any lines it would speak would limit its effect to a determinate intersubjective relationship, which Zukofsky wants to avoid in order to bring the limit-point into relation with the subject. What happens to the subject when it steps beyond the intersubjective relation?

Zukofsky's film provides a metaphor for the moment when the subject steps beyond the intersubjective relation, as well as beyond the subject–object relation of Marx's model of labour. Let me develop this metaphor in connection with Lacan's optical model of identification, which has been so productive for film theory.[187] According to Lacan, the subject is 'photo-graphed' in the gaze of the Other, which within the limits of political economy is embodied in the historical agent of the paternal will. The moment in which the subject is photo-graphed is a radically split one: the subject is embodied in an image in the very same moment that the identity of the image and the subject is questioned by the Other. In Lacan's terms, this split moment 'isolates the function of the screen' and provides the distance allowing the subject to play with the screen as mask.[188] The picture on the screen is a (nonself-conscious) strategy of camouflage that resists interpellation by the Other, even as it seems to submit to it.[189] Mickey Mouse is the picture in the gaze of the Other, a projection of the 'pulse of time' and the 'crick of a second'. At the same time as the relation to the Other constitutes it, the picture is adopted by the subject of the mimicry in order to conceal itself from the gaze of the Other. However, the relation to the picture on the screen is ambivalent. It may be a mimicry, a game of hide and seek, but the distance from the image is not simply a liberating distance from a false image. The distance is in effect no distance.[190] Zukofsky elaborates absolute fetishization in terms of such masking: *A*-9 presents commodities in their most utopian yearning as 'mask[s] espying / That, as things, men want in us...' (*A* 107). Yet this masking of the subject in the sphere of consumption or commodities, the very condition of 'espying' that which is of most value, acknowledges the impossibility of overcoming the ambivalence towards the Other within the limits of paternal and melancholic identification. The ambiguity of the enunciative positions in the mimicking of Mickey Mouse reflect the fact that the suspicion directed towards the Other ('why do you have to ask..?'), since it assumes that Other is in possession of the answer, is structurally coincident with a belief and a faith in the Other, thus repeating what we have seen as the ambivalent relationship to the paternal instance. Yet this belief and faith are also a condition of the utopian challenge to the economy of the master, of the fetish, that is to say, a condition of the Enlightenment at its most radical.

The notion of camouflage does not rely on identifying that which is camouflaged; it is enough to say, with Zukofsky, that 'something – a constant' persists, an 'idle concomitance' that runs through all 'variation'. This constant is the object of Zukofsky's political concerns. As I argued above, this constant assumes the name of that which preserves it in the economy of the fetish (for example, labour), but is not reducible to it. It is camouflaged in the name, but is not deployed in the economy arranged about the name. To say that the subject is camouflaged is to say that identification is restricted within but at the same time resistant to the historical framework of the 'image' that would regulate it in the economy of the master. At the same time, however, the economy supported by the 'image' is the condition of the articulation of this constant. The constant is a limit-point within historical economies, but it is a limit-point that marks and reserves the object of the modernist political impulse.

Zukofsky demonstrates more clearly than any other modernist, I think, the way in which this limit is articulated in the political discourse of modernity. The question remains, however, whether or not the camouflage of the subject is a survival technique, or if it bears with it any of the utopian political possibilities of modernity. That is to say, is the strategy of camouflage in any sense also a means of transformation, or has Zukofsky resigned himself to the incapacity of political discourse and practice to change the fundamental structure of the economy of the fetish? Let me return to his example of Chaplin, where this idea of camouflage emerged most explicitly. It will be recalled that Zukofsky cites Dante in his discussion of Chaplin, in order to raise two significant themes: the rationality of the species (beyond its individuals) and the concomitant desire for justice, for 'what is right'. What first becomes apparent is the implied faith in the Other – and therefore ultimately in the possibilities of political economy – as guarantor of that which is reserved and of its eventual restitution, which suggests that Zukofsky does not escape the economy whose pervasive effects he has traced. However, something else has surfaced, which cannot, I think, properly be called political or economic.

The 'material intelligence' and 'inventive existence' Zukofsky detects in Chaplin suggests a manner not of standing above history or stepping aside from it in order to reflect on it as an object. Instead, it suggests the possibility of inhabiting history in a manner that I hesitate to call resistant or critical, and hesitate even more to call redemptive, though I am not able to supply an adequate term to designate it. The reason I hesitate is because this is the very crux of the issue I have been discussing throughout this book. Taking Zukofsky's relation to Marxist discourse as the main example, I have argued that Zukofsky's own critical or revolutionary politics undermines all of the foundations that historical discourses of revolution or transformation have relied upon and those they have in turn made available; that is to say, there is no fulcrum or outside or other to which Zukofsky appeals to ground any new possibilities for the social. The power of Zukofsky's critical and emancipatory perspective is made possible by his refusal to subsume historical economic forms of exchange into normative social, political or moral relationships. Unlike Pound, he does not attempt to transcend market economics by isolating one of its features – for example, the contract – and transforming it into a normative relation to a paternal leader. The political discourse of the revolutions of modernity has in effect been exhausted. Zukofsky has not of course accomplished this in *A*-8, which hardly incorporates the entirety of modernity's politics, but the implications of his citation of Marx is that all such discourse is fundamentally unfounded in a philosophical sense. More importantly, however, all such discourse is premised on the very economic structures that drive capitalism (that is, fetishism and melancholia). It would seem therefore that there is no way outside the contradictions of political economy. According to Zukofsky's analysis, the historical conditions of practical activities and social relations in the emerging post-industrial economy are entirely subsumed by the law of value. But the law of value does not know itself entirely, and retains within itself that which is of most value, which has been represented in universalizing terms such as Labour and the human. For Zukofsky, therefore, the law of value is not in the final instance a universality founded on a sacrificial negativity. Though camouflage as a way of living is not transformation, it reserves the condition of transformation, namely, the thing that is of most value, the substance of universality that in recent history has gone by the name of the human. One might say that it is a form of survival, but a survival that is not predicated on scarcity, need and hunger.

Instead, it is what Kant in his analysis of the dynamical sublime calls 'a kind of self-preservation', in which what is at stake is not an object that is identifiable within any one of the discursive formations of the Enlightenment, such as politics or economics.[191] That is to say, it is not identifiable within 'the philosophy of the subject', to use Seyla Benhabib's terms, but appears only in terms of the hybrid object of poetico-'political economy', which exceeds the differentiations upon which the cognitive powers of Enlightenment reason are based. What camouflage reserves, withholds and guarantees is that which is at stake in the Enlightenment itself, that which is of value yet not subject in the final analysis to valuation, escaping as it does such systems of representation. That which is neither political nor economic may now, after modernism, be assuming the name 'community'. Whether the thought of community after modernism can exceed, displace or transform the limits of the poetico-political economy of modernity may for historical reasons not be a question to address to Stein, Zukofsky and Pound.[192] Nonetheless, their work does make apparent the conditions of its possibility as well as of its travesty: what makes community possible is an undetermined relation to the Other conceived not as the sacrificial universality of the law (for example, the law of value); its travesty is the determination of the relation to the Other in political-economic terms (for example, the paternal will). Meanwhile, traces of the undetermined relation remain camouflaged in, not negated by, the political economy of modernity.

Notes

Introduction

1. Wallace Stevens, *Opus Posthumous* (New York: Vintage, 1989), p. 252.
2. See Tönnies, *Community and Society* (New York: Harper and Row, 1963), pp. 33–64. One of the most significant examples of this modernist symptom is Marcel Mauss' essay *The Gift: the Form and Reason for Exchange in Archaic Societies* (New York: Norton, 1990; originally published 1925) which has been influential in recent critical thought (especially in the work of Georges Bataille, Claude Lévi-Strauss, and subsequently in the work of Jean Baudrillard and Jacques Derrida). In his conclusion to *The Gift* Mauss claims that, despite the modern differentiation of society, economy, religion, the aesthetic, etc., the shadow of the '"total" social phenomena' of archaic societies is still with us. The totality implicit even in the social phenomena of modernity holds out the promise of a total and non-alienated community, or what Tönnies calls *Gemeinschaft*. See especially Mauss' 'Moral Conclusions', pp. 65–71, where he ambiguously asserts that 'we can and must return to archaic society and to elements in it' without giving up the benefits of modernity.
3. David Carroll provides a useful discussion of the legacy of Enlightenment universality in postmodern political thought. In a reading of Hannah Arendt's notion of the public sphere, he summarizes what persists of the Enlightenment into postmodernity: 'Traditional political theories and strategies ... in one way or another assume or explicitly posit a "world which is common to all" and project an ideal or real public space in which such "commonness" could or must inevitably manifest or realize itself.' Today, Carroll argues (following Jean-François Lyotard's reading of Kant), 'this "commonness" can only be thought in terms of a radical heterogeneity or alterity, of a potentially infinite number of common or public spaces...'. I would also add that, as Carroll is well aware, the vocabulary for thinking 'community' in such a way has yet to overcome the legacy of the Enlightenment, and the predominantly economic discourses of commonality, which can be seen in such economically problematic notions as the 'sharing' of public space. (I discuss 'sharing' in more detail in the reading of Stein's 'Before the Flowers of Friendship Faded Friendship Faded' that concludes Chapter 3.) See Carroll, 'Community after Devastation: Culture, Politics, and the "Public Space"', in Mark Poster, ed., *Politics, Theory, and Contemporary Culture* (New York: Columbia University Press, 1993), pp. 165, 174.
4. Seyla Benhabib has argued that such economies of reappropriation characterize the post-Enlightenment 'philosophy of the subject'. In

the post-Hegelian (predominantly Marxist) form of the philosophy of the subject, 'history is... viewed as a *unitary* process of the unfolding of the capabilities of a collective subject, and social emancipation is... understood as the *reappropriation* by a specific social class of this heritage. The particular demands of this class coalesce with the universal demands of humanity to become the subject of its own history. Even when there is no social class at hand whose emancipatory demands can be viewed by the critical theorist as fulfilling this promise, the search for a revolutionary subject whose very particularity is to act in the name of universal mankind is not given up'. *Critique, Norm, and Utopia* (New York: Columbia University Press, 1986), p. 54.
5. In an excellent argument about the emergence of the mass subject of consumption from the Enlightenment promise of universality in the public sphere, Michael Warner claims that '[p]ublic discourse from the beginning offered a utopian self-abstraction, but in ways that left a residue of unrecuperated particularity, both for its privileged subjects and for those it minoritized'. But the benefits of abstraction are not distributed equally: the sacrifice of particularity, which he calls 'disincorporation', brings about a 'minoritizing logic of domination'. 'This minoritizing logic, intrinsic to the deployment of negativity in the bourgeois public sphere, presents the subjects of bodily difference with the paradox of a utopian promise that cannot be cashed in for them. The very mechanism designed to end domination is a form of domination'. See 'The Mass Public and the Mass Subject', in *Habermas and the Public Sphere* (Cambridge: MIT Press, 1992), p. 384.
6. Jean-François Lyotard has developed the notion of the invaluable 'thing' that constitutes the most powerful investment on the part of what can only incorrectly be called the social subject. He points out that the thing that inhabits the public space cannot be accounted for in the political or economic categories that attempt to regulate social needs and desires: 'If one had to situate the respect due the thing in the doctrine of justice, one would be obliged to count it among the duties rather than among the rights. It is the debt, par excellence.... If, unbeknownst to it, the mind is indebted to the thing, it is not because the thing has been contractually instituted as the mind's creditor following a request for a loan. The mind will have been dispossessed "before" being able to certify or to act as a subject. It is consigned to the unending effort to repossess itself over and against the thing, which means, to forget it.' What I am calling the utopian impulse of modernity and modernism is an act of fidelity to this thing: 'Revolutions, all revolutions [including, I would add, the revolutionary consumer economy], are attempts to approach it, to make the community more faithful to what, unbeknownst to it, inhabits it; at the same time, revolutions attempt to regulate, to suppress, to efface the effects that the thing engenders. There is a fidelity and an infidelity in the fact of revolution.' 'A l'insu (Unbeknownst)', *Community at Loose Ends* (Minneapolis: University of Minnesota Press, 1991), pp. 46, 45.

7. Freud, 'Mourning and Melancholia,' in *On Metapsychology: the Theory of Psychoanalysis*, vol. 2 of *The Penguin Freud Library* (Harmondsworth: Penguin, 1991), p. 265.
8. These reinterpretations, though based in part upon the work of Jacques Lacan, derive largely from the work of Nicholas Abraham and Maria Torok. See among other works, their *The Wolf-Man's Magic Word: a Cryptonomy* (Minneapolis: University of Minnesota Press, 1986), and Derrida's introduction, 'Fors', for a condensed presentation of some of the issues at stake in the distinction of melancholia from mourning.
9. I do not intend my argument that fetishism requires a constitutive melancholia to be a clinical one. Instead, my reading of the relation of melancholia and fetishism is intended to get to the general 'economic' conditions – which are not 'economic' in the disciplinary sense of that term – of the lived experience of certain forms of social and economic exchange. Melancholia in my vocabulary is not restricted to Freud's interpretation, but serves as a name for the refusal to accept a constitutive loss (rather than what Freud saw as an empirical loss).

   Nonetheless, the theoretical proximity of fetishism and melancholia is evident in Freud, since both were examples of a quasi-psychotic break with reality. On fetishism's proximity to psychosis, see 'The Splitting of the Ego in the Process of Defence,' in *On Metapsychology*, p. 463, and 'Fetishism', in *On Sexuality*, vol. 7 of *The Penguin Freud Library* (Harmondsworth: Penguin, 1977), pp. 355–6. The narcissistic regression characteristic of melancholia amounts to a rejection of the reality of loss. Similarly, the fetishist accedes to the symbolic order without giving anything up. Fetishism and melancholia are therefore privileged categories for an examination of what I have called the constitutive melancholic loss or, in more strictly Lacanian terms, the 'foreclosure' of the real from the symbolic. What remains of this failure to symbolize the real is a hole in the symbolic network of signifiers, a place from which a signifier is missing. The missing substance that haunts this place is what Lacan calls the Thing. See Lacan, *The Ethics of Psychoanalysis*, trans. Dennis Porter (New York: Norton, 1992), Chapters 4 and 5.

   Perhaps a more pressing issue than the relationship between melancholia and fetishism is the slippage that I allow to occur between Freud's notion of fetishism and Marx's notion of commodity fetishism. Briefly, my interpretation of the historical possibility of the former is framed by my understanding of the historicity of the latter. Without commodities, the economic structure of the Freudian fetish, with its characteristic split between that which embodies value and the abstract value that is embodied, would not be possible. Though it seems to have become mandatory to decry the theoretical imprecision of the notion of fetishism, it seems unnecessary after the remarkable work of William Pietz, which attempts to derive 'the truth of the fetish', as a theoretical object, 'from the history of fetish theory'. I cannot summarize his argument here, but will cite the four charac-

teristics of the fetish which persist throughout the three varieties of fetish theory, which are the anthropological, the historical-materialist, and the psychoanalytical: 'irreducible materiality; a fixed power to repeat an original event of singular synthesis or ordering; the institutional construction of consciousness of the social value of things; and the material fetish as an object established in an intense relation to and with power over the desires, actions, health, and self-identity of individuals whose personhood is conceived as inseparable from their bodies'. The 'fetish', Pietz argues, 'can be taken as a name for the total collective material object, at once social and personal... that reveals the truth of all historical objects...'. Most important for my point at this moment is Pietz's identification of the 'novel situation' that makes the phenomenon of the fetish historically possible: 'This novel situation began with the formation of inhabited intercultural spaces along the West African coast (especially that stretch known as the Mina coast) whose function was to translate and transvalue objects between radically different social systems'. See 'The Problem of the Fetish, 1', in *Res* 9 (Spring 1985), pp. 10, 14, 6.
10. As Freud puts it: 'In addition to its individual side, this ideal has a social side; it is also the common ideal of a family, a class or a nation. It binds not only a person's narcissistic libido, but also a considerable amount of his homosexual libido, which is in this way turned back into the ego. The want of satisfaction which arises from the non-fulfilment of this ideal liberates homosexual libido, and this is transformed into a sense of guilt (social anxiety).' 'On Narcissism: an Introduction', in *On Metapsychology*, pp. 96–7.
11. Freud does not insist very much on the difference between the ego-ideal and the ideal ego; it is Lacan who in his first seminar drew out the implicit distinctions in terminology. In the seventh seminar, he returns to reformulate his earlier reading in ethical and political terms: 'We will... define the ego ideal of the subject as representing the power to do good.... As for the ideal ego, which is the imaginary other who faces us at the same level, it represents by itself the one who deprives us.' *The Ethics of Psychoanalysis*, p. 234. Though Lacan affiliates the ideal ego with the imaginary and the ego-ideal with the symbolic, these are not hard and fast distinctions. Drawing from recent Lacanian analyses of modernity, my argument is essentially that the characteristic form of identification in modernity is imaginary, as opposed to the normative symbolic mode. In imaginary identification, which I am describing as melancholic, the narcissistic ideal ego appears as the imaginary 'other' conceived of as having the lost object or thing. (The small 'o' opposes it to the symbolic Other, the place occupied by the ego-ideal, which is associated with the name of the father or the paternal law.) In melancholia and psychosis, the imaginary other, the rivalrous image of the mirror stage, occupies the place of the foreclosed symbolic Other. This confusion of imaginary and symbolic identification is made possible by the constitutive melancholia discussed above. For an excellent analysis of what I am calling modern melancholia, see

Juliet Flower MacCannell, *Regime of the Brother: After the Patriarchy* (New York: Routledge, 1991), pp. 9–40. For a discussion of the relationships between the ideal ego and the ego-ideal in modern capitalism, one could consult Eugene W. Holland's *Baudelaire and Schizoanalysis: the Sociopoetics of Modernism* (New York: Cambridge, 1993), pp. 193–209.
12. This assumption of balanced exchange is the basis of Marx's critique of Adam Smith's notion of sacrifice. See *Grundrisse* (New York: Vintage, 1973), pp. 610 ff.
13. By 'disavowed acknowledgement' I refer to the fetishist's simultaneous denial and recognition of castration as the assertion of the paternal will. This is already implied by the Freudian term *Verleugnung*, which, like its English equivalent 'disavowal,' implies the denial of a prior avowal or recognition.
14. Though my thesis relies on a psychoanalytic interpretation of Marx's concept of surplus value as predicated not on labour but desire, this reinterpretation allows neither psychoanalysis nor Marxism the final word on the circulation of value in symbolic economies. Above all, I insist that there are specifically historical ways in which surpluses are produced, distributed and circulated; though not all surplus is surplus labour, all surplus values circulate according to historically specific codes.

1 'Enough is not enough': Consumption and Depression

15. The title of my chapter is from GHA 195; the first epigraph is cited in Lewis Mumford, *Technics and Civilization* (New York: Harcourt, Brace, and Company, 1934), p. 393; the second is from Edward A. Filene, *Successful Living in This Machine Age* (New York: Simon and Schuster, 1931), p. 38; the third is from *Brewsie and Willie*, LMN 441.
16. For Pound and Douglas, as Peter Nicholls puts it, '[e]conomic justice ... could be secured by orienting the whole system toward the consumer; this entailed "merely" a shifting of the balance of capitalism.... In this sense, economic change could be conceived of not in terms of the dialectical movement of history but as a moment of rupture within it.' In this chapter on 'The Quarrel with Marxism', Nicholls points out that the 'rupture' demanded by social credit reform 'substituted for the Marxian concept of revolution the altogether more ambiguous notion of change as the imposition of a new order'. For this reason, 'Pound adamantly rejected the concept of class-struggle. Like Douglas, he tended to view society as almost exclusively a body of consumers.' In Pound's words, class-struggle was 'not between one class and another, but between humanity at large and one of the most ignoble oligarchies the world has yet suffered'. *Ezra Pound: Politics, Economics and Writing* (London: Macmillan, 1984), pp. 53, 54. (Nicholls is quoting a 1933 essay by Pound.)
17. Henry Ford, *Moving Forward* (Garden City: Doubleday, Doran and Co., 1930), p. 86.

18. For a brief account of this aspect of the relations between capital and labour, see Stuart Ewen, *Captains of Consciousness: Advertising and the Social Roots of the Consumer Culture* (New York: McGraw-Hill, 1976), Chapter 1, 'Shorter hours, higher wages'.
19. *Successful Living in This Machine Age*, p. 60.
20. Pound is concerned also of course to preserve individual freedoms and the private life, and so must find a place in his economic programme for individualized patterns of consumption; these patterns must, however, serve ends beyond those of individual gratification. In *ABC of Economics*, Pound cites Hume, who 'already saw that "the increase and *consumption* (italics mine) of all the commodities, which serve to the ornament and pleasure of life, are advantages to society; because at the same time they multiply those innocent gratifications to individuals, they are a kind of *storehouse* (italics his) of labour ... which in the exigencies of the state, may be turned to the public service"' (SP 255).
21. According to Pound, a culture must be founded on 'certain ethical bases, or a general agreement on the relative importance of the various moral, intellectual, and material values' (SP 320); these material values should be regulated at the level of production. Pound considered Mussolini to be 'the first head of state in our time to perceive and to proclaim *quality* as a dimension in national production' (SP 230; cf. SP 262).
22. See Aristotle's discussion of the distinction in the first book of *The Politics*, edited and translated by Ernest Barker (New York: Oxford University Press, 1958), p. 18ff. For a discussion of the traditional condemnation of the merchant by the philosopher, see Marcel Hénaff, 'Le philosophe et le marchand', *Modern Language Notes*, 54, pp. 761–81. On the Jeffersonian ideal of the household economy, see the first chapter of Michael Gilmore's *American Romanticism and the Market* (Chicago: University of Chicago Press, 1985).
23. As Pound says, '*oikos* was bastardised to mean merely *agora*' (SP 280–1).
24. I will discuss this in more detail in the fourth chapter.
25. The term 'Volitionist Economics' is the subtitle of Pound's *Jefferson and/or Mussolini* (New York: Liveright, 1972).
26. *The Social Division of Labor* (New York: Free Press, 1964), p. 372.
27. I intend the phrase 'conservative reformers' to refer to critics of the effects of industrialization and proletarianization who made no serious criticism of the industrial mode of production, but sought in various ways to compensate for those effects by such means as 'general education', as Durkheim says. For a summary of the views of a number of these critics in the American tradition, see Daniel Horowitz, *The Morality of Spending: Attitudes towards the Consumer Society in America, 1875–1940* (Baltimore: Johns Hopkins University Press, 1985).
28. Pound was not opposed to the capitalist or to capital as such, and his Odysseus can best be seen as the entrepreneur, for whom he had much respect. For a good discussion of Pound's defence of the

proper use of private property in entrepreneurial capitalism, see Robert Casillo, *The Genealogy of Demons: Anti-Semitism, Fascism, and the Myths of Ezra Pound* (Evanston: Northwestern University Press, 1988), pp. 191–203. For Adorno and Horkheimer's remarkable and now classic discussion of Odysseus as proto-capitalist, see 'Excursus I: Odysseus, or Myth and Enlightenment', in *Dialectic of Enlightenment*, trans. John Cumming (New York: Herder & Herder, 1972). For their analysis of sacrifice in terms of the economy of exchange, see especially pp. 48 ff.

29. Since I am anticipating the argument of later chapters, it may seem confusing to identify the consumer and the usurer, since usury is predicated on the delay of consumption while the sailors' consumption appears to be immediate. I will be arguing, however, that a usurious delay or 'temporization' also determines the structure of what appears to be 'immediate' consumption.

30. It is unclear if this text quotes an account contemporary with the founding of a bank in the fourteenth century, or if the parade is contemporary with Pound. It is difficult to determine the tone of this passage: Pound may see the parade cynically as organized from above by the state, or by the bank (a state institution, in this case), rather than seeing it (from his distance as foreigner, as bourgeois, etc.) nostalgically as a 'licit' kind of 'popular' culture that is part of an organic society with which the bank and the state are continuous. Pound critics tend to read Pound as if his values are clearly determined and always in line with his theoretical pronouncements, but this and numerous other examples demonstrate the inadequacy of such an assumption. Almost all of his economic slogans, for example, contain ambiguous rifts. I will discuss an example of such a rift at the end of the chapter.

31. *The Social Division of Labor*, pp. 372–3.

32. *Suicide: a Sociological Study* (New York: Free Press, 1966), p. 321. For a discussion of Durkheim and mass consumption, see Rosalind H. Williams, *Dream Worlds: Mass Consumption in Nineteenth-Century France* (Berkeley: University of California Press, 1982), pp. 322–42.

33. Bataille's concept of the 'noble' expenditure without reserve is complicit with certain class divisions, though he is very deliberately trying to present noble consumption as a model for a democratic or generalized consumption. One of his motives, however (and in this he resembles Pound), is to resist the form of consumption he sees emerging from the bottom up. I cannot offer more than suggestions of the complexities of Bataille's concept of consumption, but it is clear that it is opposed both to bourgeois and to 'proletarian' patterns of consumption. Bataille's discussion of the Marxian politicization of the working classes is interesting in this regard, in that it reveals Bataille's own perception of what I am calling 'purely material or economic motives' at the level of 'the proletarians, who commonly lack a sense of spiritual values'. See *The Accursed Share* (New York: Zone, 1988), pp. 140–1. Bataille's position in this is quite complex and very illuminating for the possible responses to the emerging culture of consumption. He finds it necessary, as did the avant-garde

in general, to resist the opposition of 'culture' to labour (see p. 140); but as I am arguing, the revolutionary or reformist gestures, including the gesture towards a classless 'expenditure without reserve', participate in the construction of the total culture of consumption.

34. Rosalind Williams argues that Veblen's analysis of bourgeois 'conspicuous consumption' 'was becoming obsolete at the moment he enunciated it. The international exposition of 1900, under construction as Veblen's book was being printed, revealed a much more raucous type of conspicuous consumption that appealed to a class which consumed "wastefully" but which was not leisured.' She argues that there was a new fluidity between the bourgeois imitation of the nobility and working class or 'mass consumption', which could not be understood solely on the hierarchical model Veblen employed. Common to all consumers in 'mass consumption' is a much more varied 'dream world', in which 'the consumer tries to realize fantasies through merchandise'. 'Not so much the use of merchandise but the content and variety of the fantasies themselves are what distinguish bourgeois from mass consumption.' *Dream Worlds*, pp. 107, 108, 109.

35. I will discuss this in more detail in Chapter 5. In one of his few discussions of a reformist movement (written in 1894), in fact, Veblen sees the mandate of a workers' movement in the following terms: 'The ostensible purpose of the "Army of the Commonweal" has been the creation of a livelihood for a great number of people by means of a creation of employment, to be effected by a creation of capital through the creation of fiat money. That is to say, on the face of it, the heart of the "movement" is an articulate hallucination.' 'The Army of the Commonweal,' in *Essays in Our Changing Order* (New York: Viking, 1934), p. 97.

36. See Horowitz, *The Morality of Spending*, pp. 37–41.
37. *The Human Condition* (Chicago: University of Chicago Press, 1958), p. 126.
38. *The Human Condition*, p. 130.
39. *The Human Condition*, p. 133.
40. *The Human Condition*, pp. 131–2.
41. *The Human Condition*, p. 133. I will return to this issue in Chapter 4, in reference to Pound's attitude to 'things'. Let me anticipate this by pointing out that Bataille's work, again, is highly symptomatic of the ambivalence towards 'things' that is characteristic of modernism. According to Bataille, religion is an answer to 'the desire that man always had to find himself, to regain an intimacy that was always strangely lost. But the mistake of all religion is to always give man a contradictory answer: *an external form of intimacy*. So the successive solutions only exacerbate the problem: Intimacy is never separated from external elements, without which it could not be *signified*.' For Bataille, the only form of intimacy that can escape the contradiction is based in a destruction of all mediating things, or fetishes – which destruction results in *'being in a sovereign manner'*. In his discussion of 'things', a word which Bataille charges with

ambivalence by italicizing, it becomes apparent how opposed he is to Mauss, who is much more of a fetishist when it comes to the relations of persons and things. Bataille's celebration of the potlatch is opposed to Mauss' evaluation of it as a dangerously exaggerated form of gift exchange. *The Accursed Share*, pp. 129, 131.
42. Oswald Spengler, *Decline of the West*, vol. 2: *Perspectives of World History* (New York: Alfred A. Knopf, 1928), pp. 505, 484, 465.
43. *The Coming American Fascism* (New York: Harper and Row, 1936; rpt. AMS Press, 1972), pp. 225–6.
44. Walter Lippmann, *Interpretations 1931–1932* (New York: Macmillan, 1932), p. 12.
45. Freud, 'Mourning and Melancholia', in *On Metapsychology*, pp. 261–2.
46. Daniel T. Rodgers, *The Work Ethic in Industrial America, 1850–1920* (Chicago: University of Chicago Press, 1978), p. 214.
47. Richard Sennett, *Authority* (New York: Alfred A. Knopf, 1980), pp. 46–7.
48. Rodgers, *The Work Ethic in Industrial America, 1850–1920*, p. 29.
49. *Moving Forward*, p. 83. Ford's defensiveness regarding his paternalism is evident in *My Life and Work* (London: William Heinemann, 1922), p. 130.
50. *Moving Forward*, p. 84.
51. *The Poverty of Abundance: Hoover, the Nation, the Depression* (New York: Oxford University Press, 1965), p. 3.
52. *Authority*, p. 47.
53. According to Edward A. Filene, critics of the culture of mass production fear that 'a social order of material abundance must sap the moral and spiritual fiber of humanity'; after the depression, such critics advocated a return to the ethic of restraint, or thrift, claiming that 'the standard of living had been too high, and that the masses now should be reconciled to living more simply'. A nostalgia for the days when work was its own reward was of course a central theme of anti-union rhetoric. See *Successful Living in This Machine Age*, pp. 13, 56–7.
54. 'The Ego and the Id', in *On Metapsychology*, pp. 368–70, 391 n.1, 370, 394.
55. 'Mourning and Melancholia', in *On Metapsychology*, p. 254.
56. 'The Ego and the Id', in *On Metapsychology*, pp. 374, 389.
57. On the ethics of restraint, see Horowitz, *The Morality of Spending*, passim, and the chapter 'Economizing', in Nicholas Xenos, *Scarcity and Modernity* (New York: Routledge, 1989).
58. Stein critics should be grateful to Lisa Ruddick's *Reading Gertrude Stein: Body, Text, Gnosis* (Ithaca: Cornell University Press, 1990), for taking Stein's sacrificial themes and figures seriously and for putting them on the critical agenda. But I believe Ruddick's account overemphasizes the 'ethics of the remainder', at the expense of what is in effect also an ethic of sacrifice and restraint that can be expressed politically. Ruddick's notion of 'ethics' must remain extremely abstract and even sentimental without taking into account the very

different ethics exemplified by Stein's less canonical writings. The point of taking account here is not to denounce Stein, or to suggest that she has proto-fascist tendencies, but to reveal the ways in which the force of patriarchy can operate and organize the social text even when it appears that it is being resisted or opposed. It will become evident shortly that the definition of 'sacrifice' I am using is quite different from Ruddick's.

59. The typescript of Stein's introduction to the speeches of Marshal Pétain is at the Beinecke Rare Book and Manuscript Library, Yale University; in the time since this book went into production, Stein's introduction has been published in *Modernism/Modernity* 3:3 (1996), pp. 93–6. See also, in the same issue (pp. 69–92), Wanda Van Dusen, 'The Making of a National Fetish: Gertrude Stein's "Introduction to the Speeches of Maréchal Pétain"', which parallels my discussion in many respects.

60. LMN 332. It would be more precise to say that the father is one of the brothers who has come to occupy the position of the ego ideal. Fascism and consumption are both phenomena of what Juliet Flower MacCannell calls 'the regime of the brother'. 'In the modern "artificial group" the "leader," according to Freud, is just like the other members of his group – only greater. He is not necessarily Other, in the manner of a father, not an ego-ideal, but an ideal ego.... [B]y occupying the father's (empty) place, playing his role, the Brother can simulate a symbolic order – imaginarily: he is the paternal metaphor of the artificial collective'. *The Regime of the Brother*, p. 12.

61. As Richard Godden points out in a discussion of this kind of forgetting, '[t]hose who would increase production must necessarily generalize consumption, erasing the memory of labour through the gratification of leisure'. *Fictions of Capital: the American Novel from James to Mailer* (Cambridge: Cambridge University Press, 1990), p. 14.

62. Stein concludes *Brewsie and Willie* with this advice (LMN 441).

63. *The Human Condition*, p. 134.

64. *The Human Condition*, p. 133.

65. *The Philosophy of Money*, ed. David Frisby, trans. Tom Bottomore and David Frisby (New York: Routledge, 1990), pp. 85, 83. It is important to note that in Adam Smith and Simmel, it is not only the negativity of renunciation but also the positivity of suffering (for example, the suffering of labour) that is emphasized. In the Introduction, I discussed this loss in terms of the sacrifice of the particularity that exceeds that to which the self or psyche can lay claim. In Lacanian terms, this sacrifice is 'to give up on [*céder sur*] one's desire'. My argument that mass consumption is the institutionalization of such sacrifice is supported in the work of Doris-Louise Haineault and Jean-Yves Roy, who argue (from the work of René Girard) that 'consumption... involves a sacrificial dimension. Contrary to what happens in friendly exchange, in barter, or in certain other forms of commerce, consumption (of products) only takes place on condition of the surrender of one's money – of one's power – for an

object that has just sealed the agreement. Beyond its obvious economic function, it seems to us that this surrender of power operates in an extremely significant manner on the symbolic level.... Beyond buying power, what the "I" here sacrifices is equally an important part of its object libido as of its narcissistic libido.' Moreover, this sacrifice resembles ritual sacrifice in that it serves 'the greater good of the group': 'in order to avoid the anticipated pangs of separation, the subject here mourns its individuation. Fratricide does not take place.... The "I" [consumes the product] in order to avoid attaining [its] desire and seals, with this sacrifice of self, just as with its buying power, a ritual contract that maintains the "togetherness" of the group. Such a mourning requires enormous, and constant, pressure', which is exerted by advertising as 'a *moral agency*'. See *Unconscious for Sale: Advertising, Psychoanalysis and the Public* (Minnesota: University of Minnesota Press, 1993), pp. 188–9. On Lacan's notion of 'giving up on one's desire', see *The Ethics of Psychoanalysis*, p. 321, where it is translated as 'giving ground relative to one's desire'.
66. See Appadurai, 'Introduction: Commodities and the Politics of Value', in Appadurai, ed., *The Social Life of Things: Commodities in Cultural Perspective* (New York: Cambridge University Press, 1986), pp. 3–5; and Christopher Herbert, *Culture and Anomie: Ethnographic Imagination in the Nineteenth Century* (Chicago: University of Chicago Press, 1991), p. 96.
67. The word 'sacrifice' now carries heavy theoretical baggage along with it, and I by no means want merely to exploit the polysemy of the word. However, I have not found an adequate substitute that can be used, as 'sacrifice' is by Adorno and Horkheimer, to refer to various 'economic' acts, from the ritual sacrifice to the sacrifice of present demands to future rewards. The most important reason for choosing this term is, however, to point out that what is given up never finds an adequate substitute. The reason is the asymmetry of the exchange: what is given up is not an object the value of which can be determined by the system of measure or value the sacrifice institutes. The 'adequacy' of any substitute only becomes possible after the sacrifice that makes such measurement possible.
68. See Jacques Lacan, *The Ethics of Psychoanalysis*, Chapters 4 and 5.
69. *The Body in Pain: the Making and Unmaking of the World* (New York: Oxford University Press, 1985), pp. 172, 277.
70. According to Pound, this was what Roosevelt failed to perceive, and from this failure Pound in 1935 predicts the failure of the New Deal: 'In contrast to the idiotic accumulation of debt by Roosevelt, observe that *if* such government expenditure be necessary or advisable, the direct payment of workers, etc., in stamp scrip would in eight years consume itself, and leave the next decade *free* of all debt. The Roosevelt system is either a fraud or a selling of the nation's children into slavery without the ghost of an excuse' (SP 280).

2 Gertrude Stein's Great Depression

71. Theodor W. Adorno, *Prisms*, trans. Samuel and Shierry Weber (Cambridge: MIT Press, 1983), p. 25; see also p. 56.
72. This tradition also includes the metaphysical tradition of the reserve and retention critiqued by Bataille, Heidegger and Derrida. See Derrida's well-known discussion of Bataille and Hegel in 'From Restricted to General Economy: a Hegelianism Without Reserve', in *Writing and Difference*, trans. Alan Bass (Chicago: University of Chicago Press, 1978), pp. 251–77. For a good discussion of this issue, see Rebecca Comay, 'Economies of "Experience" in Bataille and Heidegger', *Yale French Studies* 78 (1990), pp. 58–89.
73. Stein values 'money' over property because money, like her 'human mind', is without 'relation' or 'necessity'. This was also, for Stein, characteristic of 'romanticism' (see GHA 190, 220–1, 231). It is possible that Stein's notion of romanticism and romance comes from Henry James, one of only a few writers whom she recognized as 'modern'. Mark Seltzer characterizes the difference between romance and the story in James' *The American* in terms that also apply to Stein's economic conceptions: 'What characterizes the romance... is a fantasy of unrelatedness: the radical autonomy of persons. The romance, as opposed to the novel, consists of a "liberated" "kind of experience," above all, relieved of "the inconvenience of a *related*, a measurable state... at large and unrelated."... Hence the turning away from forms of relation and engagement – the turn from novel to romance – is represented as the turn from a story of exchange to a romance exempt from both story and exchange.' *Bodies and Machines* (New York: Routledge, 1992), p. 68.
74. For an excellent discussion of the implicit 'economics' of property in connection with Stein's notions of entity and identity, see Karin Cope, 'Painting after Gertrude Stein', *diacritics* 24: 2–3 (1994), pp. 196–8.

In the next section I will argue that Stein's political economy is fetishistic. Let me anticipate this argument by drawing attention to the fetishistic character of Stein's notion of materiality. As I mentioned in the introduction, William Pietz has attempted to theorize 'the truth of the fetish' from various theories of fetishism. 'The truth of the fetish', he writes, 'resides in its status as a material embodiment.... Marxism's commodity fetish, psychoanalysis's sexual fetish, and modernism's fetish as art object all in an essential way involve the object's untranscended materiality.' More specifically, fetish theory relates 'the activity of the embodied individual to the value of material objects'. This materiality becomes the locus of exchanges between the private 'inside' of the individual and the public 'outside'. The fetish 'can be taken as a name for the total collective material object, at once social and personal.... "Fetish" has always named the incomprehensible mystery of the power of material things to be collective social objects experienced by individuals as truly embodying determinate values or virtues....' 'The Problem of the Fetish, 1', pp. 7, 10, 14.

75. 'Fetishism', *On Sexuality*, p. 353. Though a master-piece 'can have no fear in it', Stein's 'most perfect example of a master-piece' is the passage from *Robinson Crusoe* in which Crusoe first sees 'the footprint of Friday'. Against all of the evidence, Stein insists that 'there is no fear' in Crusoe's abject terror before the 'footprint of Friday'. See *Robinson Crusoe* (New York: Signet, 1961), pp. 152–61. Maximillian Novak emphasizes the importance of Crusoe's fear, tying it in with the social and political-economic assumptions underlying the crisis: 'Lacking the aid of his fellow man and forced to meet every enemy alone, the isolated natural man passes his life in continual expectation of destruction. Crusoe is rescued from this condition by his tools, the symbols of learning, the arts, society, and that civilization which is the reverse of man's natural state. But as soon as he discovers the footprint in the sand, Crusoe returns to his original state in which fear rules every aspect of his life.' *Defoe and the Nature of Man* (Cambridge: Oxford University Press, 1963), p. 34.
76. I am aware that Freud sees fetishism as reserved to the male subject, but it would be wrong I think to follow him in this for many reasons, only one of which is that his judgement is based on biological difference. Fetishism is a possible position of the subject in general, whether that subject is biologically male or female. It is possible also, as I mentioned in the introduction, to understand fetishism as a historically privileged position of the subject in capitalism, if one is willing to read Freud once again with Marx. Nonetheless, 'female fetishism' is coming into prominence in feminist criticism. The history of the critical concept and of the phenomenon is the task of Emily Apter's *Feminizing the Fetish: Psychoanalysis and Narrative Obsession in Turn-of-the-Century France* (Ithaca: Cornell University Press, 1991). Sarah Kofman is one of the crucial references for a feminist reading of the Derridean concept of a 'generalized fetishism'. See 'Ça cloche' in *Lectures de Derrida* (Paris: Galilée, 1986). Naomi Schor is an important precursor to Apter's work. See for example 'Female Fetishism: the Case of George Sand', in *The Female Body in Western Culture*, ed. Susan Suleiman (Cambridge: Harvard University Press, 1986). For a reading of Freud's concept of fetishism as implying a political lesbian subjectivity, see Elizabeth Grosz, 'Lesbian Fetishism?' in Emily Apter and William Pietz, eds, *Fetishism as Cultural Discourse* (Ithaca: Cornell University Press, 1993), pp. 101–15.
77. The 'St. Therese' to whom Stein refers appears in her opera, 'Four Saints in Three Acts', *Last Operas and Plays* (New York: Vintage, 1975), pp. 440–80.
78. 'All Of It'; manuscript in the Beinecke Rare Book and Manuscript Library, Yale University.
79. The temporalization of the 'present' or the 'now' in the postwar economy of 'distribution and equilibration' is not *only* the subjection of all value to the relativity of measure determined as equivalence on the market, and thus the disappearance of the unique 'now'. This economy of exchange is haunted still by the gift or the present.

The deferral of the thing itself is a deferral of what is beyond equivalence, what is beyond the measure of exchange. The economy and temporality of distribution and equilibration harbours within it the *demand* for the thing, beyond measure, value beyond value, even as the function of the economy of exchange would seem to be to destroy its possibility. Yet if temporalization is seen to be temporization, if temporalization is seen as *giving up the thing in order to guarantee its presence*, then the function of equivalence is to guarantee the future return of the equivalent without equal, made tangible in exchange undertaken with an eye to the general equivalent, the commodity of commodities that is both within and without their circulation. For a discussion of 'temporization' and 'temporalization' in connection with Marcel Mauss' analysis of the gift, see Jacques Derrida, *Given Time*, trans. Peggy Kamuf (Chicago: University of Chicago Press, 1992), pp. 39–40.
80. Marcel Mauss, *The Gift*, p. 100, n. 29.
81. *Wars I Have Seen* (New York: Random House, 1945), p. 93.
82. I am referring to Kant's well-known example of money in his discussion of *quanta*, which appears in 'Anticipations of Perception'. Kant writes: 'If I called thirteen thalers a quantum of money, I should be correct, provided my intention is to state the value of a mark of fine silver. For this is a continuous magnitude, in which no part is the smallest, and in which every part can constitute a piece of coin that always contains material for still smaller pieces. But if I understand by the phrase thirteen round thalers, so many coins, apart from the question of what their silver standard may be, I then use the phrase, quantum of thalers, inappropriately. It ought to be entitled an aggregate, that is, a number of pieces of money. But as a unity must be presupposed in all number, appearance as unity is a quantum, and as a quantum is always a continuum.' *Critique of Pure Reason*, trans. Norman Kemp Smith (London: Macmillan, 1950), p. 204. In terms of the mathematical sublime, this distinction reappears in the difference between the logical and the aesthetic estimation of quantity. See *The Critique of Judgment*, trans. J.H. Bernard (New York: Hafner Press, 1951), pp. 89–95 (section 26).
83. See *Capital: a Critique of Political Economy*, vol. 1, trans. Ben Fowkes (New York: Vintage, 1977), p. 152. I will return to this point in some detail in Chapter 5.
84. Jean-Joseph Goux, in his study of the isomorphy between the 'symbolic economies' of Marx and Freud, has compared this stage of exchange to the oral stage of incorporation, in which 'c'est la valeur reconnue après coup à l'objet déja perdu, valeur qui ne trouve sa première expression que dans le corps de celui qui le supplée'. *Economie et symbolique* (Paris: Seuil, 1973), p. 66.
85. *Capital*, vol. 1, p. 154.
86. Alfred Sohn-Rethel, *Intellectual and Manual Labour* (London: Macmillan, 1978), p. 19.
87. Žižek has an excellent discussion of the difference between the 'classical' and the 'hard-boiled' detective that is similar to the distinction

I am making. The latter, he argues, is driven by 'a certain debt', while the classical detective, who seems to be in it only for the money, is in effect *disavowing the debt*. See *Looking Awry* (Cambridge: MIT Press, 1991), pp. 60–1.

88. Stein says that her recent lecture-tour of America demonstrated to her that 'the country had a feeling that it was most awfully sick it had so many symptoms'. A similar sickness overtook America in the nineteenth century, she says, and Lincoln responded by saying that the country needed a doctor. Americans in the thirties felt they too 'did have to have a doctor and so they all remembered where the capital is' (HWW 74).

89. The claim for the postmodernity of Stein's formal innovations has been frequently made, with good reason; but the meaning of postmodernism and of formal innovation is rarely questioned in terms of any larger social or historical categories. An exception to this is Ellen Berry's *Curved Thought and Textual Wandering: Gertrude Stein's Postmodernism* (Ann Arbor: University of Michigan Press, 1992). Berry's analysis is valuable for being forthright in defining postmodernism, though her forthrightness reveals her uncritical affirmation of the 'emerging mass culture' of the early twentieth century. As Berry writes, 'Stein's texts not only anticipate many of the forms and logics widely evident in postmodern cultural practices; they also represent one of the first attempts to articulate the modern *through* the popular rather than in reaction to it. Stein refused the rigid dividing line erected by many modernists between high and low art, a barrier that also marks the great divide between modernism and our own cultural postmodernity' (p. 134). Berry makes apparent some of the political and cultural assumptions of the numerous readers of Stein who have attempted to see her as postmodern *avant la lettre*.

90. Russell Berman, following Adorno and the Frankfurt School, has argued that the avant-garde in effect contributed to the emergence of postmodern mass culture by way of its dialectical (and thus disavowed) defence of the emancipatory values of bourgeois autonomous art. The destruction of autonomy and the subsequent 'universal aestheticization' serves as a condition for the construction of the postmodern 'popular' culture of consumption. From this perspective, Stein is both modern and avant-garde in that the human mind must be everywhere and nowhere at once. *Modern Culture and Critical Theory: Art, Politics, and the Legacy of the Frankfurt School* (Madison: University of Wisconsin Press, 1989), p. 50.

3 Value from Obligation

91. As I will argue in more detail in Chapter 4, private corporations were ahead of the public sector in attempting to develop forms of group or corporate identities. Stein complains elsewhere that there is 'too much organization' at all levels of social life. The word 'organization' in this kind of argument for self-reliance stretches back to

Emerson, but was also current during the late nineteenth and early twentieth century, when the American economy was being reorganized according to corporate structures. See Richard Hofstadter, *The Age of Reform* (New York: Vintage, 1955), Chapter VI, 'The Struggle over Organization', for a discussion of the ideological terms of the debate. See also Alan Trachtenberg, *The Incorporation of America: Culture and Society in the Gilded Age* (New York: Hill and Wang, 1982), Chapters 2 and 3, for a discussion of the ideological consequences of the rise of the corporation.

92. Robert M. MacIver, 'The Ambiguity of the New Deal' (1934), reprinted in *New Deal Thought*, edited by Howard Zinn (Indianapolis: Bobbs-Merrill, 1966), pp. 58–9.

93. George's description of 'value from obligation' brings out the structure of domination involved: 'These ways of giving an additional value to things already in existence or of bringing out value in things which may have no more tangible existence than an act of mind, a verbal promise, a paper note, an act of legislature, a decision of court or a common habit or custom, are clearly of totally different origin and nature from the ways in which value originates from the expenditure of labour in the production of wealth or services, and readily to distinguish them we need a classifying name. It is because the word obligation best consorts with existing customs, and best expresses the common character of the element distinct from production that gives value, that I speak of value from obligation as distinct from value from production. For the common character of all that I am here speaking of is that their possession enables the possessor to command or compel others to render exertion without any return of exertion on his part to them. This power to command labor without the return of labor constitutes on the other side an obligation, and it is this that gives value.

'Thus a verbal promise, a bank-account, a promissory note, or any other instrument of indebtedness, an annuity, an insurance policy, things which frequently have value, derive that value from the fact that they express an obligation fixed, unfixed or merely contingent to render exertion to the holder or assignee without return. This value may be increased sometimes even by the destruction of valuable things, as the Dutch East India Company kept up the value of spices in Europe by destroying great quantities of spices in the islands where they grew...'. Henry George, *The Science of Political Economy* (New York: Robert Schalkenbach Foundation, 1962; originally published 1897), pp. 282–3.

94. The melancholic narrative means that the father does not owe his subjects in return for what they have given up to him, as a bank would owe one for what one deposits there. However, we will see in the last two sections of this chapter how the subject (in this case the 'je' of Georges Hugnet's 'Enfances') can act as if it has placed a deposit with the father, and attempt to cash in on the promise as if there were some substance to its claims. On the Kantian metaphor of the deposit, as used by Lacan in 'Kant avec Sade', see

Juliet Flower MacCannell, *Figuring Lacan: Criticism and the Cultural Unconscious* (Lincoln: University of Nebraska Press, 1986), p. 146.

95. The context of Stein's reflections on money would go back to the periodic monetary debates that came to a head in the United States after the 1893 depression. Important discussions of the general problems of representation raised by the 'silver question' and the printing of 'greenbacks' can be found in Walter Benn Michaels, *The Gold Standard and the Logic of Naturalism* (Berkeley: University of California Press, 1987), pp. 139–80, and Marc Shell, *Money, Language, and Thought* (Baltimore: Johns Hopkins University Press, 1982), pp. 5–24.

96. As Kant writes in his acccount of the mathematical sublime, 'the concept of number must disappear or be changed' (*Critique of Judgment*, p. 98). Though this is not the place to do it, an extended comparison could be made between Stein's discussion of Roosevelt's 'electioneering' and Kant's discussion of the mathematical sublime, particularly in section 26 of *The Critique of Judgment*.

97. Hamlet's ambivalence towards this enjoyment prevents his fulfilling his task, and makes him occupy his time with detective work. Though the fact that he knows everything in advance implies that there is no need for detection, Hamlet remains in some doubt as to the authority of the paternal source of his knowledge. Hamlet's detective work is in fact a symptom of the human mind in its disavowed relation to the paternal will.

98. The economy of names and naming is crucial to Stein's work. As the epigraph to this chapter suggests, the economy of names involves value by obligation and gratitude ('Thank you for a name'), as well as the refusal of that position ('Thank nobody for the same'). In the first chapter of *Four in America* (1934), Stein reflects on the name of Ulysses S. Grant: 'Grant in his very early life was under obligation to an older man named Simpson and took his name' (FA 3): 'Hiram Ulysses' became 'Ulysses Simpson'. Stein is most 'interested' in Christian names (like Gertrude) because they 'mean more than the surname', but in the case of Grant she does not like any of the first names: 'I try to think that I like the name of Hiram or even of Ulysses but really I do not. Why do I not. Because I never had the habit of saying either one or the other as the name of some one, while I have had the habit of saying Grant, and Grant is a name' (FA 7). 'Grant' is of course not only a name, but also a common noun, as Stein makes evident by beginning with the point 'that Grant did not earn a living' (FA 8). Could the fact that he never worked for a wage be reflected in his giving up the Christian name, 'Hiram'? Workers, as we saw, could be either 'employees' or 'hired men'. Grant is not a 'hired man', a 'Hiram', because he does not earn a living. His economic position seems to be revealed by his last name, 'Grant'. His proper name implies an indebtedness; he has been 'granted' his name. The name 'Simpson' was taken because of his obligation to an older man, in order to pay off his debt, or to indicate his indebtedness. The name 'Grant' bears with it a surplus of 'value from obligation'.

Notes

99. For two brief accounts of the story of the translation, see Meyerowitz's summary in LMN 273, and Richard Bridgman, *Gertrude Stein in Pieces* (New York: Oxford University Press, 1970), pp. 201–2.
100. Stein later republished the poem in the Plain Edition under the new title, 'Before the Flowers of Friendship Faded Friendship Faded'. The first poem was published opposite Hugnet's in *Pagany*, 2:1, Winter, 1931. It appeared in its own volume in the Plain Edition in 1931, and is now collected in LMN 274–87. Hugnet's poem was later published separately. My references to Hugnet's poem in parentheses throughout this chapter are to the *Pagany* version, despite its at times faulty French, and its exclusion of the final lines of Stein's poem. My references to Stein's poem are to the Meyerowitz edition, since that is the one most readily available.
101. *Capital*, vol. 1, p. 284.
102. This has been one of the most important questions raised by contemporary Stein critics, and most thoroughly discussed in Marianne DeKoven, *A Different Language* (Madison: University of Wisconsin Press, 1983). DeKoven's stylistic analyses are useful for understanding Stein's relationship to a patriarchal language, but I agree with Lisa Ruddick that it is also important to examine the fantastic scenes or stagings of gender constructions in Stein's work. This kind of reading is best exemplified by Ruddick's analysis of the 'scene of sacrifice' staged by *Tender Buttons*. See Chapter 4 of *Reading Gertrude Stein*.
103. Julia Kristeva calls the thing, 'l'objet originaire, cet "en-soi" qui reste toujours à traduire, la cause ultime de la traductibilité.... C'est parce que le traduit est déjà là que la traductible peut être imaginé et posé comme excédent ou incommensurable.' See *Soleil noir: dépression et mélancolie* (Paris: Gallimard, 1987), p. 77.
104. Hugnet's poem follows the law of the pleasure principle, which is regulated by the law of refinding the lost object; Stein, on the other hand, says that 'it is not for pleasure that I do it'. This refusal of pleasure makes possible the emergence of the other law which, according to Lacan, obtains at the limit of the pleasure principle. With the appearance of this other law, the legality or justice of the distributions effected by the pleasure principle finds itself challenged. The thing haunts the economy like a hidden surplus, an original excess – what Hugnet calls a *don* or 'gift'. It is nearby, haunting each object that circulates in the system of exchanges set up by the pleasure principle. See the second chapter of *The Ethics of Psychoanalysis* for Lacan's discussion of the limit of the pleasure principle.
105. See *Reading Gertrude Stein*, p. 218.
106. 'Mourning and Melancholia', in *On Metapsychology*, pp. 254–5.
107. As we saw in the last chapter, Stein says that the 'first thing' in a detective story 'is the dead man or if not a dead woman' (GHA 127). In this poem, the man's life depends on the death of the woman, but that life is haunted by this 'first thing'.
108. 'The Ego and the Id', in *On Metapsychology*, pp. 394, 374, 389.
109. Stein echoes Hugnet's 'd'oubli' with her 'double' and 'doublet'.
110. See Lacan's comments on 'the limit of pain' in *The Ethics of Psychoanalysis*, pp. 59–60.

111. For example, this child appears in the sentence 'Any little one will kill himself for milk', Stein's version of 'enfance homicide' (22/280).
112. These last four lines are not included in the *Pagany* copy of the poem. The layout of the page suggests that there was simply not enough room. The lines are restored in the version printed in Meyerowitz's edition (LMN 287), and in the Plain Edition.
113. Another of Stein's important and recurring epithets appears in this poem: 'Look at me now and here I am.' The disjunction between the epithet (when this you see, *see* me) and the epitaph (when this you see *remember* me) is that between presence and absence, united in the 'this', the very act of indication. Stein's 'I' thus presents or stages itself as divided between death and life, or absence and presence. This is quite different from Hugnet's 'je' making a total claim to 'la vie', and his insistence on the return of an unmediated 'présence sans mémoire'. According to Freud, melancholia is 'the transformation of object-libido into narcissistic libido'. It is related to the demand for love: the ego is 'forcing itself, so to speak, upon the id as a love-object and is trying to make good the id's loss by saying: "Look, you can love me too – I am so like the object."' ('The Ego and the Id,' in *On Metapsychology*, pp. 368–9.) Stein's epithets and epitaphs repeat this gesture of self-presentation while at the same time acknowledging that what is presented is hollowed out by the loss.
114. Recall that he appeals to 'le droit d'être dans mon tort par plaisir, / comme la peste et la famine' (20).
115. Jacques le Goff, *Your Money or Your Life: Economy and Religion in the Middle Ages* (New York: Zone, 1988), p. 23.

4 'New Deal or Steal'

116. For excellent discussions of the institutions of the corporation and the trust as instances of Emersonian discourse, see Howard Horwitz, *By the Law of Nature: Form and Value in Nineteenth-Century America* (New York: Oxford University Press, 1991), pp. 171–91, and Christopher Newfield, 'Emerson's Corporate Individualism', *American Literary History* 3:4 (1991), pp. 657–84.
117. For the Monte de Paschi, that is to say 'the Mount of Pity (or Hock Shop)' (C 210), and Pound's most extensive discussion of banking, see Cantos 42–4, which lead up to Canto 45, the famous 'Usura Canto'.
118. R. Jeffrey Lustig, *Corporate Liberalism: The Origins of Modern American Liberal Theory, 1890–1920* (Berkeley: University of California Press, 1982), p. 139.
119. *The Education of Henry Adams* (New York: Random House, 1931), p. 455.
120. Alexis de Tocqueville, *Democracy in America*, vol. 2 (New York: Vintage, 1945), pp. 336–9.
121. Charles Francis Adams, Jr, and Henry Adams, *Chapters of Erie* (Ithaca: Cornell University Press, 1956), p. 98.

122. For Pound, of course, this need not be a contradiction, as his definition of 'Fascio' reveals: 'A thousand candles together blaze with intense brightness. No one candle's light damages another's. So is the liberty of the individual in the ideal and fascist state' (SP 306).
123. On Pound and entrepreneurialism, see Robert Casillo, *The Genealogy of Demons*, pp. 191–203.
124. As Michael North argues, fascism was attractive to Pound and others because it 'promised to fulfill the individual *and* to restrain individualism, to set free localities and professions *and* to meld every group into one great whole, to liberate the particular from iron abstractions *and* to find one great abstraction to fulfill every particular'. Michael North, *The Political Aesthetic of Yeats, Pound, and Eliot* (New York: Cambridge University Press, 1992), pp. 165–6. Leo Panitch writes that corporatism 'finds its modern roots in those versions of nineteenth-century social and political thought which reacted against the individualism and competition which characterized the emerging dominance of the capitalist mode of production, and against the industrial and political conflict of classes which was the ineluctable product of this development. Although the varieties of corporatist theory are many, the common premise was that class harmony and organic unity were essential to society and could be secured if the various functional groups, and especially the organizations of capital and labour, were imbued with a conception of mutual rights and obligations somewhat similar to that presumed to have united the medieval estates in a stable society'. 'The Development of Corporatism in Liberal Democracies', *Comparative Political Studies* 10:1 (April 1977), p. 61.
125. *Corporate Liberalism*, p. 90.
126. As the English jurist F.W. Maitland pointed out in the introduction to his translation of Otto Gierke's influential *Political Theories of the Middle Age* (Cambridge: Cambridge University Press, 1922), contract is 'the greediest of legal categories', which even succeeded historically in moving from the economic to the political sphere, to take over the state with the theory of the social contract. Anglo-American contract law developed from Roman partnership theory, the *societas* of private law; as a result of ignoring a more apt source of reflection on the state and groups, namely the notion of *universitas* from Roman public law, enlightened liberal theory is unable to conceive of organic voluntarist groups. The Roman concept of partnership also started to dominate political theory at the end of the Middle Ages, when the state was conceived not in terms of an 'act of incorporation', but as a partnership. 'The political theory reacted upon legal theory. When the State itself had become a merely collective unit – a sum of presently existing individuals bound together by the operation of their own wills – it was not likely that any other group would seem capable of withstanding similar analysis' (xxiii). Only in Germany were attempts made to maintain a concept of *universitas*. This can be attributed to 'the persistence in Germany of agrarian communities with world-old histories, to the

intricate problems that their dissolution presented, and to the current complaint that Roman law had no equitable solution for these questions and had done scant justice to the peasant' (xxv). Maitland has a hypothetical German jurist defend his position against an English or American critic: 'our German Fellowship (*Genossen*) is no fiction, no symbol, no piece of the State's machinery, no collective name for individuals, but a living organism and a real person, with body and members and a will of its own.... It is not a fictitious person; it is a *Gesammtperson*, and its will is a *Gesammtwill*; it is a group-person, and its will is a group-will' (xxvi).

127. This tendency to transcend the legal forms it is simultaneously necessary to exploit is already evident in the development of the trust, which as its name implies appealed to traditional pre-contractual personal forms of exchange in order to avoid the legalities of the contract. In his testimony before an investigating committee in 1879, H.H. Rogers found it necessary to deny that the Standard Oil Trust was an 'arrangement', since that would imply contractual obligations. As Horwitz points out, 'Rogers insists that the Standard is composed only of "harmony"'. *By the Law of Nature*, pp. 184–5.

128. Lustig, *Corporate Liberalism*, p. 67.

129. The flexibility inherent in the fiction theory of corporations was crucial to certain anti-trust cases, but this flexibility first becomes apparent in certain decisions of the Supreme Court against labour unions. As I. Maurice Wormser states, '[p]ressed to a logical extreme', the fiction theory would make it 'impossible to hold that corporations – artificial beings, both invisible and intangible, – can commit torts or be held guilty of crimes.... in Anglo-American law this point of view until recent years has largely prevailed, "though," as Judge Cardozo has noted, "rifts in its uniformity are visible here and there." An example of such a rift is the recent decision of the Supreme Court of the United States in the United Mine Workers case, ruling that a trade union may be sued in the law courts as a legal entity and personality, though unincorporated.' *Frankenstein, Incorporated* (New York: McGraw-Hill, 1931), p. 58. Recent court decisions also draw comment from Maitland, who sees them as evidence that Anglo-American law is hopelessly contradictory on the question of what is and is not a corporation. See *Political Theories of the Middle Age*, pp. xxxiii–iv.

130. Richard Sennett, *Authority*, p. 82. R. Jeffrey Lustig has an excellent discussion of this strain of thought in Andrew Carnegie, whose break with liberal traditions 'was really the first of a new species of liberalism that would entirely divorce questions of personal fulfillment from matters of work.... Carnegie's scheme ... generously promised redemption from sin, and redemption through freely given grace rather than the exclusive efforts of the sufferer. But in conceiving of man as a recipient rather than an actor and acquiescing in the devaluation of work, Carnegie demeaned the very mode of activity through which Americans had traditionally expected

Notes

to surmount existential trials and achieve personal worth.' Carnegie's challenge demonstrated that the new liberalism 'would have to follow Comte toward an organically defined individualism, a greatly diminished liberty, and a paternalism that was distinguished from domination only by the fact that workers in the new order would never be permitted to voice their own interests in the first place'. *Corporate Liberalism*, p. 103.

131. Zukofsky's line has a more disturbing, because nonironic, analogue in Pound's Canto 41, where 'the commandante della piazza' insists that he would 'get scragged for Mussolini' ('Noi ci facciam sgannar per Mussolini') (C 202).

132. In William Henry George's words, Tocqueville's individualism 'is "corporative" – a strong central power limited and checked by a distribution of authority among secondary bodies. It is administrative deconcentration and political decentralization'. 'Montesquieu and De Tocqueville and Corporative Individualism', *American Political Science Review* 16 (February, 1922), pp. 18–19.

133. According to Dewey, the fictive and concession theories of the corporation, '[i]n spite of their historical logical divergence, ... flowed together', as 'is exhibited in many decisions of American judges', particularly those against trade unions. This convergence is the source of the flexibility referred to above (see note 14). 'Corporate Personality', in *The Later Works: 1925–1953*, vol. 2: *1925–1927* (Carbondale and Edwardsville: Southern Illinois University Press, 1984), pp. 37, 39.

134. 'It is nature, the actual existence of goods, or the possibility of producing them, that really determines the capacity of the state. Yet it resides above in the will and the physical force of the people. And the will becomes concentrated in the few' (SP 312).

135. Money 'is a symbol of collaboration. It is a certificate of work done within a system, estimated, or "consecrated," by the state' (SP 311).

136. 'A single commodity (EVEN GOLD) base for money is not satisfactory. / STATE AUTHORITY behind the printed note is the best means of establishing a JUST and HONEST currency.... / SOVEREIGNTY inheres in the right to ISSUE money (tickets) and to determine the value thereof' (SP 292).

137. See SP 276–7. For an account of Pound's discovery of Gesell, see Tim Redman, *Ezra Pound and Italian Fascism* (New York: Cambridge University Press, 1989), pp. 122–52. For the record of Pound's own response to Gesell, see 'The Individual in His Milieu: a Study of Relations and Gesell', written in 1935 (SP 272–82), on which I base much of my interpretation of Pound's economics during the thirties. The other important texts for Pound's theories in this period include: 'What is Money For? (SP 290–302); 'A Visiting Card' (SP 306–35); and 'Gold and Work 1944' (SP 336–51).

138. 'In Pound We Trust: the Economy of Poetry / the Poetry of Economics,' *Critical Inquiry* 14 (Autumn, 1987), p. 152. Sieburth's is one of the best psychoanalytic accounts of the theory of *Schwundgeld*.

139. I am referring to Marx's discussion of 'the transformation of money into capital', especially Part 2, Chapter 4 of *Capital* (pp. 247–57).

For a 'libidinal' reading of post-war German inflation and the 1929 crash in this light, see Jean-François Lyotard, *Economie libidinale* (Paris: Editions de Minuit, 1974), pp. 271–86.
140. Or in the terms provided by my reading of Stein, the father is only a brother who has been permitted to occupy the place of the father.
141. Zukofsky's metaphor for the economy is primarily musical, but the 'struck bars' are also bars of gold.
142. Anson Rabinbach, *The Human Motor: Energy, Fatigue, and the Origins of Modernity* (New York: Basic Books, 1990), pp. 74–5.
143. Marx, 'The Communist Manifesto', in *Selected Writings*, ed. David McLellan (Oxford: Oxford University Press), pp. 232–3.
144. Lustig, *Corporate Liberalism*, p. 18.
145. Daniel J. Boorstin, *The Americans: the Democratic Experience* (New York: Random House, 1973), pp. 413, 421.
146. *The Americans: the Democratic Experience*, pp. 423–4. The anti-trust debate made the new concept of property familiar. As Walter Lippmann wrote in 1914, '[w]hen a man buys stock in some large corporation he becomes in theory one of its owners. He is supposed to be exercising his instinct of private property. But how in fact does he exercise that instinct which we are told is the only real force in civilization? He may never see *his* property. He may not know where his property is situated. He is not consulted as to its management. He would be utterly incapable of advice if he were consulted.... Private property will melt away; its functions will be taken over by the salaried men who direct them, by government commissions, by developing labor unions. The stockholders deprived of their property rights are being transformed into moneylenders'. *Drift and Mastery: an Attempt to Diagnose the Current Unrest* (Englewood Cliffs, NJ: Prentice-Hall, 1961; originally published 1914), pp. 45, 49.
147. Henry Adams, *The Degradation of the Democratic Dogma*, ed. and introduced by Brooks Adams (New York: Capricorn, 1958), p. 95.
148. *Chapters of Erie*, pp. 95–6.
149. In Pound's historical context, these lines must also refer to the bourgeois imitation of aristocratic leisure that Veblen called 'conspicuous consumption'. Despite the dematerialization of property into what Zukofsky calls the 'immaterial wealth' and 'intangible assets' of corporate culture, sumptuary display is still crucial to the new economy of consumer credit, which relies on the displacements of desire.
150. *The Education of Henry Adams*, pp. 338, 337.
151. My reference to 'enjoyment' comes from Zukofsky. John Quincy Adams, cited by Zukofsky, longed to build observatories in order to witness what was for him 'something / Of awful enjoyment', which included the '[p]erpetual revolution of the Great and Little Bear round the pole...' (*A* 72). The citations are made to echo with the citations concerning the revolution of the great Russian bear, and therefore also the place of 'awful enjoyment' in historical revolutions.

152. Zukofsky must have noticed that when Henry Adams encountered the dynamo, he considered that 'its value lay chiefly in its occult mechanism. Between the dynamo in the gallery of machines and the engine-house outside, the break of continuity amounted to abysmal fracture for a historian's objects. No more relation could he discover between the steam and the electric current than between the Cross and the cathedral. The forces were interchangeable if not reversible, but he could see only an absolute *fiat* in electricity as in faith.' *The Education of Henry Adams*, p. 381. The same *fiat* or appearance *ex nihilo* is what Zukofsky sees as constituting commodities as fetishistic appearance, where 'labor' is in the position of Adams' 'steampower'.

5 Animated Things

153. The original context from which Pound cites does not simplify the task of determining Pound's own relation to the utterance. The lines are spoken by New York Republican Ambrose Spencer in an argument against extending the vote to labourers, since they are in fact under the control of their employers. Pound's source is George Bancroft, *Martin Van Buren to the End of His Public Career* (New York, 1889), p. 80.
154. My italics. See *Chapters of Erie* (New York: Cornell University Press, 1956; originally published 1886), pp. 96–8, for the text borrowed by Zukofsky.
155. *Chapters of Erie*, pp. 95–6.
156. *Capital*, vol. 1, pp. 176–7.
157. I will argue this in more detail in the next section of this chapter, when I discuss Zukofsky's citation of Marx's account of labour. Suffice it to say for now that, according to Marx, 'what distinguishes the worst architect from the best of bees is that the architect builds the cell in his mind before he constructs it in wax. At the end of every labour process, a result emerges which had already been conceived by the worker at the beginning, hence already existed ideally. Man not only effects a change of form in the materials of nature; he also realizes his own purpose in those materials. And this is a purpose he is conscious of, it determines the mode of his activity with the rigidity of a law, and he must subordinate his will to it'. *Capital*, vol. 1, p. 284. On the assumptions and theoretical consequences of Marx's 'intentional-teleological' model of labour, see Seyla Benhabib, *Critique, Norm, and Utopia*, p. 134 ff.
158. See Bataille, *The Accursed Share*, vol. 1, pp. 121–7.
159. Casillo may in one sense be correct in suggesting that the courtly lover 'hopes for the ultimate realization of his investment of time and emotion: not monetary but sexual possession'. However, sexual consummation of the erotic relation is not the end of the discipline of courtly love; this is only the *representation* of courtly love. As we have seen in the case of Canto 36, the 'formèd trace', or the 'fine thing held in the mind', is itself the end of the discipline.

The kind of 'possession' that Pound has in mind reflects the dematerialization and transformation of property required of corporate culture. Robert Casillo, 'Troubador Love and Usury in Ezra Pound's Writings', *Texas Studies in Literature and Language* 27 (Summer, 1985), pp. 127, 131.

160. I borrow this formula from Lacan, who analyses courtly love in connection with suffering in order to reinterpret sublimation as the production of cultural value. See *The Ethics of Psychoanalysis*, Chapter 11. Courtly love valorizes and eroticizes suffering, or, in Simmel's terms, *sacrifice*. Such love would seem to go to the extreme of self-abasement, an exhaustion of narcissistic reserves in the gamble of the *merci*, or the *don d'amour*. Yet what this total expenditure – even if it be to the death – leads to is the preservation of one's investment in the object as a guarantee. This is exactly what Zukofsky portrays as the extreme moment of commodity fetishism. The libido in love is object libido; it is, however, founded on a reserve of narcissistic libido 'bound' in the ego ideal.

161. Though there is almost no sign of it in the seamless final published version of *A*-9, the two halves of the poem were written eight years apart, and Zukofsky was circulating mimeographed copies of the 'First Half', with notes and a commentary, in 1940. My reading suggests, incidentally, that the two halves of the poem not be read as synchronous, the first as the poem of light and the second of love. They should rather be read diachronically, the second revising or translating the first, which nonetheless contained the implications that would only be drawn out in the second half. The most extensive reading of *A*-9, which however fails to take at all seriously the Marxism and its revision, can be found in Peter Quartermain, *Disjunctive Poetics: from Gertrude Stein and Louis Zukofsky to Susan Howe* (New York: Cambridge University Press, 1992), pp. 70–90. An excellent reading that does consider the Marxism as well as the gap between the two halves is Michael Davidson, 'Dismantling "Mantis": Reification and Objectivist Poetics', *American Literary History* 3:3 (1991), esp. pp. 528–37.

162. *Capital*, vol. 1, pp. 548–9.

163. The argument that Marxism relies on the economic forms it subjects to critique leads to 'the paradox of an emancipatory movement which claims to suppress capital even while preserving what it draws its nourishment and strength from: labour as it has developed since the industrial revolution.... [It continues] to express the themes of the extraction of value from scarce resources and the primacy of production and consumption over other social activities'. Jean-Marie Vincent, *Abstract Labour: a Critique* (London: Macmillan, 1991), p. 51.

164. As Marx writes in a discussion of Aristotle's failure to identify labour as the source of value: 'The secret of the expression of value, namely the equality and equivalence of all kinds of labor because and in so far as they are human labor in general, could not be deciphered until the concept of human equality had already acquired the per-

manence of a fixed popular opinion. This however becomes possible only in a society where the commodity-form is the universal form of the product of labor, hence the dominant social relation is the relation between men as possessors of commodities.' *Capital*, vol. 1, p. 152.

165. Despite his very useful discussion of Zukofsky's Marx and Spinoza, Jeffrey Twitchell has not considered the problem of conceiving of a notion of 'equality' that is not tied historically to the forms of equality determined by the requirements of capital. The division and abstraction that characterize modernity are not simply ideological errors, but are historically imposed, and cannot be overcome with more accurate theories of immanence or with the ethical response of love. By making both of these claims on Zukofsky's behalf, Twitchell denies Zukofsky's critical fetishism and makes him over into a Poundian fetishist: rather than being a symptom of fetishism, 'love lays bare the false semblance of commodity fetishism or of abstraction'. Moreover, the equivalence made possible by love 'is the standard of value when the eye of love conceives, seeing a world of men's labor where abstractions are tangible, or in Spinozian terms, where thought and body are understood as identical. "Related is equated" is the same as seeing the resemblances among diverse things ("all hues") according to their "natural use," which in one sense refers back to their use-value: all made things are related in the sense that they are desirable, fulfill some natural human desire or need which motivates the labor expended on them in the first place'. How can this be true rather than merely sentimental when labour has historically become abstract and commodities bear only the traces of the violence done to specific concrete forms of labour? See Jeffrey Twitchell, 'Tuning the Senses: Cavalcanti, Marx, Spinoza and Zukofsky's *A*,' *Sagetrieb* 11:3 (1992), pp. 81–2.
166. Both essays appear in *The Place of Science in Modern Civilisation* (New York, 1932).
167. *The Place of Science in Modern Civilisation* (New York, 1932), p. 22.
168. *The Place of Science in Modern Civilisation* (New York, 1932), pp. 6–7.
169. *The Place of Science in Modern Civilisation* (New York, 1932), pp. 6–7.
170. *The Place of Science in Modern Civilisation* (New York, 1932), p. 7.
171. *The Place of Science in Modern Civilisation* (New York, 1932), p. 16.
172. *The Place of Science in Modern Civilisation* (New York, 1932), pp. 34–5, n. 2.
173. In his comments Adorno cites the relevant passage: 'All the happiness which for [Veblen] is excluded by dreamless realism, by pliant adaptation to the conditions of the industrial world, is reflected in the image of a paradisical golden age. "The conditions under which men lived in the most primitive stages of associated life that can properly be called human, seem to have been of a peaceful kind; and the character – the temperament and spiritual attitude of men under these early conditions of environment and institutions seems to have been of a peaceful and unaggressive, not to say an indolent

cast. . . . Under the circumstances of the sheltered situation in which the leisure class is placed there seems, therefore, to be something of a reversion to the range of non-invidious impulses that characterise the ante-predatory savage culture. The reversion comprises both the sense of workmanship and the proclivity to indolence and good-fellowship"'. 'Veblen's Attack on Culture', *Prisms*, pp. 87–8.
174. *Capital*, vol. 1, p. 284.
175. *Capital*, vol. 1, p. 289.
176. John Dewey points out the ground shared by the attitude that separates means and ends: 'The cases in which ends and means fall apart are the abnormal ones, the ones which deviate from activity which is intelligently conducted. Wherever, for example, there is sheer drudgery, there is separation of the required and necessary means from both the end in view and the end attained. Wherever, on the other side, there is a so-called "ideal," which is utopian and a matter of fantasy, the same separation occurs, now from the side of the so-called *end*. Means that do not become constituent elements of the very ends or consequences they produce form what are called "necessary evils" . . .'. John Dewey, *Theory of Valuation* (Chicago: University of Chicago Press, 1939), p. 49. Dewey's account of the separation of means and ends finds its exemplar in industrial production, in which Dewey's two cases are intricated one with the other: where there is drudgery and the separation of ends and means, as in industrial production, there will be compensation, the sphere of consumption providing 'a so-called "ideal," which is utopian and a matter of fantasy'.
177. In his discussion of 'the change in the functioning of capitalism in the information age', Brian Massumi reads Deleuze and Guattari's concept of 'surplus value of flow' as 'a kind of surplus value that is created in the process of circulation itself.' He revises Marx's formula (M – C – M') in terms of the commodity (C) and its *image* (I), to conclude that the value of the commodity 'is now defined more by the desire it arouses than by the amount of labor that goes into it'. See *A User's Guide to Capitalism and Schizophrenia* (Cambridge: MIT Press, 1992), pp. 199–202.
178. Quoted in Stuart Ewen, *Captains of Consciousness*, p. 79.
179. What William Carlos Williams called 'the gist'. 'Money: Uranium (bound to be lead) . . . – the radium's the credit'; 'radium / THE GIST / credit: the gist.' Williams, *Paterson* (New York: New Directions, 1963), pp. 182–5.
180. Henry Adams, *The Education of Henry Adams*, p. 433.
181. Zukofsky turns Pound's 'white light that is allness' into the light of film technology. Pound's 'diafan' ('Where memory liveth, / it takes its state / Formed like a diafan from light on shade' [C 177]) in Zukofsky's text becomes the 'first motion picture in America, / Made in 1870, it was called "Diaphanous," / And shown in the opera houses. / One reel depicted the Minnesota Massacre . . .' (*A* 54).

182. This genre body is linked to the universalizing drive of both fascism and the culture of consumption. In the discussion of 'specie' above, an argument could also have been made for Pound's fetishization of the 'genre body', which appears tangentially in Canto XXXIII by way of a quotation from Marx: 'That this possessor be kalos k'àgathos, theocrat, baron or rich man matters very little', immediately after referring to John Adams' use of 'AGATHOS' to mean 'eternal and self-existent' (C 161). The ambivalence to the specie appears here also as an ambivalence to the body of the universal as the presentation of beauty. The Canto begins with a discussion by John Adams of 'despotism', and is an excellent example of the ambivalences and contradictions of Pound's political economy. In this connection, see Adorno and Horkheimer's discussion of *kalos kagathos* in *Dialectic of Enlightenment*, pp. 233–4.
183. A passage in *A*-8 returns to the topoi of this discussion in an eerily allusive fashion, picking up on the theme of film and light in connection with the 'animation' provided by the spirit or anima, the 'breath' that 'lives / with the image each lights'. In a quotation from Jefferson to his granddaughter Anne the gaze embodied in Chaplin's 'irising out' appears in a natural object, a flower: '"The houses and trees stand where they did . ./ the flowers come forth . ./ reproducing their like . ./ the irises giving place to . ./ as your mama has . . to you, / my dear Anne . . ."' (*A* 103; my italics).
184. For a brief discussion of the Gilbreth chronometer, see Ewen and Ewen, *Channels of Desire*, p. 36. Ewen and Ewen cite *The Book of Progress*, published by *Scientific American* in 1915: 'Every film [frame] reveals the successive positions of a workman in performing each minute operation of the task entrusted to him. The position of the chronometer pointer in successive films indicates the length of time between successive operations. These films are studied under a microscope, and a careful analysis of each operation is made to develop the standard time for each. . . . Any workman may, for a time, deceive an inexperienced efficiency engineer . . . but *the camera cannot be deceived*. . . . The film records faithfully every movement made, and subsequent analysis and study reveals how many of these movements were necessary and how many were purposely slow or useless.' However, as we will see, in 'the crick of a second', Zukofsky sees the possibility of a subversive deception of the camera.
185. Monique David-Ménard has attempted 'a metapsychology of movement' that analyses various pathological tics and cricks as both inscription and staging of an 'instinctual topology'. She says that '[m]ovements . . . seem to be a form of thought, the only one, as it happens, that can designate the subject in the place where he loses himself, in the operation of the primary repression.' *Hysteria from Freud to Lacan: Body and Language in Psychoanalysis* (Ithaca: Cornell University Press, 1989), p. 140.
186. See Zukofsky's reference to Disney's 'animated things' in his 1943 essay on Ogden and Richards' *Basic English: Introduction and Rules*: 'Animated every split second they can perhaps never be absorbed

as any stationary picture. They do not *tend* to confine thought like a name' (P 156).
187. Lacan's first extensive discussion of identification in optical terms was in his 'Remarque sur le rapport de Daniel Lagache', in *Ecrits* (Paris: Seuil, 1966), esp. pp. 667–84. He returns to it frequently in his seminars, the best-known example being in chapters 6 to 9 of *The Four Fundamental Concepts of Psychoanalysis* (New York: Norton, 1978) where he develops it again in terms of the gaze, to which I will turn in a moment. A very lucid exposition of the optical model can be found in Jacqueline Rose, *Sexuality in the Field of Vision* (London: Verso, 1986), Chapter 7.
188. On the function of the mask, see *The Four Fundamental Concepts of Psychoanalysis*, p. 107. Kaja Silverman argues that the distance of the subject from the 'photo-graphed' mask on the screen emphasizes an awareness of the pictured image as artifact, as non-natural – that is, as fetish. See *Male Subjectivity at the Margins* (New York: Routledge, 1992), p. 149.
189. The notion of camouflage that I am deriving from Zukofsky's analysis of Chaplin could also be discussed in terms of what Zukofsky in *A*-8 calls 'rapprochement with an aggressor' (*A* 70); this also appears in a reference to 'Nazis lured by *super-Nazis* – / "Become super-Nazis" in order the more quickly / To destroy the régime by its own excesses' (*A* 99–100). I intend my reading of camouflage to parallel Adorno's notoriously complex and indeterminate notion of mimesis, which is founded on a relation to otherness that is prior to the subject–object or even subject–subject relation. The critical capacity of such mimicry or mimesis, as Michael Cahn argues, operates by suspending the possibility of critique: what Cahn calls Adorno's 'subversive mimesis' is 'the instance in which the distinction between affirmation and negation, or between mimesis and subversion, is suspended, and therefore subversive mimesis *is* mimetic subversion in a precise structural simultaneity of affirmation and negation. It is subversive not of a governing rationality, but of the distinction between affirmation and critique. Being a critique of critique it is subversive of the mimetic which can only maintain its critical relevance by mimetically giving it up.' 'Subversive Mimesis: T.W. Adorno and the Modern Impasse of Critique', in *Mimesis in Contemporary Theory*, vol. 1, ed. M. Spariosu (Philadelphia: J. Benjamins Publishing Co., 1984), pp. 49–50.
190. In her discussion of the Lacanian concept of the gaze in the context of film theory, Joan Copjec emphasizes the importance of mimicry and masking, and thus of the coincidence of suspicion and belief that requires the insistence of the gaze as the guarantee of the real. The real is constituted as a gaze from outside: 'When Lacan says that the subject is trapped in the imaginary, he means that the subject can imagine nothing outside it; the imaginary cannot itself provide the means that would allow the subject to transcend it. When he says, on the other hand, that a painting, or any other representation, is a "trap for the gaze," he means that the repre-

sentation *attracts* the gaze, induces us to imagine a gaze outside – and observing – the field of representation. It is this second sense of trapping, whereby representation appears to generate its own beyond... that prevents the subject from ever being trapped in the imaginary.... For, beyond everything that is displayed to the subject, the question is asked: what is being concealed from me? What in this graphic space does not show, does not stop *not* writing itself? This point at which something appears to be missing from representation, some meaning left unrevealed, is the point of the Lacanian gaze. It marks the *absence* of a signified; it is an *unoccupiable* point, the point at which the subject disappears. The image, the visual field, then takes on a terrifying alterity that prohibits the subject from seeing itself in the representation. That "belong to me aspect" is suddenly drained from representation, as the mirror assumes the function of a screen.' 'The Orthopsychic Subject: Film Theory and the Reception of Lacan', *October* 49 (1989), pp. 68–9.

191. For Kant, that which is of most value, the object of the new form of 'self-preservation', goes by the name of 'humanity'. But this kind of self-preservation really has little to do with a political or economic 'self' or subject. It is 'a kind of self-preservation entirely different from that which can be attacked and brought into danger by external nature'. Having 'felt the proper sublimity of its destination', the mind can regard 'as small the things about which we are solicitous (goods, health, and life)'; therefore, 'humanity in our person remains unhumiliated, though the individual might have to submit to this dominion'. *Critique of Judgment*, p. 101 (section 28).

192. One of the most powerful responses to this question can be found in Jean-Luc Nancy's essay, 'The Inoperative Community', the thesis of which runs contrary to the post-Enlightenment nostalgia for communal relations lost to *Gesellschaft*: 'Community has not taken place, or rather, if it is indeed certain that humanity has known (or still knows, outside of the industrial world) social ties quite different from those familiar to us, community has never taken place along the lines of our projections of it according to these different social forms.... Nothing, therefore, has been lost, and for this reason nothing is lost. We alone are lost, we upon whom the "social bond" (relations, communication), our own invention, now descends heavily like the net of an economic, technical, political, and cultural snare. Entangled in its meshes, we have wrung for ourselves the phantasms of the lost community.' *The Inoperative Community*, ed. Peter Connor (Minneapolis: University of Minnesota Press, 1991), p. 11.

Index

Adams, C.F. 13, 143, 151–2, 191, 200
Adams, J. 158
Adorno, T. 22, 71, 223
Alighieri, D. 238–9
Appadurai, A. 47
Arendt, H. 27–9

Bataille, G. 25, 26, 204
Benhabib, S. 251
Boorstin, D. 188, 189

Casillo, R. 206
Chaplin, C. 14, 238–42
Comte, A. 149, 155
consumption 4, 7–10, 16–51, 60–71, 186–97, 199, 205, 226–35
contract 13, 152, 160, 171–4
corporation 142–74, 187–92, 200
courtly love 14, 206–14
Crevel, R. 95–6

Dennis, L. 32–3, 43, 50
Dewey, J. 160
Douglas, C.H. 16
Durkheim, E. 20, 21, 24–5, 40, 155

fascism 30–5, 54, 142–3, 150–74
fathers 9–11, 41–50, 55–8, 71–6, 90–1, 172
fetish, fetishism 6, 10, 11, 14, 56–7, 67–8, 76, 81, 84, 91–2, 110–11, 173, 170–7, 201, 205–6, 207, 246, 248–9
Filene, E.A. 16, 17, 20, 230
film 14, 236–50
Ford, H. 17, 20, 35, 42
Franklin, B. 23
Freud, S. 6, 33, 37–9, 75, 115

George, H. 10, 104–5
Gesell, S. 165

Gilbreth chronometer 243–4

Hamlet 114–16
Herbert, C. 47
Hoover, H. 8
Horkheimer, M. 22
Horowitz, D. 26
Hugnet, G. 116, 118–41

Jefferson, T. 158, 168, 171, 191

labour 12–14, 19–20, 44, 104, 151, 178–85, 193, 202, 208, 226–33
Lacan, J. 47–8, 248
le Goff, J. 140
Lippmann, W. 33
Lustig, R.J. 146, 152, 156, 187–8

MacIver, R.M. 102–3, 142
Maitland, F.W. 160
Marx, K. 10, 13, 16, 31, 47, 86–7, 173, 183–6, 202, 208, 213–15, 226–7
Mauss, M. 48, 73
melancholia 4, 5, 10, 11, 33, 37–9, 46, 50–5, 81, 86, 88–90, 103, 110–11, 118, 121–2, 173
money 65–91, 93, 105–14, 168, 170–2
Mouse, M. 14, 245–8
Mussolini, B. 8, 31, 32, 54, 153

Pétain, Marshal 4, 6, 9, 41, 76
Poincaré, H. 149
Pound, E. 1–12 passim, **16–33**, 40, 50–1, 144–5, 153–4, 161–96, 198, **202–8**

Rabinbach, A. 178
Rodgers, D. 34
Romasco, A. 36

Roosevelt, F.D.   8, 9, 43, 45, 55, 75, 100, 106–9

sacrifice   3, 4, 8, 10, 11, 39, 41, 42, 46, 48, 49, 77, 91, 93, 96–7, 103, 150, 169, 182–3, 191, 193
Scarry, E.   49
Schrödinger, E.   179–80
Sennett, R.   34, 158
Sieburth, R.   171
Simmel, G.   10, 28, 46–7, 186, 212
Sohn-Rethel, A.   87
Spencer, A.   158
Spengler, O.   30–1, 37, 43
Stein, G.   1, 2, **3–11**, 16, 29, 35, 36, **39–49**, **52–141**, 143, 168, 171; works: *Before the Flowers of Friendship Faded Friendship Faded* **116–41**
Stevens, W.   1, 8
Sumner, W.G.   149

Tocqueville, A. de   159–60
Tönnies, F.   2

Veblen, T.   26–7, 29, 153, 216–28

Wallace, E.   92, 94–5
Weber, M.   40

Zukofsky, L.   1–6 passim, 12–15, **142–251**; works: *A* 8   13, 15, 143, 145, **150–68**; *A* 9   14, 15, **175–81**